EXCELAND

Handy Excel Tips and Solutions for Inquisitive Minds

By *Ryszard Raciborski*

There are over 120 Excel-related topics covered here - from data entry to art work - for learning and for use. Every user of Excel can discover in this book some new ways of performing and presenting their work.

CREATED WITH EXCEL

Contents

Stock Portfolios Tracking with Yahoo Finance in Excel - Part 1
Stock Portfolios Tracking with Yahoo Finance in Excel - Part 2
Stock Portfolios Tracking with Yahoo Finance in Excel - Part 3
GRAPHICS / ARTS / GAMES
Picture in Picture in Excel Worksheet
Colourful Randomized Worksheet Creations
Creating Graphs Based on Data Table; the Easy Way
World of Fractals - Beauty of Recursion
Create your own Lottery
Creating Pixel Art - Iterations
Animation - Flying Objects
Animation - Swinging Objects
Pick Your Lucky Lotto Numbers
SUDOKU Solver and Creator

INTRODUCTION

Overview

MS Excel program is a powerful data organization, analysis and visualization tool. Although it is primarily used for number-crunching and charting, its functionality has become so versatile now that you can use it as a sophisticated problem solver, a statistical tool, a database, a basic programming tool, a very good graphics tool, as well as generator of reports. And it's still evolving, in fact becoming a true programming language.

The content of this book can help you stay organized, find solutions and answers to some of your tasks, save time, and make better decisions, both in your personal life and at work.

The instant of Julia set picture created in Excel and displayed below is just one instant of creative potential inherent in the program. You can learn here how to utilize some of its most useful features for your specific needs. I hope, you'll find what you're looking for.

Here are some of the most useful applications of Excel program for personal use:

- **Data Analysis**: Quick sorting, filtering, and analysing large amounts of data. Perform statistical analysis, create pivot tables, and generate charts and graphs. Analysis and visualising data in creative arts and social sciences; e.g., analysis of survey data, creating charts and graphs to visualize patterns in the data, and to identify trends and correlations.
- **Tracking personal finances**: Tracking of your personal finances by creating spreadsheets for creating budgets, complex financial models and statements, calculating taxes, controlling your bank balances, investments, loans, monthly bills, credit card payments and other expenses.
- **Inventory management**: Creating an inventory of your personal belongings. Creating a spreadsheet to track the items you own, their value, and their location.
- **Personal productivity**: Creating to-do lists, tracking personal goals, managing personal finances, creating personal lists for various purposes, such as shopping lists, travel packing lists, etc. Managing personal projects by tracking tasks, timelines, and milestones.
- **Planning and scheduling**: Planning and scheduling tasks, events, and appointments. Creating calendars or schedules that include important dates, deadlines, and reminders. Planning events, such as weddings, parties, and other gatherings. Creating worksheets for tracking guest lists, seating arrangements, and other details.

- **Tracking fitness and health**: Tracking your fitness and health goals by creating worksheets for monitoring your weight, exercise routines, workouts, and nutrition. Planning your meals, creating shopping lists, storing your favourite recipes and ingredient lists.
- **Research and data organization**: Organizing your research data. Creating databases of research articles and managing data collection.
- **Visual design**: Creating visual designs in creative arts, such as charts, graphs, and tables for presentations and reports.

Workbook Design: Basic Principles

Design your workbook for both EFFICIENCY and LOOK & FEEL.

- First of all - **plan it well for your specific purpose**, in order to avoid complications down the road. In cases where there is complexity of data and calculations, use multiple worksheets within the workbook and label them properly (name them by their purpose) to separate clearly data input, assumptions, calculations, output, tables, charts, etc.

- Use highlighting/shading to differentiate, in particular, data entry parts (input) from output (results, report).

- If you design the workbook for multiple users, add instructions and documentation, record of changes, wherever needed.

- Use *Comments* or *Callouts* features to add meaningful explanatory notes to some cells, e.g., to explain more complex calculations, especially for external users.

- Break formulas involving complex calculations into multiple cells to make any troubleshooting much easier. Use cell references rather than numbers (constants) to avoid errors related to input. Any assumptions must be clearly visible in worksheet layout.

- Organize your worksheets vertically rather than horizontally. This improves flow of calculations.

- Plan for logical constraints on data entries to avoid results that don't make sense or appear false. Use *= IF(logical test, value if true, value if false)* formulas and highlight cells resulting in *false* for further review.

- Use also *Data Validation* feature to create certain restrictions for user input. E.g., include some limits for entering dates, other numbers, or text data). This will improve accuracy of data being entered.

- Be clear and consistent about used units and number formats!

- Avoid blank rows and columns within ranges of data. They can be treated as the end of your data in some cases.

- Sort your data, where possible, in a logical order. This will make some calculations easier.

- FORMATTING - keep it efficient and SIMPLE.

    - Use the *Format Painter* (available in the ribbon) to automate formatting where possible. Do not overuse formats!

    - Change the gridlines in your workbook to a light colour, or even turn them off, for better look (*File>Options>Advanced>Display options for this worksheet>Gridline colour*). Use *Borders* formatting tool where necessary.

    - Avoid merging cells; it causes all kinds of problems. Use "*Center across selection*" instead.

    - Avoid hiding data. This increases risk of errors.

- Preferably, use 12-point Calibri font, because it is well readable for both numbers and text. Limit use of different fonts to minimum.

- Pay attention to formatting Dates, especially if they will be used in formulas.

- Bold the font of headings.

- Keep *Conditional Formatting* simple, if you need to apply it, at all.

- Always use Excel's solutions before resorting to VBA macros. If possible, avoid the use of macros.

- Protect (Lock) cells used for formulas, functions and calculation details. Usually, the only unlocked cells should be those used for user input. Remember that cells protection takes effect only then when you protect the worksheet afterwards.

- Protect also the whole workbook if you consider it necessary. Keep in mind, however, that if you forget your password, its recovery in Excel may not be possible due to a very strong encryption.

Use Excel Workbook <u>Templates</u> to Boost Your Productivity

Before you even start with designing your new workbook you need to be aware of assistance that Excel program provides in the form of **templates**. They can greatly facilitate your workbook design and use. To check if there is a template that fits your project, open Excel and click on "File" in the top left corner; in the upper part of the page, you'll see all kinds of templates you can choose from. Click on the "**More templates**" at the right and there you can browse by category or search for a specific template using keywords to find the most relevant to meet your needs.

You can also search online for Excel workbook templates. There are many websites that offer free or paid templates, such as **MS Office Templates, Vertex42, or Smartsheet**.

Once you've found a template you like, you can customize it as needed. This may involve adding or removing columns, changing the formatting, or adjusting formulas. To do this, simply open the template in Excel and make the changes you need.

If you create a customized workbook that you think you may need to use again in the future, you can save it as a template. To do this, simply click on "File" and then "Save As." Choose "Excel Template (*.xltx)" from the "Save as type" dropdown menu and give your template a name. The next time you want to use this template, simply open it from the "New" menu in Excel.

INTERFACE / FEATURES

Excel offers a very abundant interface (ribbon) and wide range of features and tools for data management, analysis, and visualization. The most useful of them include:

- variety of built-in formulas and functions,
- PivotTables, enabling users to summarize, analyse, and visualize large amounts of data quickly,
- variety of chart types, to represent data visually and make it easier to interpret,
- creation and use of macros and user-defined functions, allowing automation of repetitive tasks,
- Solver add-in tool, enabling users to optimize solutions to many constrained tasks,
- Goal Seek tool, allowing users to find the input value required to achieve a specific output,
- Power Query tool, that allows users to import, transform, and merge data from external sources.

Those are just a few of the many special features and tools available in Excel. Here I'm just touching on some of them.

Excel Interface – Hide or Restore

Normally, Excel application displays user interface (ribbon standard) like this (*top* and *bottom* parts):

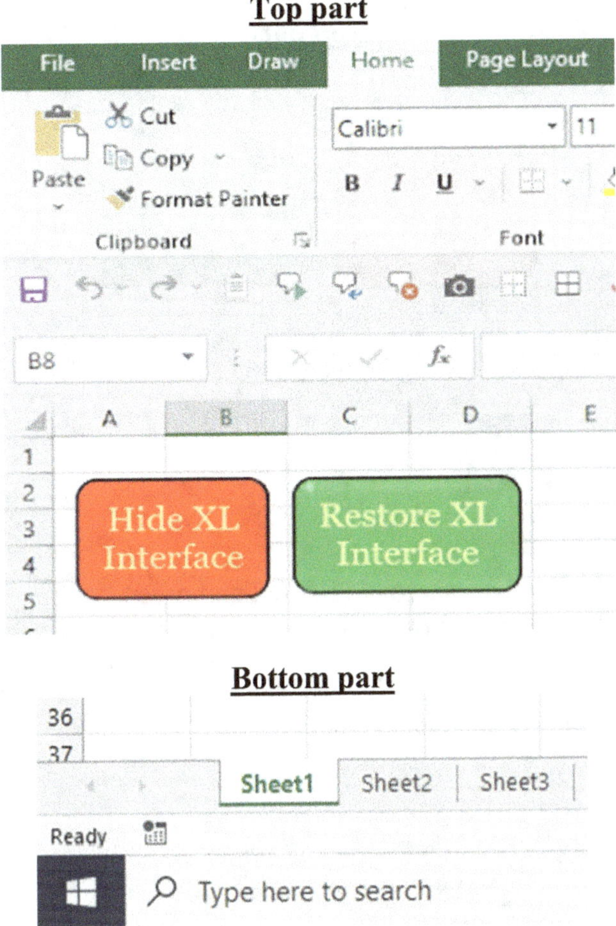

The ribbon and other elements of the interface (upper Tabs, Headings, Scroll bars, Formula bar, Status bar) take quite a bit of screen surface area. When working on a workbook, there are situations when the functionality of Excel can be utilized better in a static view, without all the bars and ribbon in view. Wouldn't it be nice to have only the title bar and clean worksheet (even without gridlines) visible on some occasions; e.g., during some presentations...

Obviously, we can use Excel Options dialog for hiding some bars, headers and tabs. To do that, we can select **File>Options>Advanced>Display options for this workbook/worksheet** and uncheck e.g., scroll bars, sheet tabs, row and column headers, gridlines etc.

However, in many cases it is more convenient to utilize short macros to hide or unhide these Excel features, with a single click on a Control button. We would use in such a case the following two macros, one for hiding and the other for restoring (*if you're not familiar with Excel macros, please see "**Working with macros in Excel**" in this book*):

```vba
Sub HideXLiface()
'Hide Excel interface
ActiveWindow.Caption = ""
ActiveWindow.DisplayHeadings = False
ActiveWindow.DisplayWorkbookTabs = False
ActiveWindow.DisplayGridlines = False
Application.DisplayScrollBars = False
Application.DisplayStatusBar = False
```

Application.DisplayFormulaBar = False
Application.ExecuteExcel4Macro "show.toolbar(""Ribbon"",False)"
End Sub

The result of running the macro would look like this (*top* and *bottom* parts):

Top part

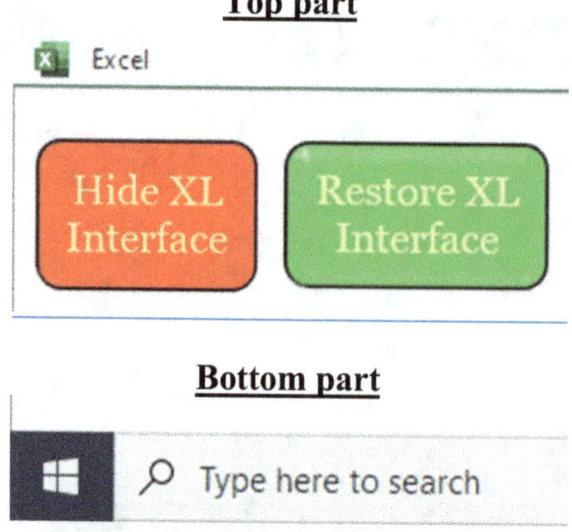

Bottom part

In this example I've assigned my two macros to the red and green buttons. The buttons can be located, obviously, somewhere else (out of the way) in your workbook.

To hide the elements of Excel interface I click on the red button, and to restore the interface I click on the green button. The macro assigned to the green button looks like this one:

Sub UnhideXLiface()
'Restore Excel interface
ActiveWindow.Caption = ThisWorkbook.Name
ActiveWindow.DisplayHeadings = True
ActiveWindow.DisplayWorkbookTabs = True
ActiveWindow.DisplayGridlines = True
Application.DisplayScrollBars = True
Application.DisplayStatusBar = True
Application.DisplayFormulaBar = True
Application.ExecuteExcel4Macro "show.toolbar(""Ribbon"",True)"
End Sub

Basics on CELLS: Blank, Empty, Space, Zero

What's the meaning of all these basic terms in Excel?

BLANK cell: empty or not? Not quite, it may contain **""** (*zero length text string*)

EMPTY cell: nothing is there (no text string, no zero); always *evaluates* to zero

Cell with **SPACE**: contains 'space' character (=" ")

Do you know that:

- Cell containing **Text** can never equate to a cell containing **Number** (**""**<>0), even if formatted as Number.
- Value of a cell with **zero length text string** is 'worth' more than **zero** (**""**>0), i.e., not equal to zero.
- Function **ISTEXT** confirms that *EMPTY* cell is 'worth' more than zero (>0), i.e., not equal to zero, as well.

- Both **EMPTY** cells and cells with **zero length text strings** are counted in Excel as **BLANK** cells.
- Cell with '**0**' value is <u>**not**</u> *BLANK*, but **equal to** *EMPTY* cell. E.g., if A2 contains **0**, and cell A3 is **EMPTY**, then formula **=A3=A2** results in **TRUE**.

It's **very important** to be aware of all those definitions and statements when using Excel, especially when working with statistical functions, like *Average, Max, Min, STDEV, etc.* It's quite easy to draw wrong conclusions about your data set. Avoid mixing the blank and empty cells, or text and space characters, with numbers.

CELL "tricks"

What is the Excel cell? Essentially, it is a "rectangular-shaped box on a worksheet", located at the intersection of any column and row, where you can enter some value - number or text. But it is much more than that.

First of all, it can be shaped rectangularly as well as squarely. Secondly, you can enter into each cell not only any kind of text or/and any kind of graphics, but also pictures and drawings, and enter them in many layers, displayed or hidden (*within specified computer memory limits*). The layering feature allows placing multiple objects on top of each other, with each object being partially or fully visible.

E.g., you can place in any single cell:

- Some text on top of any Excel Shape (by selecting *Insert>Text Box*)
- Multiple Shapes stacked on top of each other (by right-clicking and selecting *Bring to Front* or *Send to Back*) - to create custom graphics
- Any Shape on top of any image, again - to create custom graphics
- Multiple Text Boxes with different content and formatting (e.g., heading, subtitle, normal text)
- Excel Chart on top of an image (create chart normally and move to a position over the image)
- Conditional Formatting on selected data, based on selected Excel Rules of formatting
- Joined or overlapping Charts

Here is just an example of content fitted in a SINGLE cell, in multiple layers and displays.

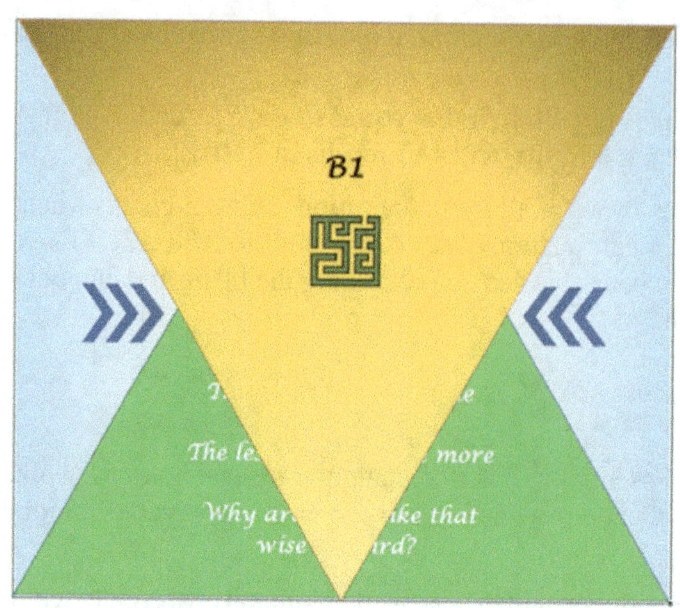

One CELL in Excel

I'm connected to it

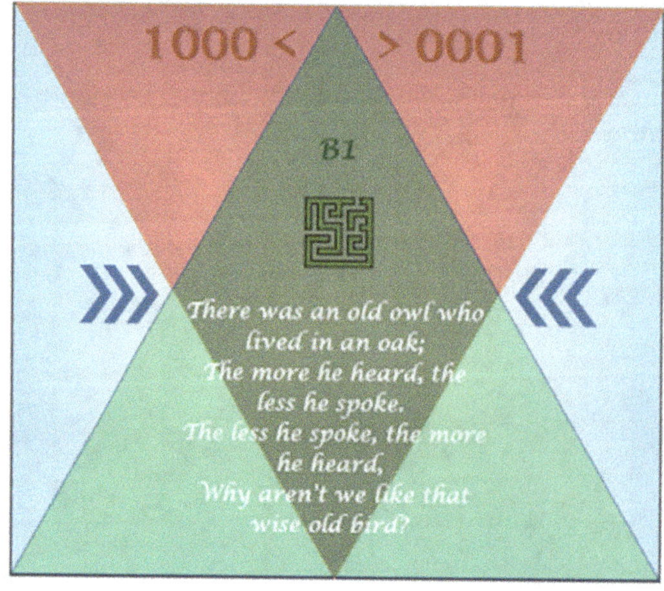

You can create unlimited variety of such multi-layered formations. Try to unveil *your* own creativity using this kind of Excel cell features. Every single Excel cell can contain lots of different types of information, both alphanumeric and graphics, and even Excel Charts.

Unhide SOME of hidden Rows/Columns

It's quite easy to unhide *a whole range* of hidden columns or rows in a worksheet (simply select the adjacent visible columns or rows, right-click on them, and select **Unhide** from the menu).

But what if you want to unhide just one specific row or column, or a couple of them only.

Let's say, you've hidden columns from M to W, and rows from 30 to 40. Now you need to unhide columns S-T and rows 35-38 only. In such situation probably the best way is a macro way. The following two macros can be very helpful:

```vb
Sub UnhideSomeRows()
'Unhide one or more of the hidden rows
Dim sRows As String
Repeat:
sRows = Application.InputBox("Enter row number(s) to unhide", "Unhide row(s)", "e.g., 12 or 20:25")
If sRows = "" Then Exit Sub
On Error Resume Next
If Err.Number <> 0 Then
        On Error GoTo 0
        Err.Clear
        MsgBox "Please input valid row(s)."
        GoTo Repeat
End If
Rows(sRows).EntireRow.Hidden = False
MsgBox "Row(s) " & sRows & " is/are visible now", vbOKOnly, "Unhide specific Row(s)"
End Sub


Sub UnhideSomeColumns()
'Unhide one or more of the hidden columns
Dim sCols As String
Dim rRng As Range
Repeat:
sCols = InputBox("Enter column(s) to unhide", "Unhide some of hidden Column(s)", "e.g., H or K:M")
If sCols = "" Then Exit Sub
On Error Resume Next
Set rRng = ActiveSheet.Columns(sCols)
If Err.Number <> 0 Then
        On Error GoTo 0
        Err.Clear
        MsgBox "Please input valid column(s)"
        GoTo Repeat
End If
rRng.EntireColumn.Hidden = False
MsgBox "Column(s) " & UCase(sCols) & " is/are visible now", vbOKOnly, "Unhide specified Columns"
Set rRng = Nothing
On Error GoTo 0
End Sub
```

I've assigned the macros to distinct Control buttons and gave them names "**Unhide Rows**" and "**Unhide Columns**". If you need help to do that, see "**Working with macros in Excel**" in this book.

I've then combined the two buttons into one, by moving and grouping them together as illustrated in this figure:

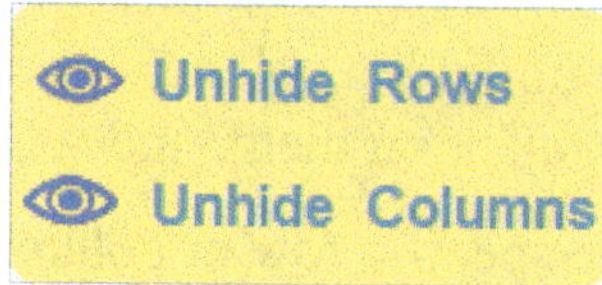

To unhide any columns or rows in my worksheet I just click on corresponding line of text on the button.

TIPS for CLICKS: Using Mouse in Excel – Mouse Shortcuts

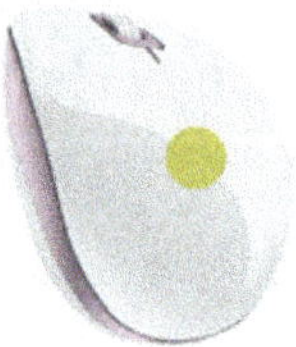

"**Click**" - means here **left** button click.

"**Fill Handle**" - in Excel means: small black rectangle in the lower right corner of a cell/range selection.

The following table provides **30** helpful tips related to the use of mouse in the Excel program. It covers the most useful mouse "shortcuts" enhancing user's skills and productivity, and explains how to use them. It's worth to utilize them in your work.

WHAT TO DO	HOW TO DO, WITH MOUSE
Snap a shape/image to Excel grid or to a cell size	Insert the selected object into a worksheet. Hold down **ALT+click and drag** to a cell/range border. Release.
Apply formatting of selected cell/range to other area(s) in a worksheet	**Click on Format Painter** in the Ribbon and select one cell or range. **Double-click on the Format Painter** and select consecutively multiple areas to format.
Select multiple non-adjacent cells/ranges	Hold down **CTRL key** while selecting
Zoom In/Out the whole worksheet area	Hold down **CTRL key and scroll** the wheel Up or Down to zoom.
Select/group multiple worksheets (*non-adjacent* or *adjacent*) together and apply any action to them	Hold down **CTRL key and select tabs of** non-adjacent worksheets. Hold down **SHIFT key and select tabs of** adjacent worksheets.
Add multiple arguments in a function (like e.g., Sum, Vlookup) **without typing commas** between the arguments	Hold down **CTRL key** while adding the arguments.

Add to a worksheet multiple copies of any selected shape/chart/image	Hold down **CTRL key and move/drag** the object to a new place many times.
Copy a selected range of cells to any **position** and as many times as needed	Hold down **CTRL key and drag** one of the **borders** of the selection in a desired direction.
Change formatting or formulas in selected multiple **ranges of cells simultaneously**	Hold down **CTRL key** while **selecting different ranges**, then act on them as needed; also copy & paste elsewhere.
Expand/reduce the Formula Bar size vertically by as much as needed	**Drag the lower edge** of the Formula Bar. Click on the top-right 'v' to minimize its height.
Copy/Cut and Paste a range of cells using one of **available formats**	**Select a range** and use the **right-click to copy/cut and paste** the range **in** one of displayed **menu options.**
Open the 'Activate' sheet menu to select one of the numerous worksheets in a workbook	**Right-click** on **one of the small arrows** to the left of the workbook sheet tabs.
Expand selection of cell(s) and apply one of the options presented in displayed menu	**Right-click the Fill Handle** on any cell/range of cells **and drag** to expand selection. After releasing the button, a list of available options appears for use.
Copy the format of any selected cell to another cell or range of cells	**Double-click** on the **Format Painter** and **click** on a target cell; **drag** to select a range of cells.
Draw numerous numbers of a selected Shape, of the same or different dimensions, as needed	**Right-click on selected shape** in the Shapes (on Ribbon) and **click on the 'Lock Drawing Mode'** option. **Click in the worksheet** to insert and resize (if needed) copies of the shape. Use **ESC key to exit** the mode.
Auto-fill series of data or formulas in a column of some table (suggesting where to stop filling), **with a given / initiated pattern/format**	**Double-click on the Fill Handle** of selected cell/range. Filling stops down the column based on the size of filled column to the left.
Open the Format Chart Area or Format Plot Area pane (with menu)	**Double-click on the chart/plot area.** When the pane is already displayed, **single click** on the chart/plot area **switches the pane.**
Hide/Unhide the Ribbon; or display it temporarily	**Double-click any Ribbon menu tab** to hide the Ribbon; **now click once to display it** (but without Formula Bar) until you click on any cell. **Double-click again** any menu tab and the **Ribbon reappears.**
Rename any worksheet	**Double-click on worksheet's tab** and enter a new name.
Select the whole worksheet	**Click on the** half square looking **button at the top left corner of Excel screen** (to the left of Col. A and above Row 1).
Change any menu docked to the side of active workbook (e.g., *Format Shape*) **to a**	**Click on the title of the docked menu and drag it** to a chosen position. **Double-click the title again** to return the

floating window, and position it conveniently in the worksheet	menu to its original position.
Select the first word, then extend the selection of text/sentence further	**Double-click on the first word and** - keeping the left button depressed – **drag to select more text,** as needed.
Move a selected range of cells to a new position, in any direction	**Hold down the SHIFT key and drag one of the outside borders** of the range to position the selection in new area.
Extend selected range of filled cells in a desired direction to continue filling cells with related additional data / formulas	**Click on the Fill Handle of the selected range and drag it** in a desired direction.
Select the whole cell content	**Triple-click or quadruple-click** on the cell.
Auto-scroll in horizontal and vertical directions	**Click the wheel button.**
Keep an eye on some of the cells in a workbook, while working with a workbook	**Click on Formulas** tab>**Watch Window. Add cells/ranges to be displayed** in the Window floating above the worksheet. The Window can be dragged to the side or to the top of the workbook screen.
Get Excel Help immediately while entering a complex function or formula into a cell	**After entering '=' sign and the function name** followed by '(', **click on the hyperlink** (underlined function name). The relevant **Help pane** will be **displayed** at once.
Browse quickly between Excel menu tabs (except for the File tab) without the need to click on each of them	**Use the scroll wheel** anywhere in the Ribbon, scrolling **Up** or **Down.**
Add a <u>mouse-over</u> helpful tip to any shape or other object on a worksheet	The **mouse-over** is an action (tip) that is displayed when the user stops or hovers the mouse pointer above the object. To add it, follow these steps: 1. **Click the object**, then use **CTRL+K** shortcut. 2. In **Insert Hyperlink** window, click **Screen Tip...** (top right) and **enter text** you want to display when the user is hovering the mouse pointer over the object. Click OK. 3. Next, select Link to: **Existing File or Web Page** and click **Bookmark...** button; enter **A1** in the **Type in the cell reference** field. Click OK. 4. Click OK in the **Insert Hyperlink** window.

Keyboard Functions: Cheat Sheet

All in one place, practical reference to your keyboard functions. Very helpful for every user of Excel, especially in situations when you can't use your mouse.

This is what you can do with your keyboard **Function Keys**, when combined also with **control keys** (Ctrl, Alt, Shift).

Key Shortcuts	Description of the Effect
F1	Display the **Help** Task pane or associated Help topic
Ctrl+F1	Expand or collapse the **Ribbon**
Alt+F1	Create an **embedded chart** using currently selected data
Alt+Shift+F1	Insert new **worksheet**
F2	**Edit** active **cell**. Within the VBE, display the **Object Browser**.
Ctrl+F2	Display **Print Preview** area on Print tab of Backstage View
Alt+F2	Display the **Save As** dialog box
Shift+F2	Insert or edit a **cell Comment**
F3	Display the **Paste Name** dialog box (if defined names are available)
Ctrl+F3	Display the **Name Manager** dialog box
Shift+F3	Display the **Insert Function** dialog box
Ctrl+Shift+F3	Display the **Create Names** from Selection dialog box
F4	**Repeat last command / action**, when possible. Also, **toggle** between available combinations of **absolute & relative** references
Ctrl+F4	**Close** current selected **workbook window**
Alt+F4	**Close** current active **Excel window**
Shift+F4	**Repeat** last **find** action / **Find next** match
Ctrl+Shift+F4	**Find previous** match
F5	Within the VBE, **execute macro**
Shift+F5	Display the **Find and Replace** dialog (with the Find tab selected)
F6	**Switch between panes** in the following order: worksheet, Ribbon
Ctrl+F6	**Alternate** between active and next **workbook windows**
Shift+F6	**Switch** between **panes**. Includes split panes in a split worksheet
F7	Display the **Spelling** dialog box
Ctrl+F7	Apply **Move** command on workbook window (when not maximized)
Shift+F7	Display the **Thesaurus** dialog box or task pane
F8	Turn **Extend Selection** mode **On/Off**, using only the arrow keys
Ctrl+F8	Apply **Resize** command on **workbook** window (when not maximized)
Alt+F8	Display the **Macro dialog** box
Shift+F8	**Add non-adjacent range(s)** to current selection
F9	**Calculate all** worksheets in all open workbooks
Ctrl+F9	**Minimize** current selected **workbook window**
Shift+F9	**Calculate** the current **active worksheet**
Ctrl+Alt+F9	**Calculate all** worksheets in all open workbooks
F10	**Turn key tips** (Ribbon keyboard shortcuts) **On/Off**
Ctrl+F10	**Maximize/restore** current selected **workbook window**
Shift+F10	Display the **Context/Shortcut menu** for the selected item
Alt+Shift+F10	Display **menu / message** generated by **error background checking**
Shift+F10+m	**Insert / delete cell comment**
F11	**Create chart** in a separate Chart sheet using currently selected data
Ctrl+F11	Create **New Macro sheet**
Alt+F11	**Open/Toggle** between **Excel and VBE**
Shift+F11	**Insert** a new **worksheet** in the current workbook
F12	Display the **Save As** dialog box
Ctrl+F12	Display the **"Open"** dialog box
Shift+F12	**Save** file using **current file name & format**, in current file location

How to Navigate in Excel Worksheet

Moving around a worksheet made easy. Just fix in memory several intuitive shortcuts/clicks, as illustrated in this sketch, and you can move swiftly to any place in your even very large data range, and beyond.

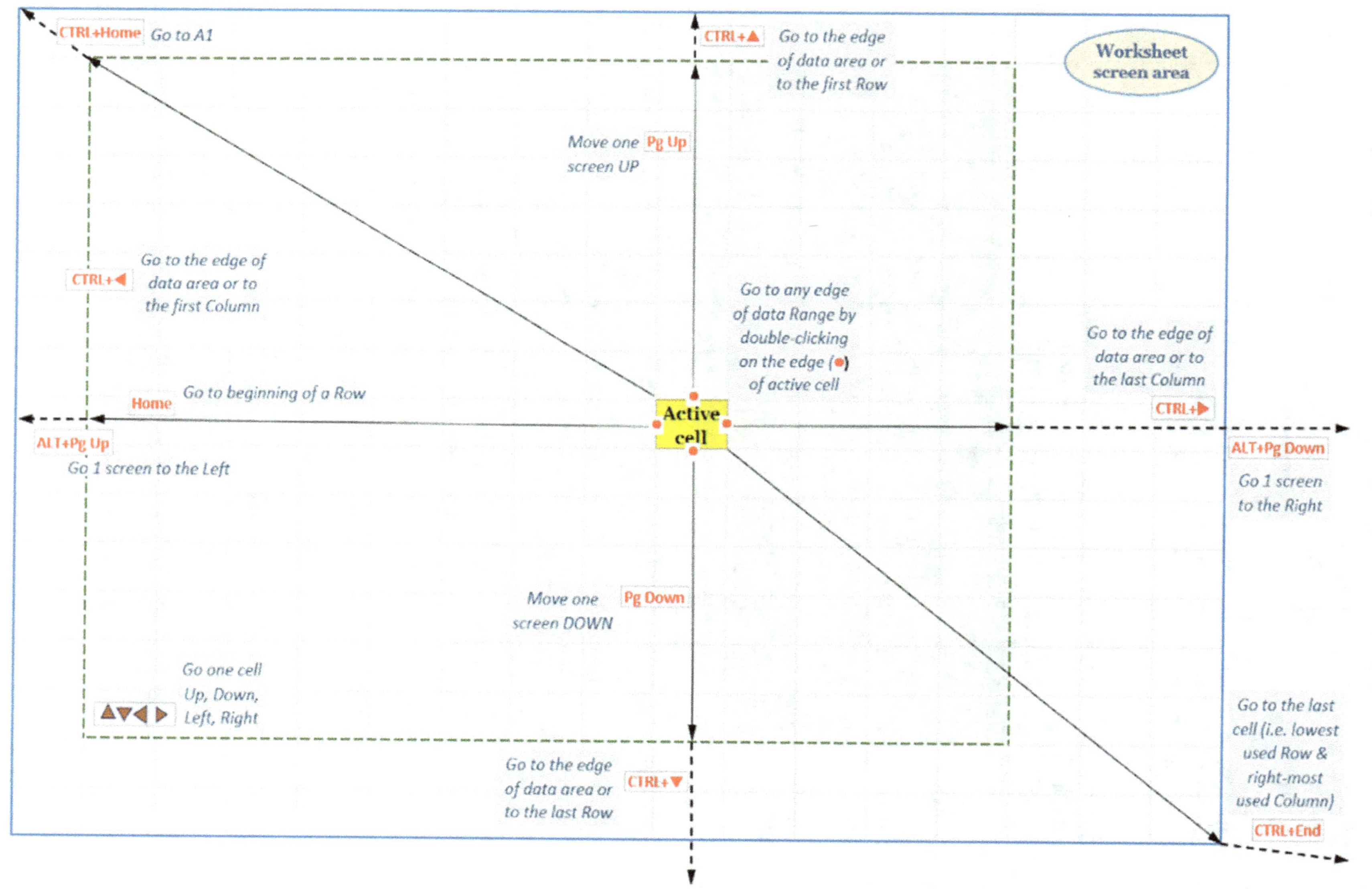

Current data range area (a table) is shaded in light green colour here.

In a list format these shortcuts can be summarized as follows:

- **Arrow keys** (right, left, up, down)   *- move by one Cell*
- *ALT+Pg Up / Pg Down*   *- move by one screen to the Left/Right*
- **CTRL+Arrow keys**   *- go to the edge of data range*
- **CTRL+End key**   *- go to the last cell boundary (Row/Column)*
- **CTRL+Home key**   *- go to cell A1*
- **Home key**   *- go to the beginning of a Row*
- **Pg Up / Pg Down key**   *- move by one screen Up/Down*
- **Double-click on any edge of active cell**   *- go to any edge of current data range*

Set Worksheet CELLS to SQUARE Shape

There are situations, especially in graphic design area, when it's convenient to work with worksheet cells that are square in shape. You can get such effect in many ways, including a macro. However, the best method is probably the one I'm suggesting here. Just follow these easy steps:

1. Start with the main Menu strip; click on **View** and select **PageLayout**. Select a range or the whole worksheet, whichever you want to format.

2. While in the page layout, click on **Home** in the main Menu and select **Format** in **Cells** group.

3. Click on **Row Height** and enter the height value you want, e.g., **5** mm (if mm is your default or preferred display option). The unit can be changed to cm or inch, if necessary, by clicking on **File>Options** (*at the bottom of vertical strip*)>**Advanced>Display** and selecting one of the **Ruler units**.

4. Go back to **Format** and click on **Column Width**; enter the same value as you entered for the row height.

That's it. You've got square cells. Return to the **Normal** workbook view.

Your worksheet display format could now look like this one:

How to Make Square Cells for Grid Paper in MMs or CMs

No macro needed here. Just follow these steps to fill your worksheet with **square cells**:

- select the whole worksheet, or any part of it (your choice)
- in the ribbon, select **View > Page Layout**, then

- select **Home > Format >Row Height**, and enter e.g.:
- 0.03937 for 1mm grid (= 1 / 25.4), or
- 0.19685 for 5mm grid (= 5 / 25.4), or
- 0.3937 for 1cm grid (= 1 / 2.54), and so on (your choice)
- select **Home > Format > Column Width**, and enter the same value as for row height
- return to the **Normal** View.

Your grid is displayed and ready for use on your computer screen.

Here are examples of created this way **1mm** and **1cm** grids:

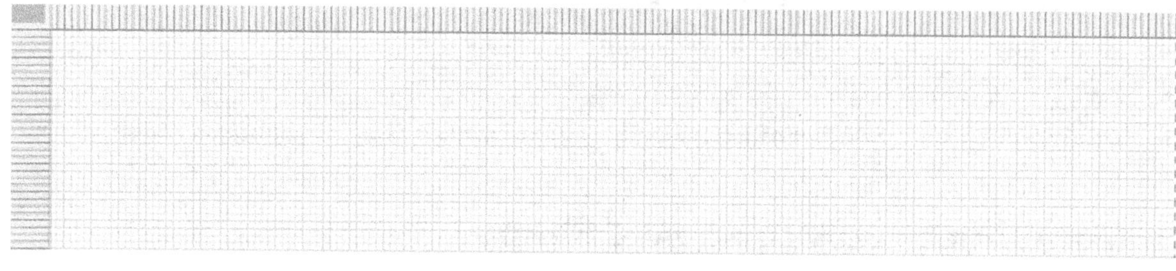

If you want to get **printout of your grid on paper**, the next steps depend on the size of paper, selected margins, printer settings etc. Here I'm providing just one example. Let's say that you use *letter-size paper* and set *2.5 cm custom margins* on each side. You would proceed as follows:

- enter anything in one of the cells on the worksheet; otherwise, you may get error message like this one: "*We didn't find anything to print*"

- in Normal view, select one full page in the worksheet (as shown by page breaks)

- go to **File > Print > Page Setup > Sheet > Print**, and select **Gridlines** option

- in **Print Settings**, select **Print Selection**, then set **Custom Scaling Options** to: Adjust to **335%** of normal size.

Some tweaking may be necessary, depending on printers and Excel version, to fit the page size. I had no problem with printing the page filled with exactly 1mm size grid.

Other grids can be printed in a similar way, just with different % adjustments of normal size (e.g., I've used **262%** adjustment for 1cm grid).

Some tweaking may be necessary, depending on printers and Excel version, to fit the page size. I had no problem with printing the page filled with exactly 1mm size grid.

Other grids can be printed in a similar way, just with different % adjustments of normal size (e.g., I've used **262%** adjustment for 1cm grid).

How to Enhance Cell Borders with Shapes

Borders around Excel cells make worksheet contents visually enhanced and easier for evaluation. They clarify the format and layout of the data, make it appear more orderly and, also highlight important information. Drop-down menu of Borders provides multiple pre-built options for that, as you can see some of them here.

However, some Excel users sometimes would like to apply different type of borders (e.g., rounded-corner borders) instead of the square-cornered ones. There is no such an option in Excel. Fortunately, there is a workaround available for such unconventional type of 'borders'.

So, if you see any good reason for using a different kind of cell '*borders*' (e.g., for presentations, reports), you can create them quite easily with the help of many different Shapes provided by Excel. Here are some of my creations:

Shape with rounded corners

Rectangle with rounded corners				
461	273	459	509	410
226	283	313	379	233
458	475	373	284	483

Octagon Shape

Octagon				
ab	*cd*	*ef*	*gh*	*ij*
55	*efg*	*ghij*	225	*tu*
55	*ghij2*	*225tu*	225	*tu*

Beveled Shape

Beveled rectangle				
1.939519	1.732394	1.612784	1.518514	1.716003
1.60206	1.934498	1.897627	1.78533	1.623249
1.518514	1.414973	1.662758	1.690196	1.863323

Oval Shape

Oval				
11.27	13.42	13.30	10.95	13.15
12.92	13.53	11.49	11.87	13.78
14.07	11.70	13.04	11.87	13.82

Frame Shape

Frame				
ò	¶	í	¡	×
Ú	°	Ã	œ	»
ì	Ê	å	Î	ñ

What does it take to place such cell '*borders*' in your worksheet?

It is possible to create a Shape/drawing object the same size as your cells and format it so it has no fill colour. Then, you can copy the '*border*' to as many cells as you need to.

Here's how to format your selected '*border*':

1. Click on **Insert** tab > **Shapes** and select the shape you want from **Rectangles, Basic Shapes**, etc., e.g., Plaque.

2. Go with cursor (showing '+' sign) to a cell of your choice, press and hold the **ALT key** and resize the shape so it covers exactly the cell size.

3. Right-click on the shape and select '**Format Shape...**' from drop-down menu.

4. Click on '**Size & Properties**' in '**Shape Options**', then on '**Properties**' and make sure that '**Move and size with cells**' option is selected.

5. Click on '**Fill & Line**' in '**Shape Options**', then on '**Fill**' and select '**No fill**'. You can also select there the '**Line**' properties (e.g., colour and width), if you want.

Your cell '*border*' is ready.

Now you can select and copy the cell with your '*border*'. Be careful, select the whole cell, not the shape only, to copy it (you may need to use arrow keys to select the whole cell). Use ***CTRL+C*** and ***CTRL+V*** to paste your cell to other cells in your worksheet.

IMPORTANT: You'll notice at some point that the '*border*' is floating (can be freely moved around) in a layer *above* the cell layer, so leave it alone. If you want to fill the underlying cell with a specific colour or pattern, you can do this separately by selecting the cell itself, not the '*border*'. Remember also that you can't add fill colour to your shape. Only the shape's *line* can be formatted (width, colour) if needed.

To enter any value or formula to your '*bordered*' cell, click on the cell and enter whatever you want. Your typing should appear in the *Formula bar*. If it is not there, then it means that you are entering data into the '*border*' layer instead into the cell layer. You couldn't use such entries in any calculations.

The entry into the cell layer can be referred to by other cells, and formatted (colour, font, alignment) to your liking, as usually.

DATA ENTRY, ORGANIZING & ANALYSIS

Working with data includes data collection, data entry, storage, organization, as well as using the essential tools and features for the analysis of datasets and presenting the outcomes, which usually means visualization of data and proper reporting. This requires good knowledge of the "anatomy" of workbook and worksheets, and relevant experience in using at least:

- Excel functions
- Conditional formatting
- Data validation
- Sorting and filtering
- PivotTables
- Data visualization, charting

Data Entry Tips: Formulas and Dates

You might learn from some sources that when you enter a **formula** into a cell in Excel, you have to start your entry always with the equal sign. *This is not true.* You can, but DON'T NEED to start with the '=' sign.

Each formula can be started also with either '+', or '-' (if you mean negative number/expression) signs. When you press the ENTER key, Excel will voluntarily add the equal sign for you.

Here are couple of examples to illustrate what happens:

	A	B	C
	Your FORMULA entry	After presing ENTER key (displayed in formula bar)	Result
2	+SQRT(43)*0.75 ➡	=+SQRT(43)*0.75 ➡	4.9181
3	-LN(A1)-INT(6.876)➡	=-LN(A1)-INT(6.876) ➡	-7.5929
4	+0.333*52 ➡	=0.333*52 ➡	17.316

Similarly, entering **dates** (especially multiple dates) into your worksheet cells can be made easier/faster by following these exemplary patterns:

	A	B	C
	Your DATE entry	After pressing ENTER key	Result (displayed in formula bar)
2	9-3 ➡	09/03/2021 ➡	09-Mar-21
3	10-10-2010 ➡	10/10/2010 ➡	10-Oct-10
4	8-15 ➡	01/08/2015 ➡	01-Aug-15
5	12-21 ➡	21/12/2021 ➡	21-Dec-21

Just make sure that you get values you intended to enter. Please note that you must format cells in *column C* to your own formatting pattern. I've used my custom date format: **dd-mmm-yy**.

Wonders of Excel: FILL HANDLE

As you probably know, Excel **Fill Handle** is located at the bottom right of any active cell or the bottom right cell of a selected range. It's a quite **small** black square visible in this snip:

Small it is, but it's very important to know how to utilize it, as it can be really helpful in eliminating lots of manual typing and saving time in working with data entry... and much more than this. It can be used for filling any range of cells with increments of any choice you want to select.

To utilize the Fill Handle, first you need to fill one or more cells with values (numbers or text, incl. dates and other custom lists). **Hover** your mouse pointer over the small square until it changes to a small black cross, then you have couple of choices: you can left-click, right-click or double-click (in some situations); **click and drag** the mouse in the direction you want to fill up the range of cells with series or custom lists that follow your pre-defined pattern.

In simple cases the pattern can be defined with just two numbers or two text entries. In case of more complex patterns, you may need to enter values in three or even more cells to define your pattern.

Custom patterns, like days of the week or months are identified even with just one entry (e.g., Mon, Feb).

All patterns are auto-filled with some increments (or decrements). E.g., pattern *1, 3* will continue filling up with 5, 7, 9, etc.; pattern ***Jan, Mar*** will continue filling up with May, Jul, Sep, etc. You can use e.g., a weekly increment (*28-Mar-22, 04-Apr-22*) to fill your list of dates with consecutive Mondays only, as illustrated here:

	Dates
1	**Dates**
2	28-Mar-22
3	04-Apr-22
4	11-Apr-22
5	18-Apr-22
6	25-Apr-22
7	02-May-22
8	09-May-22
9	16-May-22
10	23-May-22
11	30-May-22

But there is more to it. What if you define your pattern using values entered in ***three*** cells, and what if the values are not in incremental or decremental order? Here are just three examples of such patterns (cells with yellow fills), defined randomly:

A	B Rand3_1	C Step	D	E Rand3_2	F Step	G	H Rand3_3	I Step
n1	4			2.7			6	
n2	6	2		3	0.3		4.5	-1.5
n3	9	3		2	-1		8	3.5
n4	11.33333	2.33333		1.86667	-0.13333		8.16667	0.16667
	13.83333	2.5		1.51667	-0.35		9.16667	1
	16.33333	2.5		1.16667	-0.35		10.16667	1
	18.83333	2.5		0.81667	-0.35		11.16667	1
	21.33333	2.5		0.46667	-0.35		12.16667	1
	23.83333	2.5		0.11667	-0.35		13.16667	1
n4	11.33333			1.86667			8.16667	
Step >n4	2.5			-0.35			1	

Look at the fragments of series located below them, and the increments/decrements shown to the right of them. It doesn't matter, how the numbers in the patterns vary - increase or decrease, linearly or not - all the subsequent numbers - *with exception of n4* - created by the patterns increase/decrease **linearly** and in **specific steps** (increments/decrements) predetermined by each of the patterns.

In all instances of these 3-number patterns we can determine the value directly following the pattern (i.e., **n4**) using the following formula:

$$n4 = n3 + SUM(n1{:}n3) / 3 - n1$$

where n1, n2, n3 are consecutive numbers of the specific pattern.
And the value of the increment/decrement (**step**) can be determined using this simple formula:

$$step = 0.5 *(n3 - n1)$$

Just couple of the "wonders" possible with using that *small* Fill Handle.

Using Drop-down Lists for Data Entry

This is an excellent helper for data entry in Excel. When we create worksheets with tables of data or databases, in many cases there are text entries, expressions or phrases that we need to enter repeatedly many times. In such situations we can create lists of entries, like people names, phone numbers, cities, days of the week, months, whatever is included in tables, and then create drop-down lists based on the entries. Later, instead of typing the entries one by one in our table we just select the entries from the drop-down list.

Here is an example, based on the list of fruits. Follow the steps below to create the list.

First, create (somewhere in the vicinity of your planned table, e.g., in the $X$1:$X$24 range) the list of potential entries and sort them A to Z for easy selection. Create table by selecting the range of listed values and pressing **CTRL+T**:

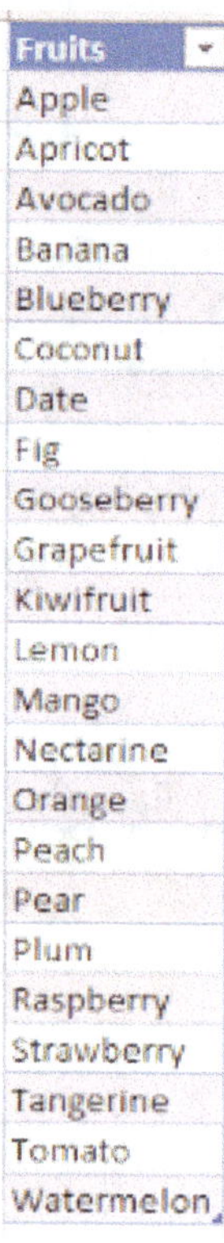

Select the first data cell in your table column designated for the names of fruits, e.g., cell **C2**, and click **Data** tab on the ribbon, then select **Validation>Settings>Allow>List>Source: $X$2:$X$24** . Click OK.

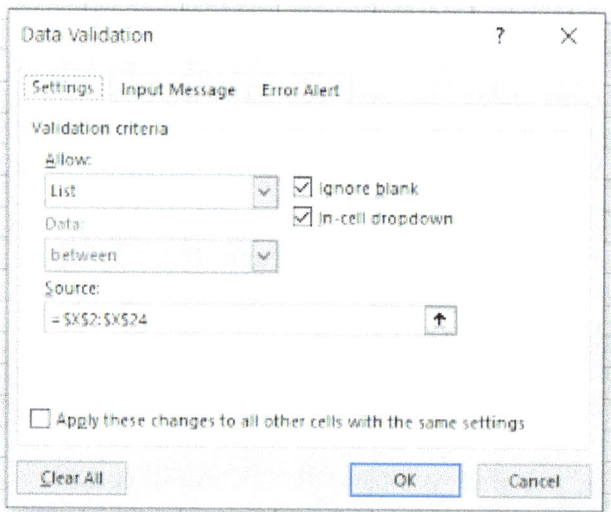

Your drop-down list is created in the cell **C2**. Now extend (copy) the **C2** selection down the column as far as you expect your table size will need. From now on you won't need to type any entry in the column; you'll just select appropriate item from the list.

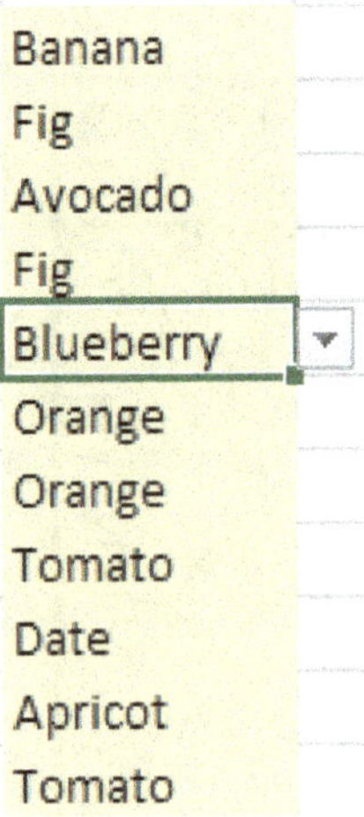

There is one small problem with this approach. The standard Excel drop-down list size is limited to eight lines. What if your list contains more entries? You have to use a vertical scroll bar to select items listed below the eight's line. This isn't convenient and takes additional time, so we need to find a remedy for that inconvenience.

To display more than eight lines in the drop-down list we can use a *Combo Box* from *Form Controls*. Click on **Developer** tab in the ribbon, then select **Insert>Form Controls>Combo Box**. While pressing **ALT** key (in order to fit the box into the cell size) draw a Combo Box in cell **C2** (in our example).

Right-click on the box and select **Format Control>Control>Input Range**, and then:

enter the range with your values to be displayed (**$X$2:$X$24** in our case) in the drop-down list, and enter also the number of lines you want to display in the drop-down list (**23** in our case) in the **'Drop down lines'** box, as shown below. Click OK.

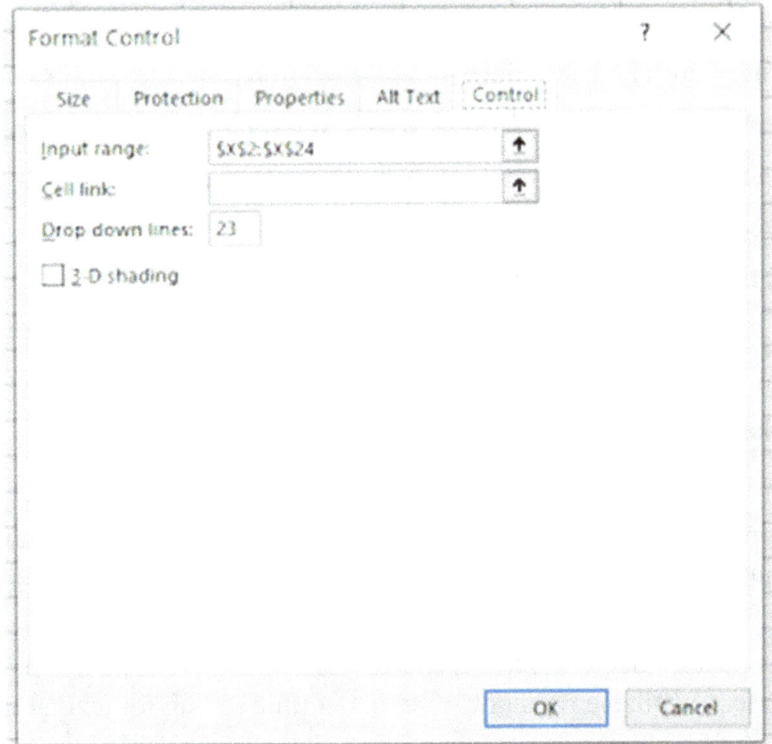

Now extend (copy) the **C2** selection down the column as originally intended above. From now on you will see the whole list of fruits for selection in cells beneath cell C2. You'll just select appropriate item from the list without any scrolling.

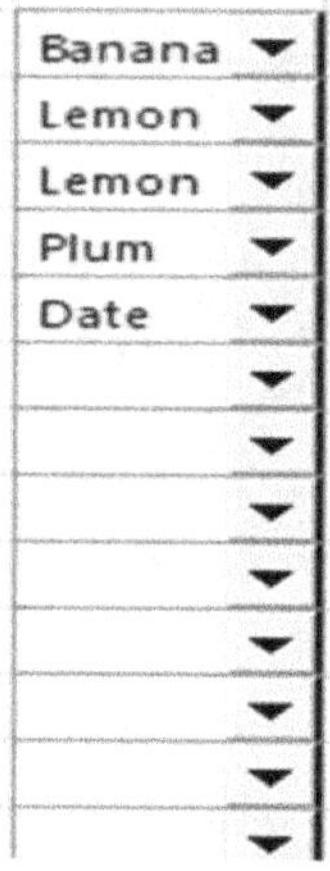

This way you can prepare and use drop-down lists for any column in your table, wherever you need to enter the same text in some of the cells; without the limitation to eight lines.

More on Data Entry

There are plenty of **shortcuts** provided in Excel program for data entry. Their purpose is twofold:

- to reduce data entry time, and
- to reduce data entry mistakes, to avoid errors

I don't think that average Excel user can remember or need to use all of them. However, several of those shortcuts are helpful for almost all users and are worth remembering.

Here is my very short list of shortcuts for data entry and basic editing.

Press **CTRL** key together with:

; (semicolon) - to insert current date

: (colon)   - to insert current time (*need to use SHIFT key simultaneously to use* <u>colon</u>)

" (quotation mark) or letter **d** - to copy the cell from above the active cell

c - to copy the selection

r - to copy the cell from the left of the active cell

v - to paste the recent selection

x - to cut the selection

y or press function key **F4**   - to repeat the last action, *e.g., format a cell, copy cell value, etc.*

z - to cut the selection

By the way, if it happens that you enter lots of textual data in Excel or Word, I'd recommend installing and utilizing on your computer or laptop the **"PhraseExpress"** or **"Wordtune"** software that you can download and use.

They are excellent data entry helpers, text expanders and proofing/autocorrecting tools. Probably the best kind of 'shortcut' available right now in terms of time saving for textual data entry people. You can type long blocks of text with just a few keystrokes. It's available for both Windows and Mac users. Try it for yourself in Excel or Word etc.

Calculating an AVERAGE of Values Between Any Two Dates

You've created a table which contains a column with dates. Now you need to do some calculations on numeric data included between some two selected dates. E.g., you want to calculate average of some 'Output' numbers falling within one month, December 2021, like in this example:

	A	B	C	D	E
1	Date	Output		Start Date	End Date
2	27/11/2021	700		01/12/2021	31/12/2021
3	13/10/2021	1103			
4	04/12/2021	1101			
5	30/10/2021	698			
6	07/01/2022	649			
7	02/12/2021	345			
8	08/11/2021	520			
9	03/12/2021	349			
10	11/12/2021	427			
11	06/12/2021	353			
12	12/11/2021	959			
13	23/10/2021	1191			
14	28/09/2021	403			
15	21/10/2021	800			
16	08/12/2021	553			
17	12/12/2021	1195			
18	13/12/2021	578			
19	01/01/2022	476			
20	16/11/2021	861			
21	05/01/2022	784			
22					
23		612.625		Result using sorted dates	
24		612.625		Result using the formula	

If your table is **sorted** by the 'Date' column, the simplest way to get your average 'Output' is as follows:

- select the range in the 'Output' column falling between the two dates ('*Start Date*' and '*End Date*'),
- in the **Status Bar** at the bottom of your worksheet you'll see, among others, the **Average** value displayed; click on it, and then
- if you want to save it for later use, select any empty cell and **Paste** (using *CTRL+V* shortcut) that Average value there.

If the table is **NOT sorted** by the 'Date' column, you can use the following formula to get the same result:

=SUMPRODUCT((A2:A21>=D2)*(A2:A21<=E2)*(B2:B21)/(COUNTIFS(A2:A21,">=01/12/2021",A2:A21,"<=31/12/2021")))

This is an example formula only, so you need to edit it, to reflect the ranges and the Start and End Dates applicable to your table and your specific purpose.

Hiding/Unhiding Sheets in a Workbook

The number of sheets in a workbook is limited by your available computer memory only. So, in some cases you may have to work on projects that include a very high number of sheets, e.g., for some weekly routine testing and analysis of data. In such cases you don't need to see and access most of the sheets. You'd rather like to remove them from the scroll bar to make selections easier and faster. This is normally not necessary if you're dealing with just several sheets. You can simply right-click on any of the tabs and hide it. But **what if you have e.g., 100 or more sheets in your workbook?** It would be better to automate the task of hiding and unhiding most of them.

Here's an example how the scroll bar with sheet tabs would look like before showing all the sheets/tabs and after hiding unnecessary tabs:

Bar with unhidden tabs

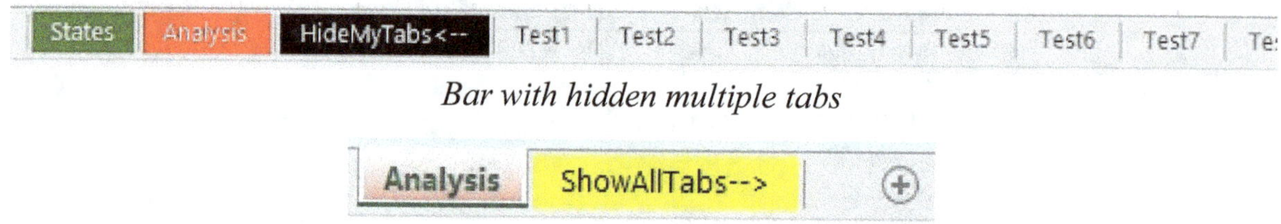

Bar with hidden multiple tabs

The following steps will guide you through the procedure of creating such a result for your project.

- Start with adding a new sheet in your multi-tab workbook. I named it **"Views"** in my workbook. It will remain empty, serving just as a *button tab*. I click on the tab of this sheet (renamed within my macro to either **"HideMyTabs←"** or **"ShowAllTabs→"**) to *hide* or *unhide* designated tabs/sheets.

- First, hide all the cells in the sheet by clicking on the **Select All** (small box with triangle) at the upper-left corner of the sheet, right-clicking on the sheet and selecting **Hide** in drop-down options.

- Add the following VBA code to its Worksheet Activate event. Do this by using **ALT+F11** shortcut, then opening **Project Explorer** in the **View** menu and selecting the newly created sheet in the list of your workbook objects. Double-click the sheet to bring a blank window for the sheet code. Paste this code into that window:

```
Private Sub Worksheet_Activate()
'Code to be entered for 'Views' worksheet in VB editor
Dim wsh As Worksheet
Application.ScreenUpdating = False
If Views.Name = "ShowAllTabs→" Then
        'Unhide all tabs
        For Each wsh In ThisWorkbook.Sheets
                wsh.Visible = xlSheetVisible
        Next wsh
        Views.Name = "HideMyTabs←"
        Sheets("HideMyTabs←").Tab.ColorIndex = 1     'black
        'Tab you want to see after the hidden sheets are unhidden
        Sheet11.Activate
Else
        'Hide all tabs except those you need to see
        For Each wsh In ThisWorkbook.Sheets
                If (wsh.Name <> Analysis.Name And wsh.Name <> Views.Name) Then
                        wsh.Visible = xlSheetVeryHidden
                End If
        Next wsh
        Views.Name = "ShowAllTabs→"
        Sheets("ShowAllTabs→").Tab.ColorIndex = 6   'yellow
        'Tab you want to see after the sheets become hidden
        Analysis.Activate
```

End If
Application.ScreenUpdating = True
End Sub

- This code must be edited for your needs because the names of sheets I've used refer to *my* specific workbook. You need to replace e.g., the names **Views**, **Sheet11**, and **Analysis**, so that the names refer to the sheets in *your* workbook. You may need to add some more names, as needed. The image below - related to my project - may give you a better idea how to apply necessary changes (especially regarding *Names*) in **Properties** window related to the created "button" sheet (*"Views"* in my case).

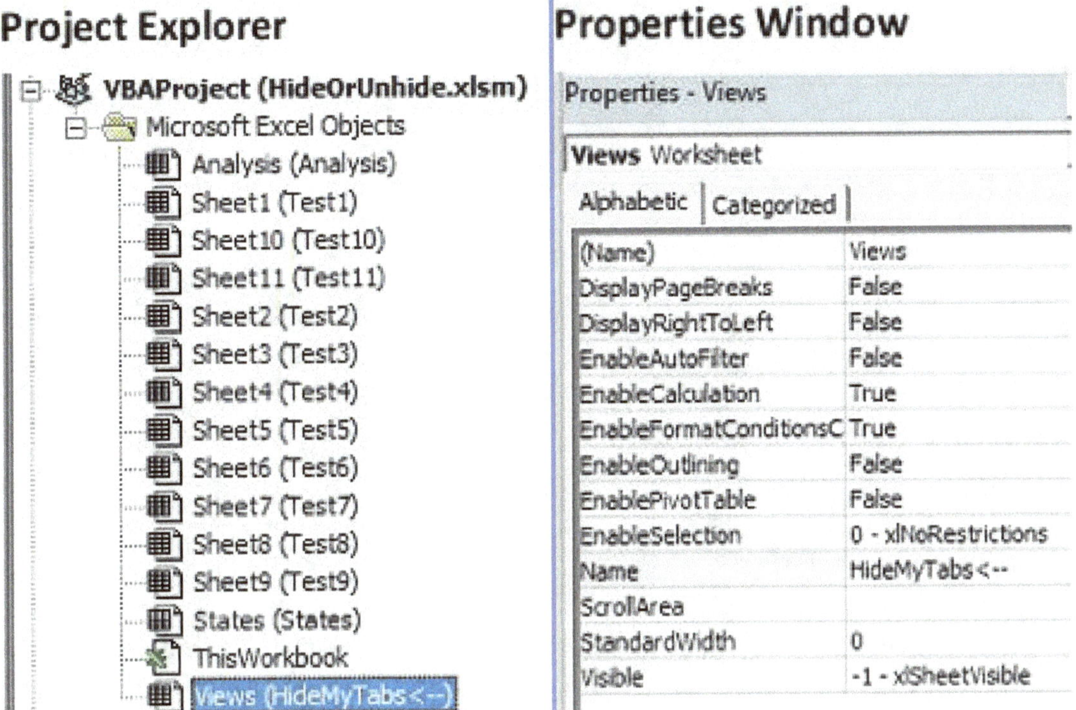

- Select those of your sheets that you want to stay visible while the rest is hidden. Customize the VBA code to display maybe more than two tabs/sheets, but keep showing only the most frequently used sheets. I'm providing here just one simple example. You can build on it and make even more customization according to your specific project.

You can go now back to your workbook main window and test if everything works as you expected.

Template for Basic Data Summary/Analysis

If you have collected and organized some data in table(s) or list(s), the first thing you might need to do could be to get quick general analysis/evaluation of that data - before going any further with some math, statistical or graphic analysis.

The following example provides easy solution, kind of a template, for that preliminary summary and basic analysis.

Here's just illustrative table of random data. Let's say you want to know "everything" about this set of values.

	colB	colC	colD	colE	colF	colG	colH
1	Named ranges			tabA			
3	6	0.1	311	50	-16	220	-51
4	58	13	45	-35	-119	-58	-78
5	71	75	77	-154	78	-83	10
6	16	49	78	-71	-175	-194	-12
7	49	51	rrr	-62	69	97	-54
8	64	17	59	-45	-33.3	-25	-76
9	-73	-8	2.8	63	69	-36	-47
10	-93	97	61	-57	13	67	-14
11	10.32	44	19	61	22	47	33
12	-64	-14	48	39	70	0	-14
13	76	-10	81	0	71	69	-89
14	183	45	77	73	73	17	49
15		90	-15	68	29	23	24
16	293	-37	yyy	78	77	22	3
17	166	-25	-12	0.6	0.1	35	20
18	-31	-70	-40	8	75	56	5
19	277	85	-12	0.8	sss	47	-36
20	186	-99	62	69	19	60	59
21	201	-37	-78	47	0.5	37	22
22	180	37	-40	72	0.6		38
23	-8.08	-86	96	26	-97	14	33
24	182	36	-93	79	144	-19	70
25	199	12	-68	31	28	156	41
26	115	-73	73	55	265	-22	35
27	-34	-50	87	16	-44.8	41	-28
28	zzz	-80	8	66	-69	35	16
29	55	24	65	48	-16	66	-47
30	60	27	61	39	-7	-2	14
31	14	52	36	87	85	82	7

As you can see, the table (range) is named 'tabA' (using **Formulas-Define Name** in the ribbon). All columns have also Defined Names (colB, colC etc.) for easy referencing, if needed for the analysis.

And here is the **template**, including essentially all relevant **Excel functions** and the **results** based on formulas using those functions, and some **comments** explaining the purpose/meaning of the formulas:

Excel Function / Formula Used	Result	Comment on Use/Return
=AREAS((B3:D14,E15:F22,G2:H8))	3	Note double parentheses for multiple references used here
=AVEDEV(tabA)	55.6801	Average of absolute deviations of data points from their mean
=AVERAGE(tabA)	25.2115	Arithmetic mean of numbers in the range
=AVERAGEA(tabA)	24.7098	Average of the values in the list of specified arguments
=AVERAGEIF(tabA,">0")	63.2562	Average of cells that meet specified criteria
=AVERAGEIFS(tabA,tabA,">0",tabA,"<100")	45.0583	Average of cells that meet specified multiple criteria
=CHOOSE(3,C15,E17,F9,D5,C4)	69	Uses index_num to return one of the listed arguments

Formula	Result	Description
=COLUMN(F3)	6	Column number of the given cell reference
=COLUMNS(B3:H3)	7	Number of columns in the reference or an array
=COUNT(tabA)	197	Number of cells containing numbers in the range
=COUNTA(tabA)	201	Number of cells that are not empty in the specified range
=COUNTBLANK(tabA)	2	Number of empty cells in the specified range
=COUNTIF(tabA,">0")	132	Number of cells meeting a criterion (e.g., numbers-0)
=COUNTIF(tabA,"*")	4	Number of cells meeting a criterion (e.g., containing text)
=COUNTIFS(tabA,"<0",tabA,">-15")	11	Count of numbers or dates based on multiple conditions
=COVAR(colB,colD)	-3174.5389	Covariance; determines relationship between 2 data sets
=COVARIANCE.P(colC,colF)	-676.4893	Covariance; determines relationship between 2 data sets
=COVARIANCE.S(colE,colH)	1052.4810	Covariance; determines relationship between 2 data sets
=FORMULATEXT(E9)	=7*9	Formula from the specified cell returned as a string
=KURT(tabA)	2.2227	Kurtosis; relative peakedness/ flatness of the data set
=LARGE(tabA,10)	182	k-th largest value in the specified data set (k=10 here)
=MAX(tabA)	311	Largest value in the specified set of values
=MAXA(tabA)	311	Largest value in the specified list of arguments
=MAXIFS(tabA,tabA,"<11.5",tabA,">0")	10.32	Maximum value meeting given criteria/conditions
=MEDIAN(tabA)	24	Number located in the middle of the set/range of numbers
=MIN(tabA)	-194	Smallest number in the specified set of values
=MINA(tabA)	-194	Smallest value in the specified list of arguments

=MINIFS(tabA,tabA,"<-20",tabA,">-100")	-99	Minimum value among cells, specified by set of criteria
=MODE(tabA)	-78	Most frequently occurring value in specified range of data
=MODE.MULT(tabA)	-78	On multiple modes returns multiple results; array formula(!)
=MODE.SNGL(tabA)	-78	Most frequently occurring value in specified range of data
=PERCENTILE(tabA,0.05)	-83.6	k-th percentile in the specified data set (k=0.05 here)
=PERCENTILE.EXC(tabA,0.05)	-86.3	k-th percentile in the specified data set, exclusive
=PERCENTILE.INC(tabA,0.05)	-83.6	k-th percentile in the specified data set, inclusive
=PERCENTRANK(tabA,65)	0.75	Rank of specified value in dataset as %-age of the set
=QUARTILE(tabA,3)	65	Finds 0,25,50,75,100 % (0,1,2,3 or 4) quartile value
=QUARTILE.EXC(tabA,3)	65.5	Finds the quartile value of dataset range, exclusive
=QUARTILE.INC(tabA,3)	65	Finds the quartile value of dataset range, inclusive
=RANK(B7,tabA)	68	Rank (size) of a number in a range of cells
=RANK.AVG(E10,tabA)	171	Average rank, if more than one value has the same rank
=RANK.EQ(G9,tabA)	158	The top rank, if more than one value has the same rank
=ROW(D23)	23	Row number of the referenced cell
=ROWS(B19:B33)	15	Number of rows in the specified reference/array
=SMALL(tabA,23)	-68	k-th smallest value in the specified data set (k=23 here)
=STDEV(tabA)	76.6950	Estimate of standard deviation based on specified sample
=STDEV.P(tabA)	76.5001	Standard deviation based on population (ignores text)
=STDEV.S(tabA)	76.6950	Estimate of std deviation based on sample (ignores text)

=STDEVA(tabA)	76.0062	Estimate of std deviation based on sample of values
=STDEVP(tabA)	76.5001	Standard deviation based on population (ignores text)
=STDEVPA(tabA)	75.8169	Standard deviation based on population (includes text)
=SUM(tabA)	4966.66	Sum of cell values in specified range/references
=SUMIF(tabA,"-5")	8336.32	Sum of cell values meeting the criteria in specified range
=SUMIFS(tabA,tabA,">'=60",tabA,"<'=70")	1171	Sum of cell values meeting multiple criteria in spec range
=SUMPRODUCT(F:F,G:G)	47352.5	Sum of the products of two corresponding ranges/arrays
=SUMSQ(tabA)	1278113.71	Sum of the squares of numbers in specified range
=TRIMMEAN(tabA,0.6)	25.3765	The mean of the interior of dataset (trimmed by % fraction
=VAR(tabA)	5882.1270	Variance based on sample (specified range of data)
=VAR.P(tabA)	5852.2685	Variance based on entire population (ignores text)
=VAR.S(tabA)	5882.1270	Variance based on sample (ignores text)
=VARA(tabA)	5776.9439	Variance estimated based on the sample
=VARP(tabA)	5852.2685	Variance based on the entire population (specified range)
=VARPA(tabA)	5748.2029	Variance based on the entire population

The table content can be copied/entered into your worksheet and used as a template for your specific analytical needs. To utilize it, all you need to do is to **Define Name of the range** that your data set covers (*and Names of table columns, too, if needed*), and eventually replace 'tabA' name with your own favourite one. No other major modifications are needed, unless you want to use different options supported by some of the functions, or different cell addresses used in some of the formulas.

Working with Excel Tables

Excel Tables are one of those basic, most useful features used for data recording and analysis. Excel makes its tables smarter, more versatile, cognitive, and easy to use all the time.

However, if you spend lots of your time working with Excel tables it's worth to remember all the keyboard and mouse *shortcuts* available for tables. They help to use the tables more efficiently and save some time. Here is my collection of the most frequently used **keyboard** and **mouse** shortcuts for use with tables:

Action ↓ Shortcut →	Using **Keyboard** press	Using **Mouse** select/click in the ribbon
Create Excel table (display dialog box)	CTRL+T or CTRL+L	Click on **Insert** > **Table**
Select table row	SHIFT+SPACEBAR	Hover cursor near the row left border until you see →, and click.
Select table column	CTRL+SPACEBAR	Hover over the column's header until you see ↓, and click. Double-click to select also the header.
Select table data (press twice to include headers)	CTRL+A	Select any cell in your table and hover over any header until crosshair (✛) symbol appears, and click.
Insert table row(s) or column(s)	CTRL++	Select row(s) or column(s), then select **Insert > Insert Table Rows Above** or **Columns to the Right/Left**.
Delete table row(s) or column(s)	CTRL+-	Select row(s) or column(s), then select **Delete > Delete Table Rows/Columns**.
Activate Sort & Filter menu (select header first)	ALT+▼	With a selection in your table, click on **Sort & Filter** in the ribbon.
Toggle Autofilter (On/Off)	CTRL+SHIFT+L	With a selection in your table, click on **Sort & Filter > Filter**.
Resize width of column(s) (select columns first)	ALT+H+O+I	With selected column(s) click on **Format > AutoFit Column Width**.
Bring up menu of table formatting options	ALT+H+T	With a selection in your table, click on **Table Tools** above the ribbon.
Toggle the Total Row of the table (On/Off)	CTRL+SHIFT+T	With a selection in your table, click on **Table Tools** (above the ribbon) and turn On/Off **Total Row**.
Bring up PivotTable (and PivotChart Wizard)	ALT+D+P	With a selection in your table, click on **Insert > PivotTable** in the ribbon.
Rename a table (get focus on Table Name box in the ribbon)	ALT+J+T+A	With a selection in your table, click on **Table Tools** above the ribbon and select **Table Name** box at the left side of the ribbon. **Rename** (and **resize**) your table, if needed.
Use Quick Analysis of table data	CTRL+Q	Right-click anywhere in your table and select **Quick Analysis** from displayed dropdown menu, or any other option you need to use.

Essential Statistics on Coronavirus Covid-19

Official news reports on Covid-19 pandemic are sometimes 'fake news'. Tending to be dark and gloomy, hiding the real picture. The real picture, based on records provided by **https://www.worldometers.info/coronavirus/**, tells us that the highest death rate is not in Brazil or India or Mexico, but in Europe, especially in Central Europe, with Hungary leading the way.

I've analysed reported deaths by country, based on the Worldometers information, using Excel functions and charts. Here are my findings, as of 5th May, 2021, illustrating situation in top **20 countries with the highest rate of deaths per 1000 residents**, and 20 countries with low rate of deaths per 1000 residents but above the rate of 0.5. Here's the 2-D Pie of Pie type chart for the countries with the highest rates of deaths:

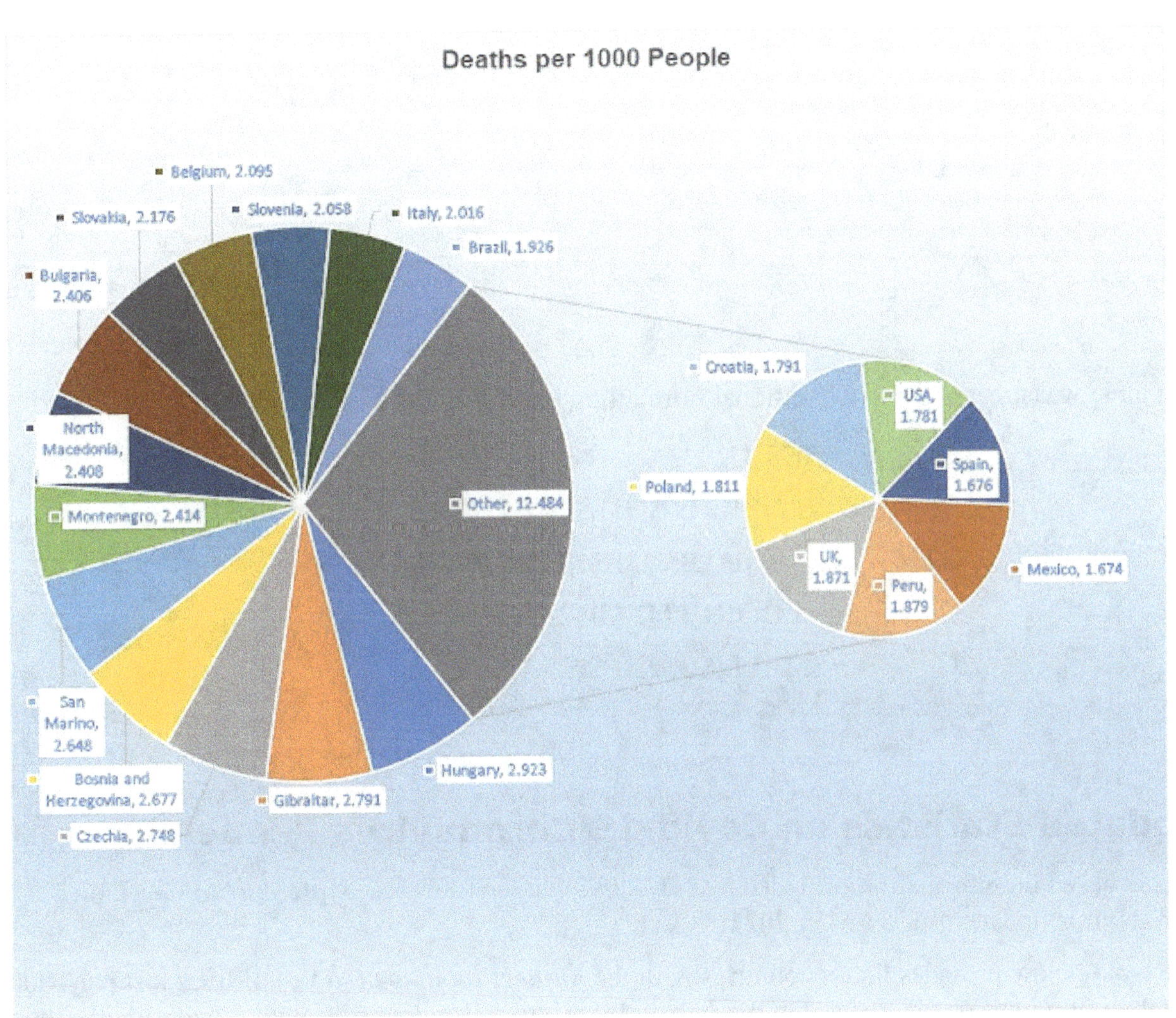

This chart is based on the following data:

	A	B	C	D	E	F	G	H	I	J
	No.	Deaths per 1000 People	Deaths	Country Population	Country	Highest, by Country	Deaths per 1000 People	Position in World	Low, by Country (but >0.50)	Deaths per 1000 People
1										
2	1	1.78	592,456	332,632,623	USA	Hungary	2.9226	1	French Polynesia	0.499518
3	2	0.16	226,720	1,391,382,919	India	Gibraltar	2.79073	2	Bahamas	0.529773
4	3	1.93	411,854	213,827,754	Brazil	Czechia	2.74845	3	Honduras	0.536645
5	4	1.61	105,387	65,394,942	France	Bosnia and Herzegovina	2.67678	4	Eswatini	0.573389
6	5	0.49	41,527	85,099,924	Turkey	San Marino	2.64776	5	Caribbean Netherlands	0.605441
7	6	0.77	111,895	145,987,100	Russia	Montenegro	2.4135	6	Mayotte	0.610838
8	7	1.87	127,570	68,185,535	UK	North Macedonia	2.40772	7	Sint Maarten	0.623787
9	8	2.02	121,738	60,386,998	Italy	Bulgaria	2.40559	8	Wallis and Futuna	0.632168
10	9	1.68	78,399	46,770,012	Spain	Slovakia	2.17618	9	Palestine	0.637838
11	10	1.01	84,457	84,009,107	Germany	Belgium	2.09482	10	Canada	0.641666
12	11	1.43	65,202	45,543,664	Argentina	Slovenia	2.05802	11	Costa Rica	0.64483
13	12	1.47	75,627	51,337,597	Colombia	Italy	2.01596	12	Curaçao	0.674129
14	13	1.81	68,482	37,811,727	Poland	Brazil	1.9261	13	Israel	0.692464
15	14	0.87	73,568	84,893,671	Iran	Peru	1.87891	14	Serbia	0.743937
16	15	1.67	217,740	130,068,544	Mexico	UK	1.87092	15	Russia	0.766472
17	16	1.04	45,077	43,512,338	Ukraine	Poland	1.81113	16	Belize	0.80017
18	17	1.88	62,674	33,356,492	Peru	Croatia	1.79117	17	Monaco	0.810619
19	18	0.17	46,349	275,948,657	Indonesia	USA	1.78111	18	Uruguay	0.821219
20	19	2.75	29,479	10,725,686	Czechia	Spain	1.67627	19	Albania	0.835434
21	20	0.91	54,511	59,935,197	South Africa	Mexico	1.67404	20	Iran	0.86659
22	21	1.00	17,245	17,166,747	Netherlands					

The table was created using Conditional Formatting and formulas listed below:

B2	=1000*C2/D2
F2	=VLOOKUP(G2,$B$2:$E$223,4,FALSE)
G2	=LARGE($B$2:$B$223, ROWS(E$2:E2))
I2	**=VLOOKUP(J2,$B$2:$E$223,4,FALSE)**
J2	=SMALL($B$2:$B$223,150)

Updated Statistics on Covid-19 Coronavirus Pandemic

This is based on information provided by https://www.worldometers.info/coronavirus/ on Coronavirus update as of **31 May 2021**.

The table below provides list of countries with the ***highest number*s** (so far) of lives lost per 1000 people living in those countries. On the right side it shows also countries with a ***low number*** (but not the lowest) of **deaths attributed to the Covid-19**.

I've used one simple formula and the following three Excel functions to produce the table: **VLOOKUP**, **LARGE**, and **SMALL**.

This kind of statistics is not published for some reason (?) in the media. China is, in fact, not covered at all, or... am I missing something? So interesting; the truth, I mean...

Highest, by Country	Deaths per 1000 People	Position in World	Low, by Country (but >0.50)	Deaths per 1000 People
Hungary	3.085	1	Turkey	0.557
Bosnia and Herzegovina	2.836	2	Eswatini	0.575
Czechia	2.807	3	Bahamas	0.577
Gibraltar	2.791	4	Mayotte	0.613
San Marino	2.647	5	Honduras	0.629
North Macedonia	2.598	6	Wallis and Futuna	0.633
Bulgaria	2.559	7	Caribbean Netherlands	0.643
Montenegro	2.522	8	Sint Maarten	0.646
Slovakia	2.260	9	Canada	0.671
Brazil	2.160	10	Palestine	0.671
Belgium	2.143	11	Israel	0.730
Slovenia	2.104	12	Curaçao	0.741
Italy	2.089	13	Costa Rica	0.771
Peru	2.077	14	Serbia	0.789
Croatia	1.966	15	Belize	0.802
Poland	1.950	16	Monaco	0.810
UK	1.873	17	Russia	0.832
USA	1.832	18	Albania	0.853
Colombia	1.718	19	Jordan	0.919
Mexico	1.717	20	South Africa	0.941

The following 2-D Pie of Pie type chart illustrates just the left-hand side of the table.

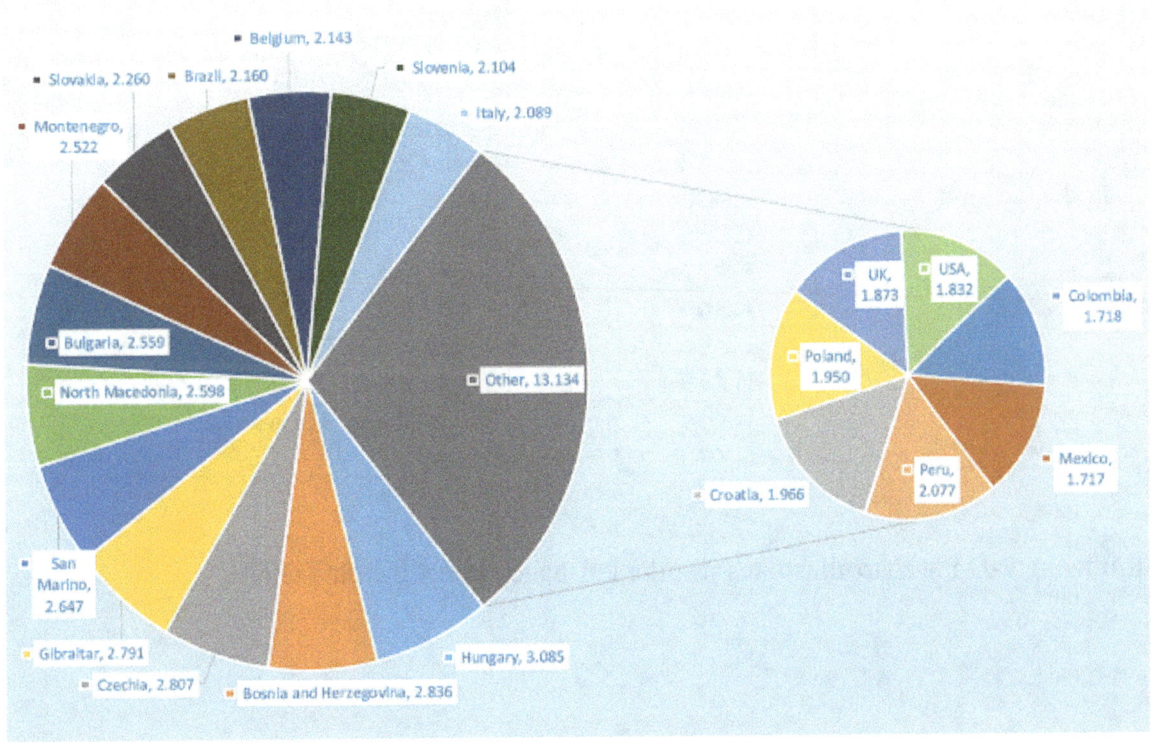

Data Analysis: UPDATE on CoVid-19 Coronavirus Pandemic

Three months later... This is the update of my analysis created previously in May this year.

The following is based on information provided by **https://www.worldometers.info/coronavirus/** as of **29 August 2021**.

The table below provides list of countries with the ***highest number*** (so far) of lives lost per 1000 people living in those countries. On the right side it shows also countries with a ***low number*** (but not the lowest) of **deaths attributed to the CoVid-19**.

It looks like there is a striking increase of deaths among Peruvians, and a relatively low number of deaths per 1000 residents in Iraq, among others.

Highest, by Country	Deaths per 1000 people	Position in World	Low, by Country (but >0.50)	Deaths per 1000 people
Peru	5.915	1	Iraq	0.500
Hungary	3.121	2	Turks and Caicos	0.509
Bosnia and Herzegovina	3.004	3	Fiji	0.530
Gibraltar	2.880	4	Bermuda	0.532
Czech Republic	2.833	5	Azerbaijan	0.538
North Macedonia	2.804	6	Channel Islands	0.541
Montenegro	2.725	7	Cabo Verde	0.547
Bulgaria	2.716	8	Kuwait	0.556
Brazil	2.702	9	Saint Lucia	0.558
San Marino	2.646	10	Libya	0.599
Argentina	2.437	11	Mayotte	0.624
Colombia	2.422	12	Caribbean Netherlands	0.641
Slovakia	2.297	13	Guatemala	0.646
Belgium	2.177	14	Turkey	0.655
Paraguay	2.170	15	French Guiana	0.699
Slovenia	2.139	16	Palestine	0.700
Italy	2.138	17	Canada	0.706
Croatia	2.042	18	Israel	0.746
Poland	1.993	19	Guyana	0.770
Mexico	1.976	20	Oman	0.772
United States	1.964	21	Bahrain	0.784
Tunisia	1.954	22	Monaco	0.834
United Kingdom	1.938	23	Serbia	0.834
Chile	1.908	24	Albania	0.866
Georgia	1.822	25	Curaçao	0.867
Romania	1.809	26	Honduras	0.876
Spain	1.796	27	Belize	0.877
Ecuador	1.795	28	Bahamas	0.890
France	1.744	29	Trinidad and Tobago	0.907
Portugal	1.743	30	Eswatini	0.909

The following 2-D Pie chart illustrates just the left-hand side of the data table...

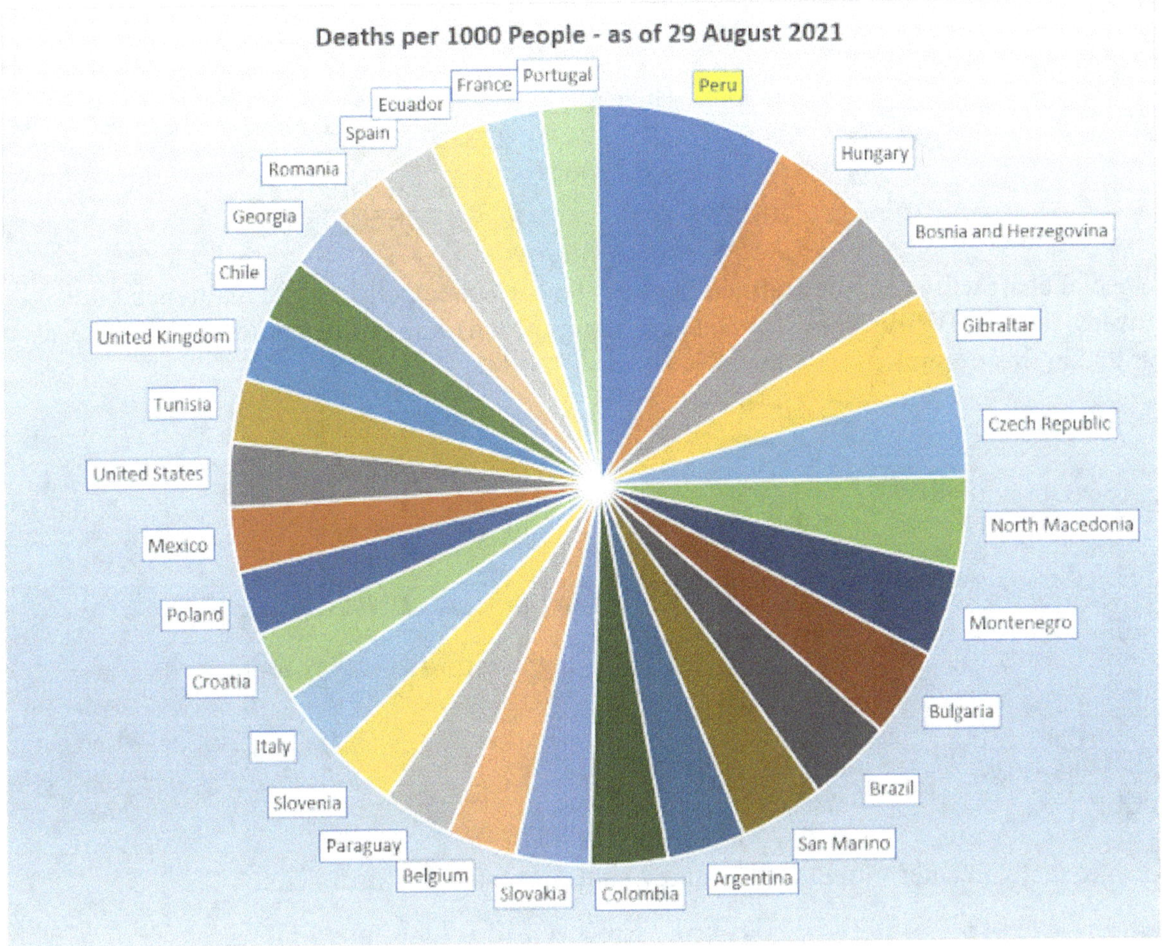

How to Create a 'Slide Show' Using a Single Formula and a Chart

If you want to make use of some **math formulas** for practical applications or just to show off your Excel creativity, you can utilize kind of slide show: i.e., refreshable charts based on some brilliant formula of yours.

Follow these steps:

- Open a new workbook. Enter any two numbers into your worksheet (Sheet1), e.g., 1 in cell A2 and 2 in B2.
- Start with creating a simple **XY scatter** chart based on your entries. This chart is named as "Chart 1".
- Delete the two numbers you've just entered. You don't need them anymore.
- Expand the width of column A to e.g., 200, move there the chart and resize it to the size of your choice.
- In cell D1, type the formula you want to chart, in the format using explicitly normal math signs and functions, e.g., x^2+5*sqrt(x)-3 .
- Enter the low and high limits (of your choice) for the **Left** value and the **Right** value of **x** axis, then also the **Low** and **High** limits for the number of **Points** you want to be plotted, as shown in the example below (cells D3:E5).
- In cells F3:F5, enter **RANDBETWEEN** formulas as shown in the example, cells F3:F5.

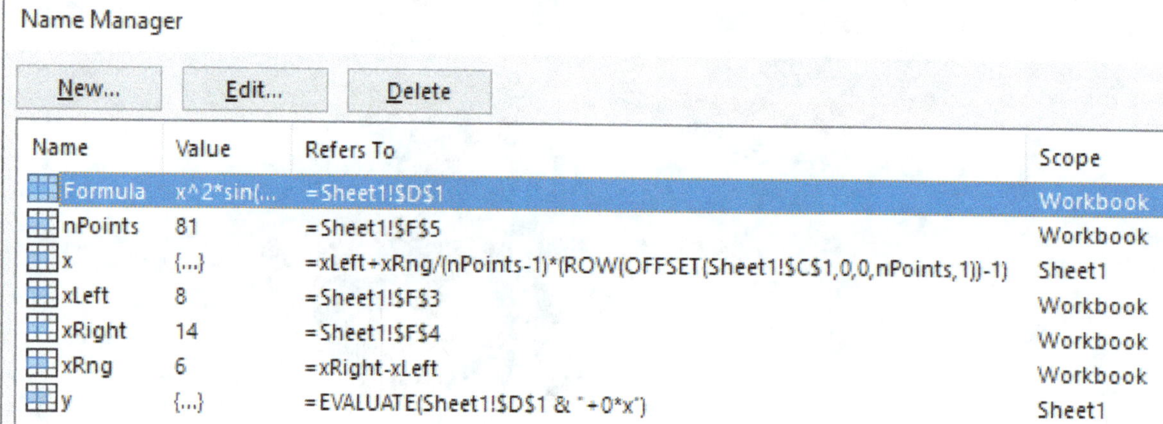

Our special chart will use some **Defined Names**. To enter them, click in the main menu on **Formulas**, then on **Define Name** (in *Defined Names* group), and define names, one by one, as illustrated in this example:

Make sure that you enter formulas for **x** and **y** names exactly as shown here:

=xLeft+xRng/(nPoints-1)*(ROW(OFFSET(Sheet1!$C$1,0,0,nPoints,1))-1)
=EVALUATE(Sheet1!$D$1 & "+0*x")

Click in the formula bar to refresh the chart.

Format Chart Area and Plot Area to your personal satisfaction, including: chart size and properties, fill and border, plot fill and border, etc. To get clear view of plotted points only, you can also delete axis values (both x and y), plot gridlines, and even titles of the axes.

Now, for additional effects, right-click on the **Plot Area** and click on **Change Chart Type...**, to select e.g., **3-D Bubble** type. Click OK.

Your chart is ready. But how can you run the 'slide show' automatically, without having to refresh it manually all the time? Well, for automation we need to employ a macro and a Button to which we will assign the macro.

Here's the macro, you need to copy and paste into a **module** of your VBA Project. To get there, select from menus: **Developer>Visual Basic>View>Project Explorer>Insert>Module**.

```vba
Sub RefreshChart()
'Refreshes Chart in a worksheet at intervals set by TimeValue
Dim i As Integer
Dim Chart As Chart
i = 0
For i = 1 To 1000'Number of chart instances to show
    Range("D1").Select
    ActiveCell.FormulaR1C1 = Range("D1").Value
    Application.Wait (Now + TimeValue("0:00:03"))   'Refresh every 3 seconds
    ActiveSheet.ChartObjects("Chart 1").Activate
    ActiveChart.Refresh
```

Next i
End Sub

The macro refreshes your chart every 3 seconds. You can change both the looping number and the refreshing period according to your specific needs.

Finally, you can add a Form Controls **Button** _or_ ActiveX Control **Command Button** in your worksheet (click on **Developer-Insert**, in **Controls** menu, and select the button). Format it as needed and assign the **_RefreshChart_** macro to it. If you select Command Button, then this code is to be added for the button to work:

Private Sub CommandButton1_Click()
RefreshChart   _'Macro name_
End Sub

If everything is set correctly, you are ready to run your show. Try it with various formulas and settings (limits) and chart types. It can be a good fun.

Don't forget to save the workbook as **macro-enabled** one.

Here's an example view of the 3-D Bubble chart:

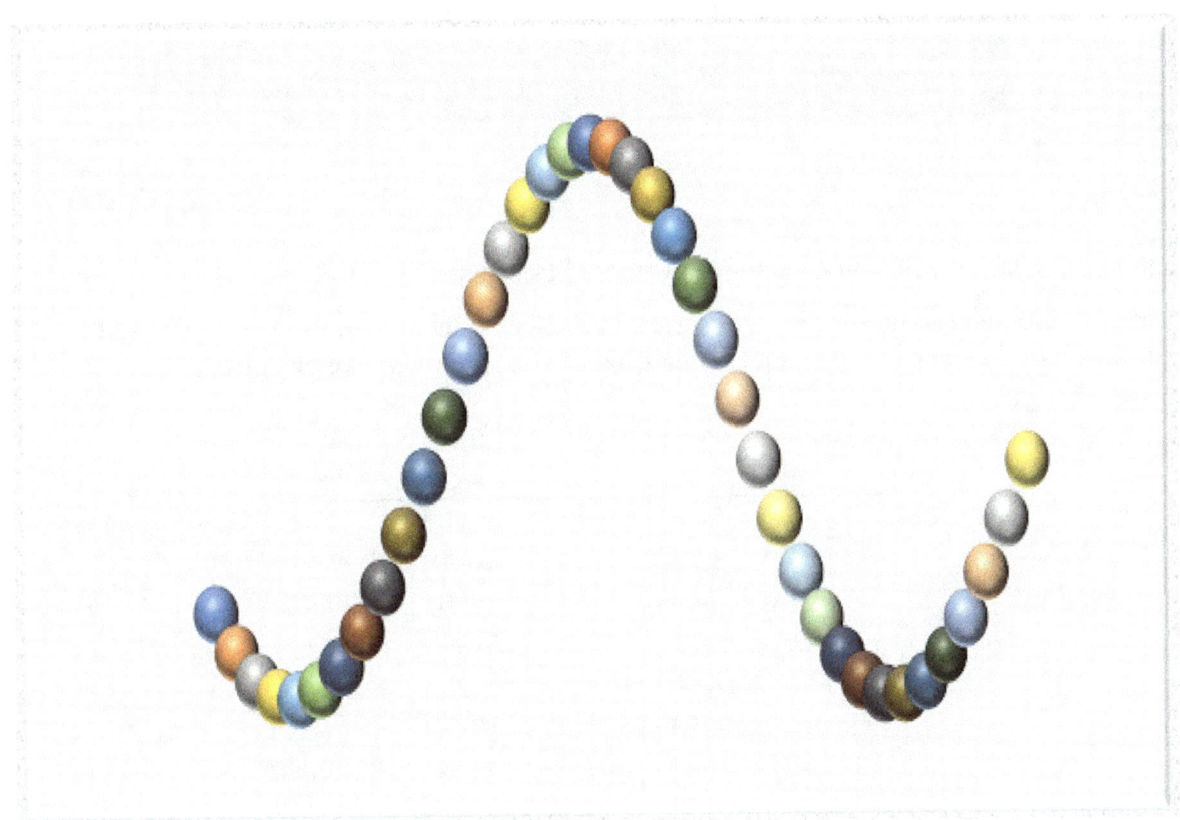

How to Highlight Space Between Two Plotted Curves/Lines

If you want to enhance your Excel charts, to fill with colour some targeted range of your data, this procedure may be helpful.

I'm providing here two examples of such enhanced charts. In addition, I've included procedure for calculation of the surface area bounded by the two curves/lines.

Chart #1

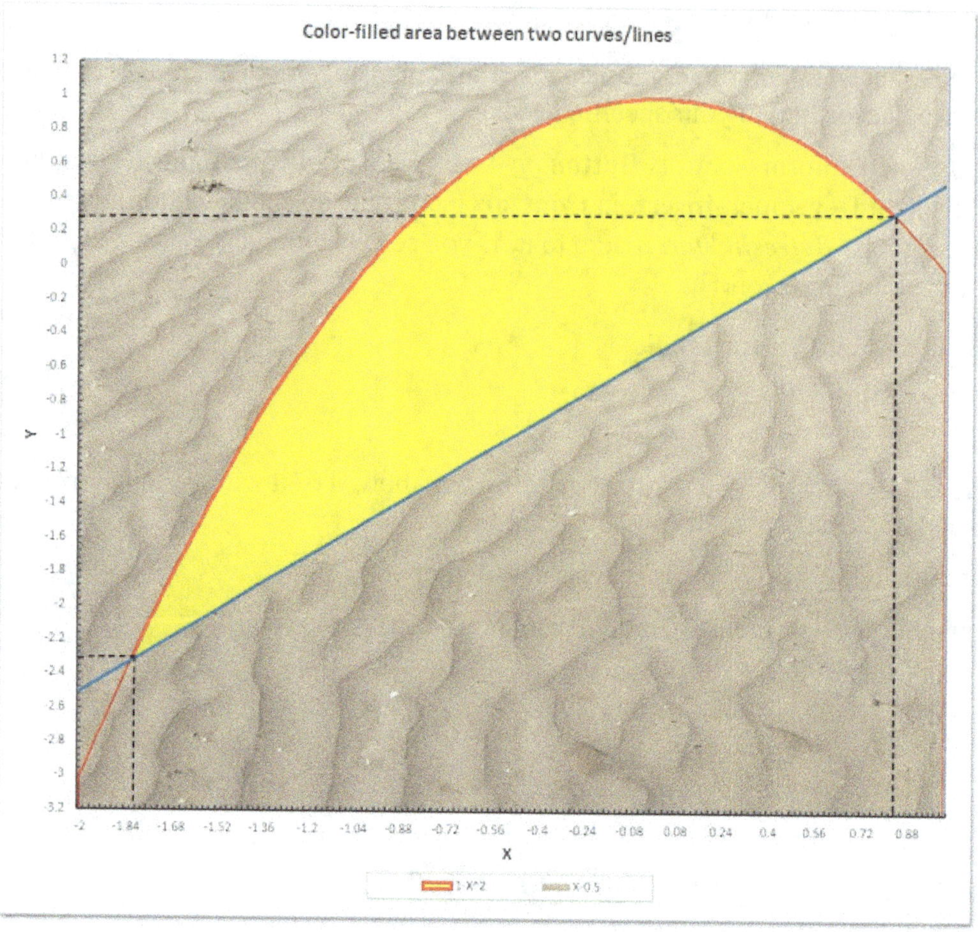

To achieve similar effects, you need to follow these basic steps:

1. Start with producing data for the chart series. I've selected the two lines: $Y = 1 - X^2$ and $Y = X - 0.5$ for the chart and prepared data table consisting of five columns, like this one:

	A	B	C	D	E
1	**X**	**1-X^2**	**X-0.5**	**1-X^2**	**1-X^2-X+0.5**
2	-2	-3	-2.5	-3	-0.5
3	-1.98	-2.9204	-2.48	-2.9204	-0.4404
4	-1.96	-2.8416	-2.46	-2.8416	-0.3816
5	-1.94	-2.7636	-2.44	-2.7636	-0.3236
6	-1.92	-2.6864	-2.42	-2.6864	-0.2664
7	-1.9	-2.61	-2.4	-2.61	-0.21
8	-1.88	-2.5344	-2.38	-2.5344	-0.1544
9	-1.86	-2.4596	-2.36	-2.4596	-0.0996
10	1.84	2.3855	2.34	2.3855	0.0455

Column E lists differences between values of Columns B and C.

2. Select the series for both curves (Columns A to C) and insert the *scatter chart* with smooth lines on your worksheet.

3. Right-click on the chart and select all the data (five Columns) and add the third line based on data in Column E.

4. Select the line representing Column C data. Right-click and select option "***Change Series Chart Type...***" to the ***Combo Stacked Area*** type. Do the same with the curve representing Column E data.

5. Select the curve representing Column B data, and click in the ribbon menu *Format - Shape Fill - No Fill* .

6. Do all the formatting, as you need to, related to the axes, gridlines, chart title, legend, labels, chart area, plot area, etc.

7. Using your algebraic knowledge, calculate coordinates of intersection points for the curves. In this specific case the coordinates are:

- X1 = -1.82288   Y1 = 2.32288
- X2 = 0.82288   Y2 = 0.32288

8. Knowing the coordinates you can calculate e.g., the surface area enveloped between the two curves/lines using the following integral function:

$$\int_{-1.82288}^{0.82288} (-x^2 - x + 1.5)\, dx = \left(-\frac{x^3}{3} - \frac{x^2}{2} + \frac{3}{2} * x\right) \Big|_{-1.82288}^{0.82288} = 0.710022 - (-2.37669) = \mathbf{3.08671}$$

Chart #2

This chart is based on two curves: **Y = X^0.5** and **Y = X^2** and the chart data table, like this one:

	A	B	C	D	E
	X	X^0.5	X^2	X^0.5	X^0.5-X^2
2	0	0	0	0	0
3	0.02	0.141421	0.0004	0.141421	0.1410214
4	0.04	0.2	0.0016	0.2	0.1984
5	0.06	0.244949	0.0036	0.244949	0.241349
6	0.08	0.282843	0.0064	0.282843	0.2764427
7	0.1	0.316228	0.01	0.316228	0.3062278
8	0.12	0.34641	0.0144	0.34641	0.3320102
9	0.14	0.374166	0.0196	0.374166	0.3545657

The coordinates of intersection points for the curves are in this case as follows:

- X1 = 1, Y1 = 1
- X2 = 0, Y2 = 0

And the surface area enveloped between the two curves is calculated using the following integral function:

$$\int_{0}^{1} \sqrt{X} - X^2 \, dx = \left(\frac{2}{3} * X^{\frac{3}{2}} - \frac{1}{3} * X^3 \right) \Big|_{0}^{1} = \frac{1}{3}$$

Simulation of the Arithmetic Mean and Data Normality

The world around us is full of uncertainties. In research, in engineering and sciences, uncertainties must be dealt with in a formalized way, using statistics. We are required to follow procedures for dealing with inevitable variation in routine testing: in laboratory, in production and construction, in relation to quality control and quality assurance issues.

Excel statistical functions help in solving many practical problems in that area, as well as in simulation and estimation of probabilities of certain outcomes. Here I just like to share with you couple of charts based on simulation I've carried out in Excel regarding the critical role of sampling frequency and the number of tested samples in evaluation of various processes and material properties.

The simulation example shown below is based on assumption of normal distribution of sampling and uses two basic statistical functions:

- **RAND()**, which returns evenly distributed random numbers from 0 to 1 (not including 1), and

- **NORM.INV**, which returns the inverse of the normal cumulative distribution for the specified arithmetic mean and standard deviation.

Here is the chart illustrating the effect of the number of tests (samples) on the value of the Mean. The data have been obtained with the formula =**NORM.INV(RAND(),2.60,0.009)**, where **2.60** is the expected arithmetic Mean and **0.009** is Standard Deviation of the population ('targets'). We can see that variability of the **running Mean** is very high up to about 15 tests. Its reliability increases with number of samples and reaches good stability starting at around 50 tests (samples). At the same time the spread of data widens up to about three standard deviations, as can be expected in any normal distribution.

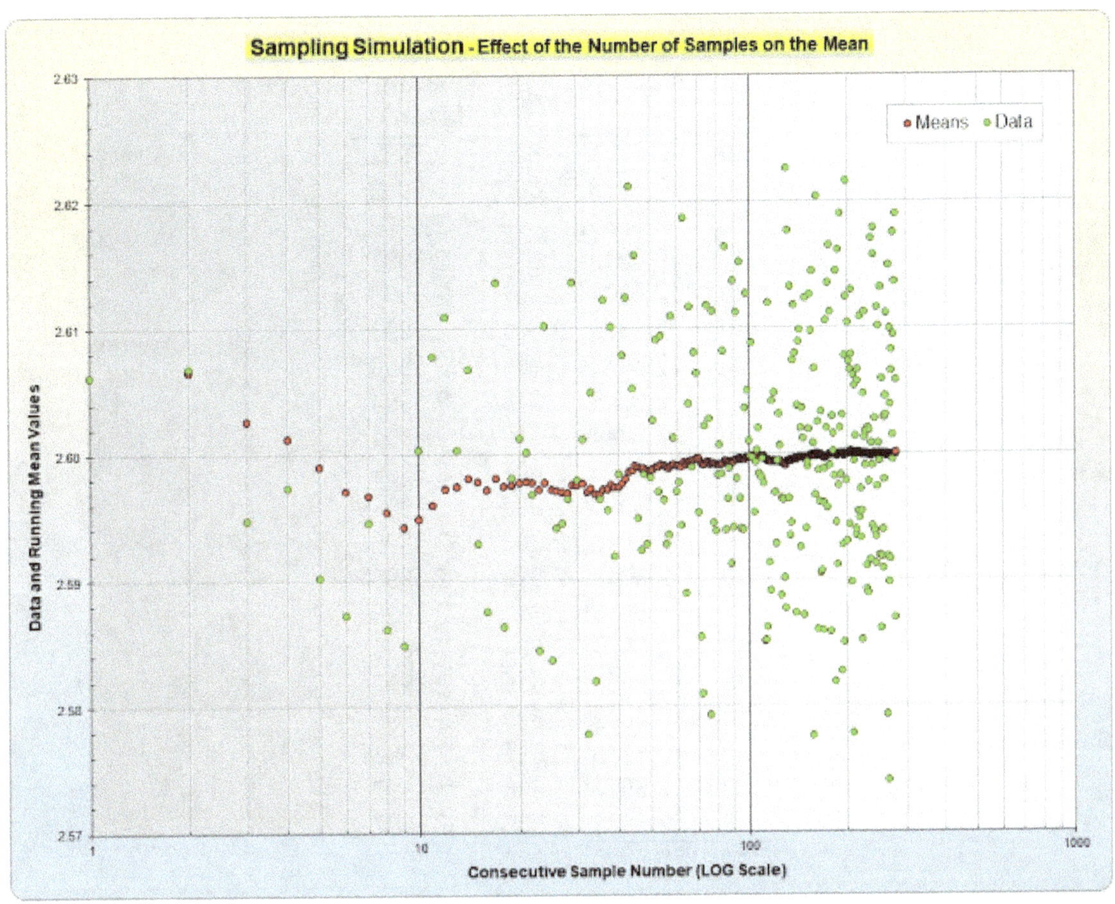

The second chart shows how the Mean of Means varies depending on the number of the Means taken into account. As we can see, 20 samples of the Means of **two** samples spread over wide range (from 2.5842 to 2.6115), while 20 samples of the Means of **10** samples (*shown in the table below*) spread much less (from 2.5949 to 2.6049). High reliability of the Mean of Means (MofM) is again achievable at around 50 'samples'.

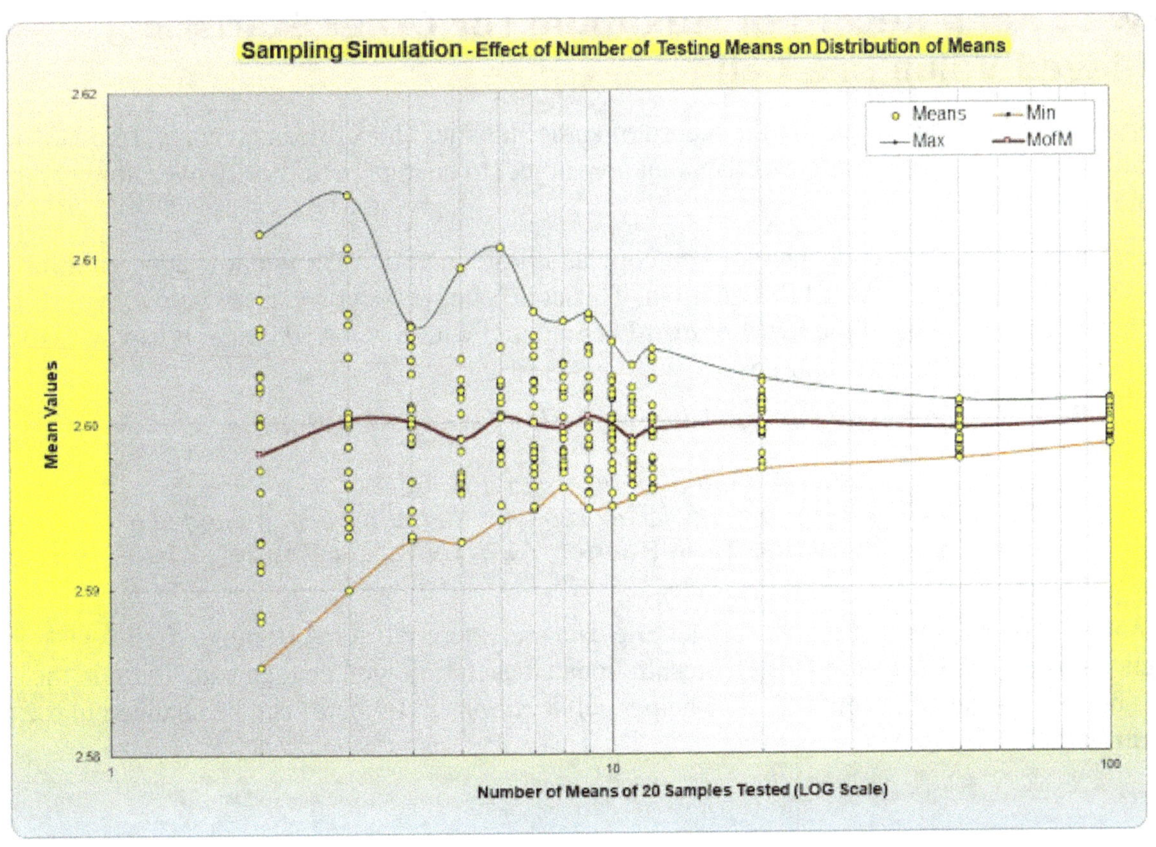

X	Y	Data	Running Mean
10	2.6001	2.602	2.5992
10	2.5983	2.605	2.5992
10	2.5991	2.602	2.5992
10	2.6019	2.612	2.5993
10	2.6004	2.604	2.5993
10	2.5995	2.601	2.5993
10	2.5975	2.590	2.5993
10	2.5949	2.610	2.5994
10	2.6014	2.610	2.5994
10	2.5996	2.607	2.5995
10	2.5993	2.602	2.5995
10	2.6015	2.606	2.5995
10	2.6049	2.599	2.5995
10	2.6016	2.611	2.5996
10	2.6027	2.604	2.5996
10	2.5957	2.615	2.5997
10	2.6002	2.593	2.5997
10	2.5989	2.597	2.5996
10	2.6024	2.608	2.5997
10	2.5971	2.596	2.5997
11	2.6009	2.589	2.5996

It's important to keep in mind these distributions at the time of preparing sampling programs and interpreting the real-world results of testing. There is no **certainty** in testing and evaluation of the results, there is always only **certain** probability of outcome, some level of confidence in conclusion.

How to Keep Record of Maximum (or Other Statistics) Achieved Value in a Cell

If you'd like to keep automatically the record of some statistics (max, mean, average, standard deviation, etc.) related to your set of data that are subject to change periodically over time, then a simple macro can help.

Here is an example VBA code that you can copy and paste in your VBE window appearing for your worksheet after using the **ALT+F11** shortcut. This code sample, as you can see below, will record just the **maximum** value of the **SUM of numbers** entered within A1:A10 range. It can be easily modified for any other special purpose.

```vba
Private Sub Worksheet_SelectionChange(ByVal Target As Range)
Dim myVar As Double
myVar = Range("A11").Value 'Sum of numbers in a range
Range("Z100").Value = myVar   'Replace Z100 with any other cell, if needed
If myVar - Range("A12").Value Then Range("A12").Value = Range("Z100").Value
End Sub
```

As shown in the fragment of my worksheet, the data are entered in A1:A10 range. Cell A11 contains formula **=SUM(A1:A10)**. The result, updated each time you change something in the worksheet, is displayed in cell A12. The helper cell *location* (Z100 here) can be changed in the code at your will.

	A	B
1	84	
2	68	
3	59	
4	52	
5	61	
6	20	
7	21	
8	21	
9	95	
10	70	
11	**551**	Actual **sum of the values** in A1:A10 range
12	**663**	The **Max sum** reached since the first use/event
13		

CHARTS / TOOLS / SPECIAL FEATURES

Radar (Called Also as Spider) Chart in Excel

Excel charts are not for numbers only... While they are not specifically designed for visualizing text entries, they can still be used effectively with some data manipulation and creativity.

	A	B
1	iks	igrek
2	3>;	3<?
3	6@;	5HH
4	6YE	2QS
5	1=4	1W:
6	8KA	8C9
7	8KZ	3WJ
8	0PT	2I8
9	1TZ	8MT
10	8XX	5JT
11	6ZN	1ZV
12	9>N	606
13	7G>	9HK
14	361	9FI
15	3B6	2B0
16	3EB	2BJ
17	9E7	0:C
18	44G	0ZC
19	0B:	06D
20	9RV	2BS
21	3P7	2O6

Here is just an example of the Radar chart type based on the presented sample of data (A2:B20).

This chart, as any other Excel chart, can be formatted, as desired, using the "Design" and "Format" tabs on the Excel ribbon.

You can customize the chart further by right-clicking on the chart and selecting "Format Data Series" or "Format Data Labels" to format axis labels and adjust the colours, fonts, and other properties of the chart elements.

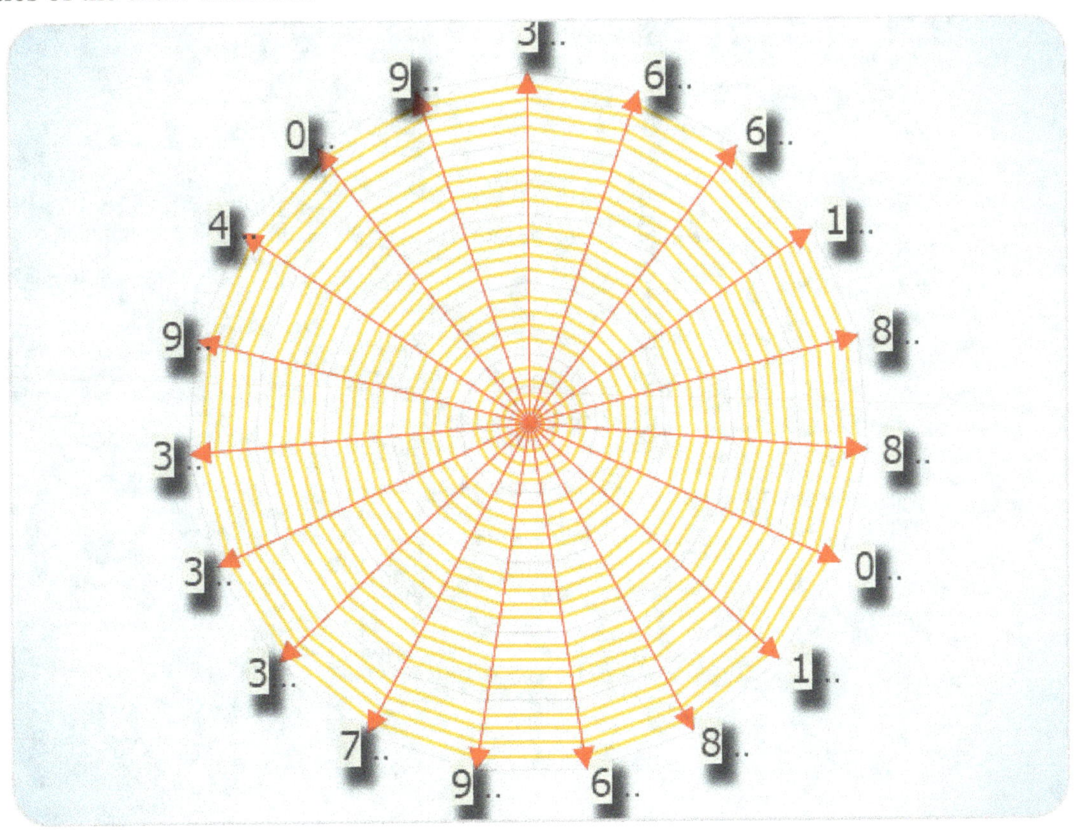

Bubbles in Excel

The Bubble and 3-D Bubble chart types are hidden within XY (Scatter) group of charts.

x	y
7.110861	8.704633
7.467311	4.904414
2.462785	5.918692
8.431328	4.424469
5.503416	0.5195
8.944619	8.248382
8.799255	8.195325
7.01476	3.19884
4.174949	2.879406
7.558052	3.055417
1.873693	9.43091
3.045835	6.881051
4.737993	2.388074
4.08867	4.058055
1.370042	5.684295

The **3-D Bubble charts** presented below are based on the series of randomized data points created with formula: **=RAND()*10**. There are 500 bubbles in each of the charts. Here is shown a small fragment of the data table representing bubble sizes.

The first chart is created with golden-coloured bubbles, with Solid fill, and sizes representing bubble width, while the second chart displays bubbles with Varied Colours and sizes representing bubble area.

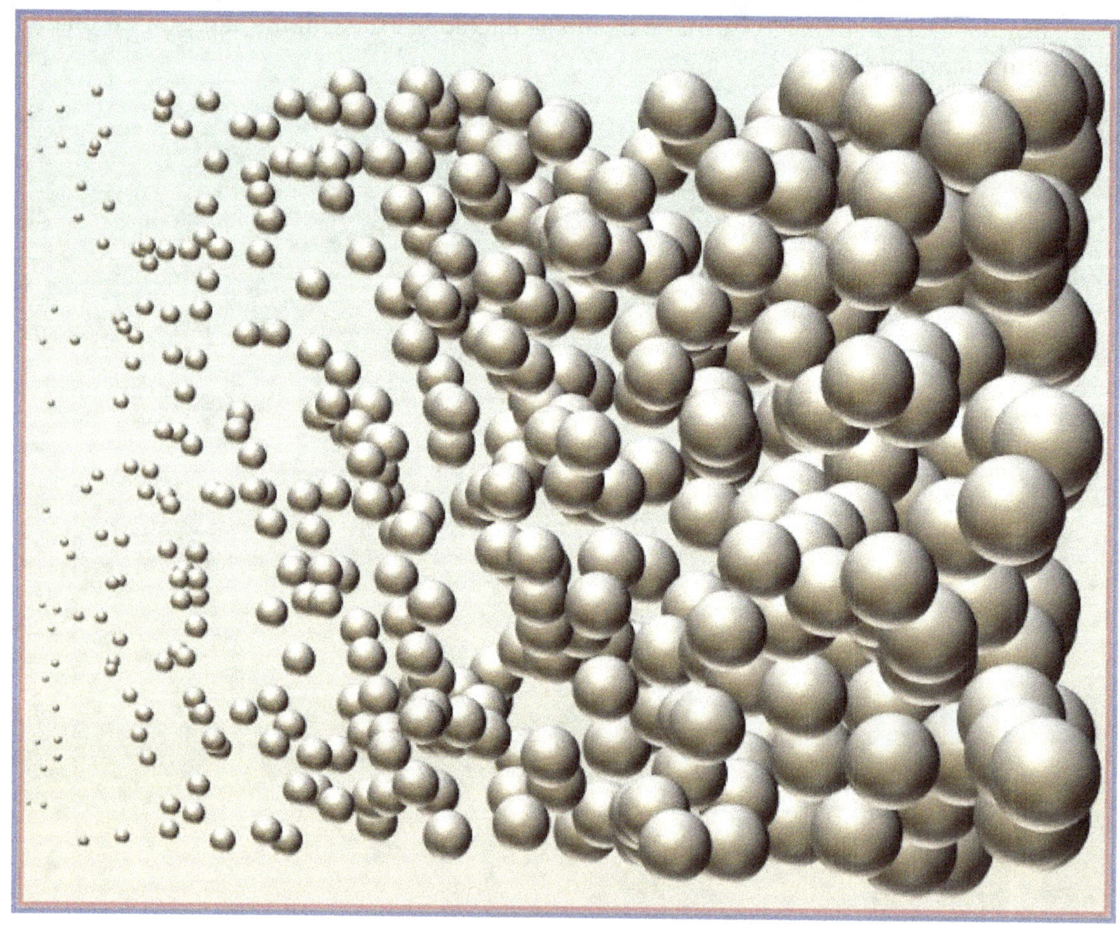

Creating Surface Charts 3D

Surface charts in Excel deserve special attention. They allow to see your data in three dimensions and can be particularly useful in engineering applications (design and control of processes) as well as in the art of drawing and painting.

Typical surface chart shows how the dependent variable (z) behaves as a function of two independent variables (x & y). In other words, the chart illustrates outcome of any nonlinear function involving two variables. E.g., we can plot speed of some technological process (reaction) as a function of pressure and temperature.

Here I'll show how you can prepare a template for creating surface charts based on equations including variety of math functions (algebraic, transcendental, periodic). Such template can be very useful in all kinds of design, as it allows you to visualize plenty of solutions in minutes.

Let's start with just one example of surface chart I've created. This is 3-D plot of equation shown in the title of this chart:

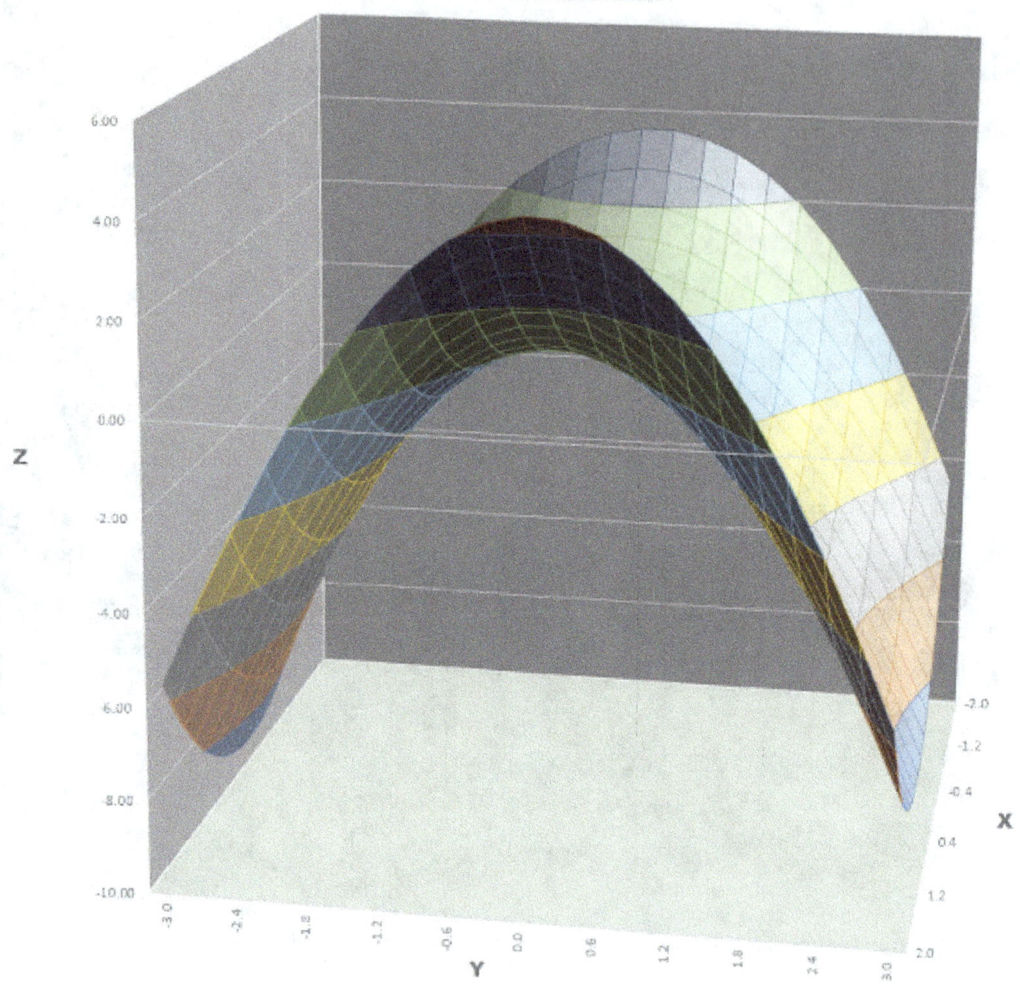

How can you create similar charts based on your own equations?

Here's the way to follow:

- First, create kind of a small table in exactly the same location on your worksheet as shown below. You can enter even the same numbers and equation, to start with.

- Now, manually prepare base for your data table. Enter the following formulas:

- in cell N23: **=A$9**
- in cell N22: **=N23+(B$9-A$9)/$E$9**

Copy cell **N22** to the **N3:N21** range.

Enter the following formulas:

- in cell O2: **=C$9**
- in cell P2: **=O2+($D$9-$C$9)/$E$9**

Copy cell **P2** to **Q2:AI2** range.

The range **O3:AI23** will be filled later with the help of VBA macro. For now, just format the table range to your liking, e.g., as shown in this worksheet fragment:

N	O	P	Q	R	S	T	
	y						
x	0.0	0.2	0.3	0.5	0.6	0.8	0.9	1.
2.0	0.00	-0.09	0.05	0.23	0.43	0.63	0.85	1.0
1.8	0.00	-0.12	-0.01	0.14	0.31	0.48	0.67	0.87
1.6	0.00	-0.15	-0.07	0.05	0.19	0.33	0.49	0.66
1.4	0.00	-0.18	-0.13	-0.04	0.07	0.18	0.31	0.45
1.2	0.00	-0.21	-0.19	-0.13	-0.05	0.03	0.13	0.24
1.0	0.00	-0.24	-0.25	-0.22	-0.17	-0.12	-0.05	0.03
0.8	0.00	-0.27	-0.31	-0.31	-0.29	-0.27	-0.23	-0.1
0.6	0.00	-0.30	-0.37	-0.40	-0.41	-0.42	-0.41	-0.3
0.00	-0.33	-0.43	-0.49	-0.53	-0.57	-0.59		

- Next, go to VBE by pressing **ALT+F11** shortcut on your keyboard, then - in **View** menu - select **Project Explorer** and double-click on **Sheet1** (or whatever name of your worksheet). **Copy** the following VBA macro code and function code (which is used by the macro) and **Paste** it in the open window:

```vba
Private Sub Worksheet_Change(ByVal Target As Excel.Range)
MinX = Range("A9").Value
MaxX = Range("B9").Value
nPoints = Range("E9").Value   'Default is 20, but can be changed
For Each P In Target
        If P.Row = 5 And P.Column = 2 Then
                If Range("B5").Value <> "" Then
                        aSt = Range("B5").Text
                        bSt = ChngStr(aSt, "x", "$N3")
                        aSt = ChngStr(bSt, "y", "O$2")
                        Range("O3").Formula = "=" & aSt
                        Range("O3").AutoFill Destination:=Range(Cells(3, 15), _
                        Cells(3 + nPoints, 15)), Type:=xlFillDefault
                        Range(Cells(3, 15), Cells(3 + nPoints, 15)).AutoFill _
                        Destination:=Range(Cells(3, 15), Cells(3 + nPoints, 15 + nPoints)), _
                        Type:=xlFillDefault
                Else
                        Range(Cells(3, 15), Cells(3 + nPoints, 15 + nPoints)).Formula = ""
                End If
                Exit For
        End If
Next P
End Sub

Function ChngStr(aStr, bStr, wStr) As String
dStr = ""
i = Len(aStr)
```

```
j = Len(bStr)
For k = 1 To i
        If Mid(aStr, k, j) = bStr Then
                dStr = dStr + wStr
                k = k + j – 1
        Else
                dStr = dStr + Mid(aStr, k, 1)
        End If
Next k
ChngStr = dStr
```
End Function

That procedure will be used to fill data table for your chart with formulas, when you enter correctly your equation into cell **B5**. Here is a fragment of the data table with the formulas shown as already entered by the macro:

	N	O	P	Q	R
		y			
	x	=C$9	=O2+($D$9-$C$9)/$E$9	=P2+($D$9-$C$9)/$E$9	=Q2+($D$9-$C$9)/$E$9
	=N4+(B$9-A$9)/$E$9	=$N3*O$2 - O$2^0.5	=$N3*P$2 - P$2^0.5	=$N3*Q$2 - Q$2^0.5	=$N3*R$2 - R$2^0.5
	=N5+(B$9-A$9)/$E$9	=$N4*O$2 - O$2^0.5	=$N4*P$2 - P$2^0.5	=$N4*Q$2 - Q$2^0.5	=$N4*R$2 - R$2^0.5
	=N6+(B$9-A$9)/$E$9	=$N5*O$2 - O$2^0.5	=$N5*P$2 - P$2^0.5	=$N5*Q$2 - Q$2^0.5	=$N5*R$2 - R$2^0.5
	=N7+(B$9-A$9)/$E$9	=$N6*O$2 - O$2^0.5	=$N6*P$2 - P$2^0.5	=$N6*Q$2 - Q$2^0.5	=$N6*R$2 - R$2^0.5
	=N8+(B$9-A$9)/$E$9	=$N7*O$2 - O$2^0.5	=$N7*P$2 - P$2^0.5	=$N7*Q$2 - Q$2^0.5	=$N7*R$2 - R$2^0.5
	=N9+(B$9-A$9)/$E$9	=$N8*O$2 - O$2^0.5	=$N8*P$2 - P$2^0.5	=$N8*Q$2 - Q$2^0.5	=$N8*R$2 - R$2^0.5
	=N10+(B$9-A$9)/$E$9	=$N9*O$2 - O$2^0.5	=$N9*P$2 - P$2^0.5	=$N9*Q$2 - Q$2^0.5	=$N9*R$2 - R$2^0.5
	=N11+(B$9-A$9)/$E$9	=$N10*O$2 - O$2^0.5	=$N10*P$2 - P$2^0.5	=$N10*Q$2 - Q$2^0.5	=$N10*R$2 - R$2^0.5
	=N12+(B$9-A$9)/$E$9	=$N11*O$2 - O$2^0.5	=$N11*P$2 - P$2^0.5	=$N11*Q$2 - Q$2^0.5	=$N11*R$2 - R$2^0.5
	N13+(B$9-A$9)/$E$9	=$N12*O$2 - O$2^0.5	=$N12*P$2 - P$2^0.5	=$N12*Q$2 - Q$2^0.5	=$N12*R$2 - R$2^0.5
	+(B$9-A$9)/$E$9	=$N13*O$2 - O$2^0.5	=$N13*P$2 - P$2^0.5	=$N13*Q$2 - Q$2^0.5	=$N13*R$2 - R$2^0.5
	-A$9)/$E$9	=$N14*O$2 - O$2^0.5	=$N14*P$2 - P$2^0.5	=$N14*Q$2 - Q$2^0.5	=$N14*R$2 - R$2^0.5
	E$9	=$N15*O$2 - O$2^0.5	=$N15*P$2 - P$2^0.5	=$N15*Q$2 - Q$2^0.5	=$N15*R$2 - R$2^0.5
		O$2 - O$2^0.5	=$N16*P$2 - P$2^0.5	=$N16*Q$2 - Q$2^0.5	=$N16*R$2 - R$2^0.5
					=$N17*R$2 - R$2^0.5

- Return to your worksheet now by pressing AT+F11 again. Enter your equation into cell **B5**. The data table should get filled immediately with numbers. Next, select the range **O3:AI23** and go to **_Insert-Charts-Surface charts_** and select **_3D Surface chart_**. Your chart appears instantly. Move it where you want it to display and format to your liking.

- There are plenty of options/choices available. Now you can try to get some preferable views of your chart, including e.g., a **_wireframe_** surface chart.

Whatever nonlinear equation you want to plot, just enter it (_remember, no equal sign_) into cell **B5**. You can also enter or change the Min and Max values of **X & Y** in **A9:D9** range. That's essentially it. Save your work. The values in the table and the chart will get updated automatically for you after entering any new equation into cell B5.

The following charts, that I've created with my template, will give you some idea about what you can do using the template and your creativity.

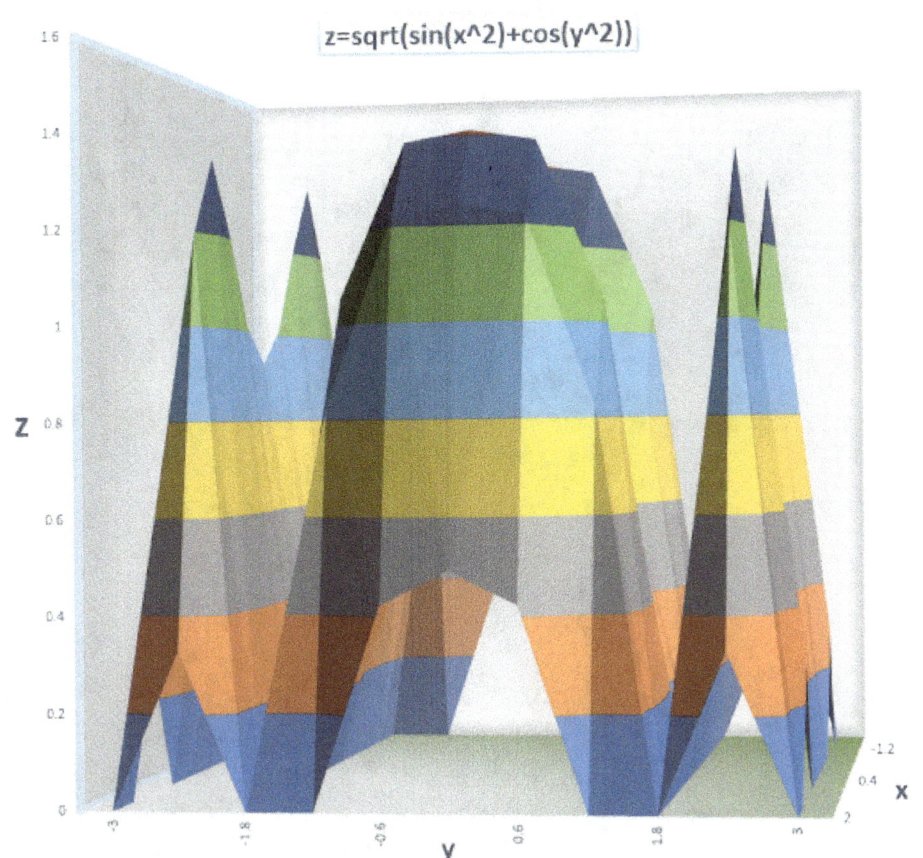

z=sqrt(sin(x^2)+cos(y^2))
z
x
y

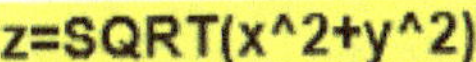

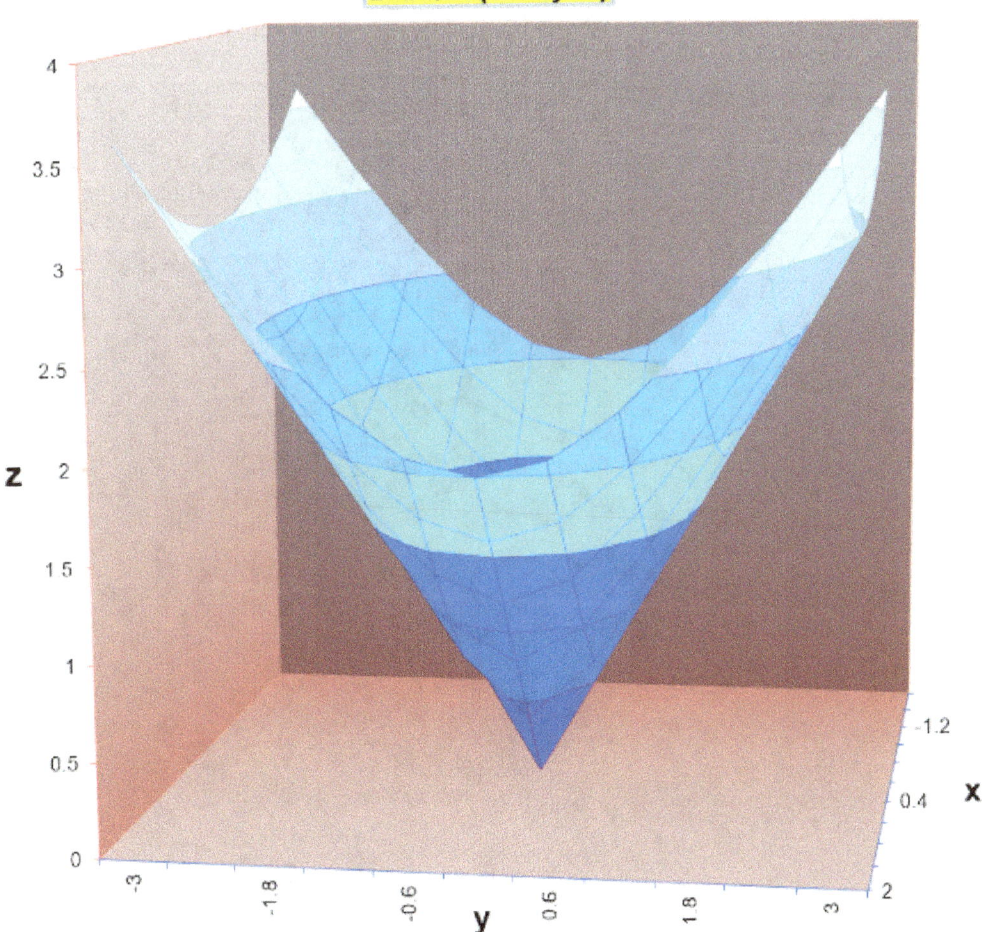

z=SQRT(x^2+y^2)
z
x
y

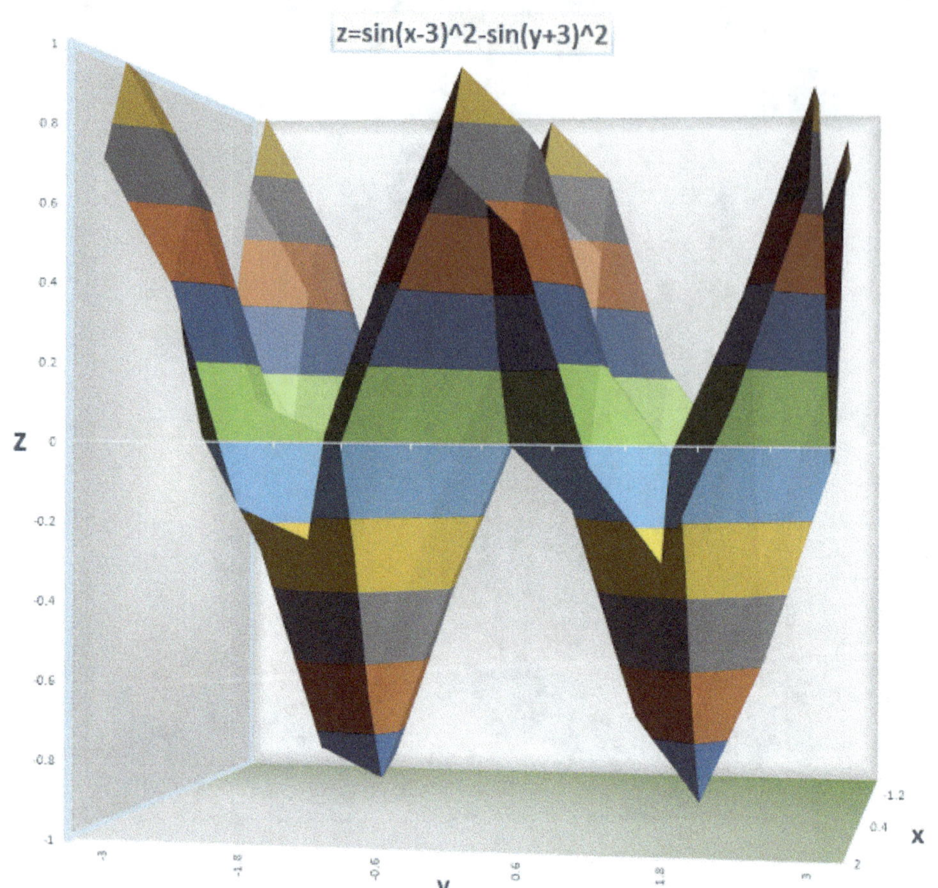

z=sin(x-3)^2-sin(y+3)^2
z
0
y
x

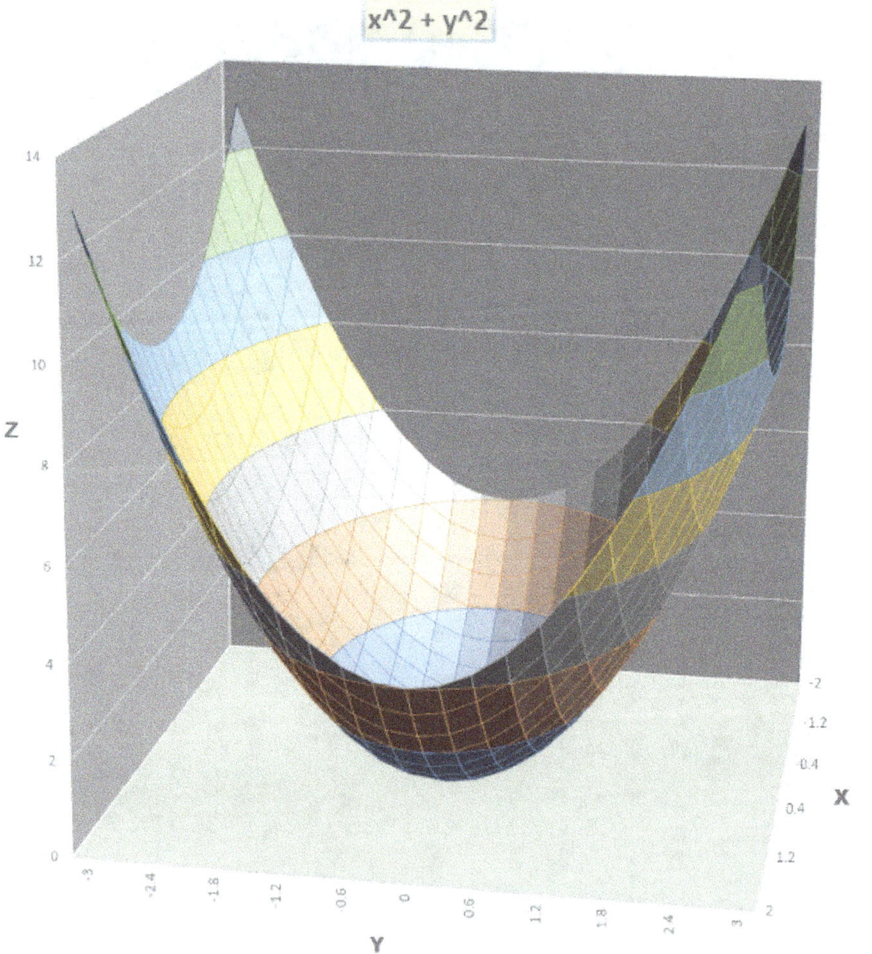

x^2 + y^2
z
Y
X

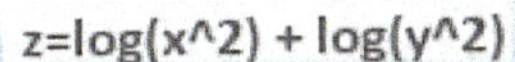

z=log(x^2) + log(y^2)

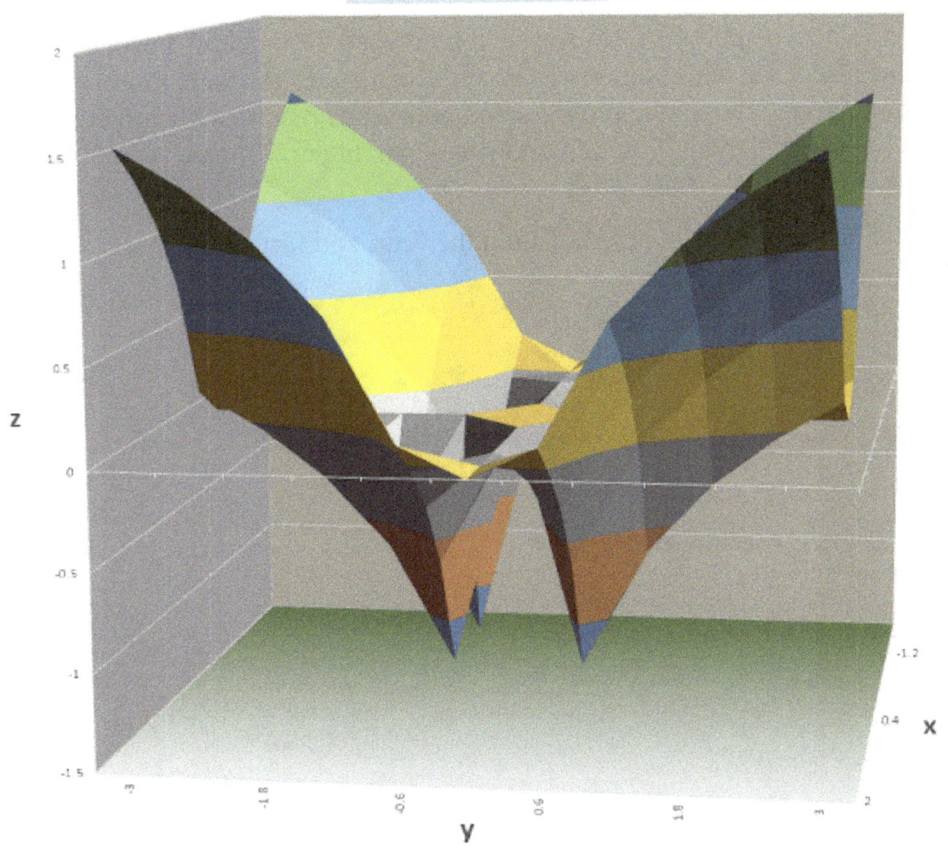

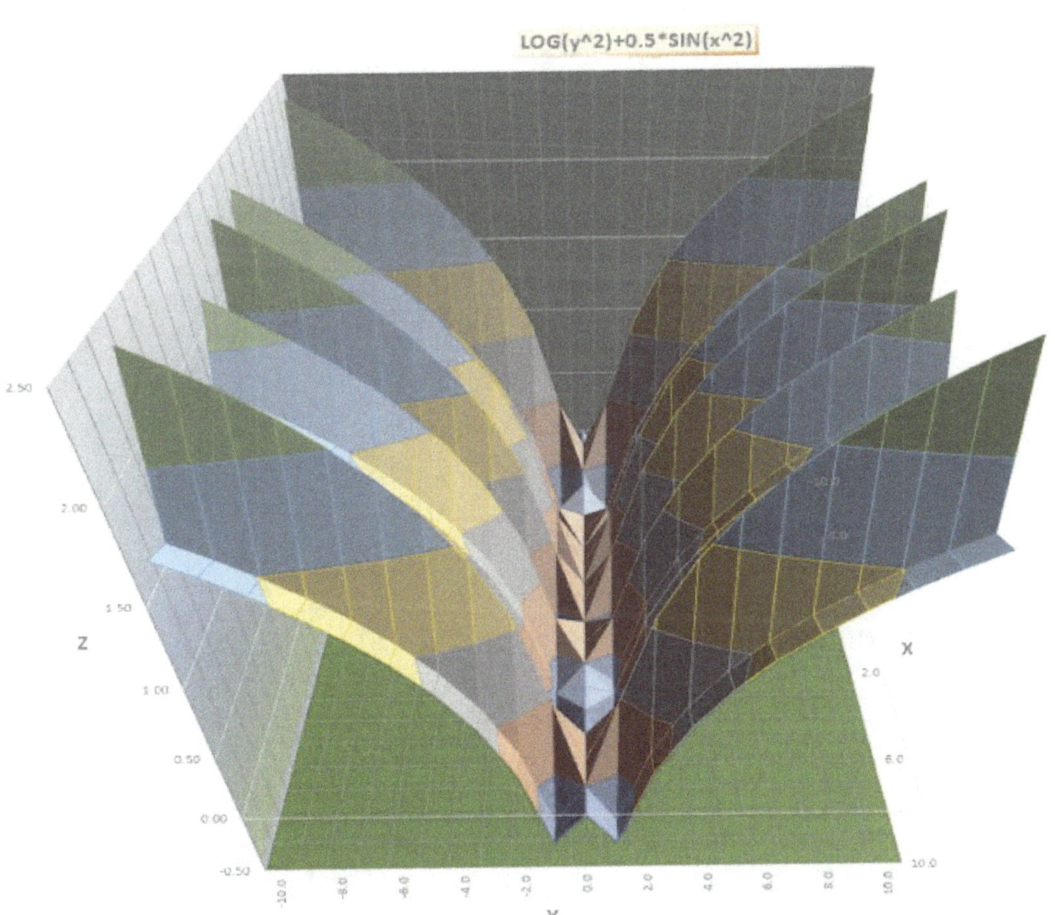

LOG(y^2)+0.5*SIN(x^2)

Excel Chart and COVID-19

In most cases a graphical display let us to see what otherwise we wouldn't be able to perceive in the structure of a table. The Line with Markers chart and fragment of the table presented below confirm this. The chart summarizes clearly the progress and number of recorded human deaths - per one million people - caused by Covid-19 within one-year span, in populations of the *five* European countries. It's easy to notice, the following:

UK: **1.85** deaths per 1000 people within the year, and further
IT: **1.84** deaths
FR: **1.48** deaths
PL: **1.45** deaths
DE: **0.92** deaths

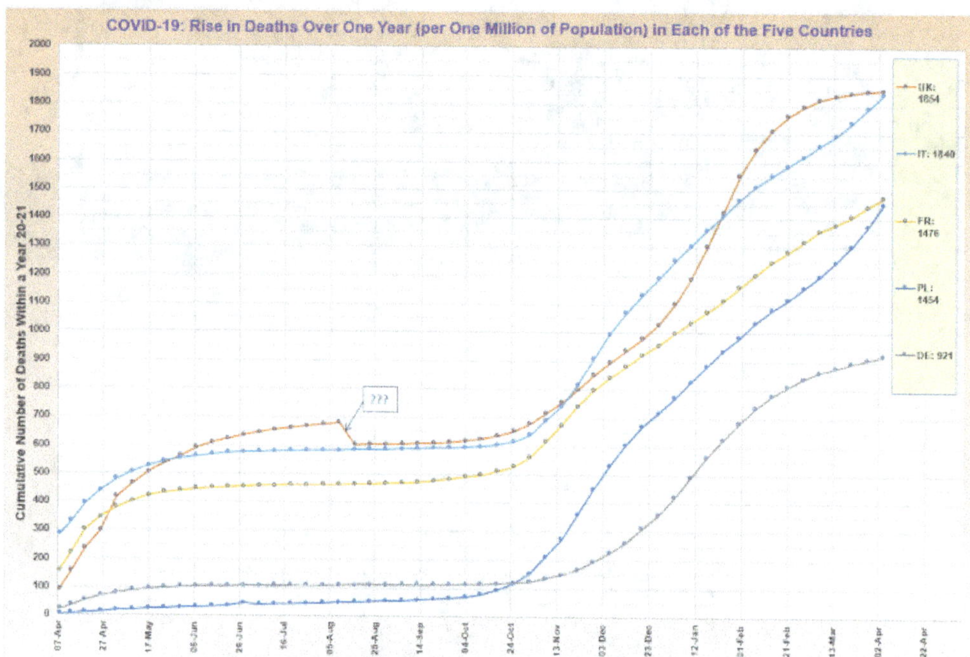

The table is based on data published on **https://www.worldometers.info/coronavirus/**

Date	Germany	Poland	France	UK	Italy
08-Apr	23.96	3.41	157.70	91.00	283.91
13-Apr	35.89	6.14	219.76	155.08	329.85
19-Apr	54.47	9.53	301.07	234.70	392.20
26-Apr	69.76	13.87	345.29	296.94	437.35
03-May	81.55	17.94	380.12	415.70	478.79
10-May	89.66	20.78	401.72	461.61	503.84
17-May	95.34	24.22	421.80	503.68	526.52
24-May	99.38	26.36	433.13	537.68	543.46
31-May	102.15	28.08	439.30	560.82	552.66
07-Jun	104.16	30.52	444.96	591.35	561.05
14-Jun	105.32	32.74	448.73	608.84	568.59
21-Jun	106.44	35.62	452.46	622.39	573.71
28-Jun	107.20	44.46	454.67	635.90	575.47
05-Jul	107.92	40.15	456.64	646.22	577.87
12-Jul	108.49	41.58	458.12	654.97	579.41
19-Jul	108.94	43.06	460.76	662.18	581.14
26-Jul	109.31	44.23	460.99	668.61	581.95
02-Aug	109.58	45.81	462.11	675.05	582.60
09-Aug	110.00	47.83	463.01	680.50	583.54
16-Aug	110.34	49.68	464.32	604.51	586.74
23-Aug	110.84	51.74	465.88	605.43	587.42
30-Aug	111.22	53.81	467.31	606.46	588.08

Plateau of deaths caused by Covid-19 is visible in several summer months, followed then by quite sharp rise during wintery weather.

Excel Secrets: Dates in Charts

Something strange happens with Excel charts when you create a chart based on data that include column of **dates** in the selected data range. Here is an example of simple data set I'm using as basis for my charts:

Date	Value
20-Feb	105
27-Feb	78
06-Mar	66
13-Mar	91
20-Mar	45
27-Mar	88
03-Apr	102
10-Apr	75
17-Apr	48
24-Apr	100

This is my first selected type of chart. Everything looks OK, dates on X axis are displayed correctly:

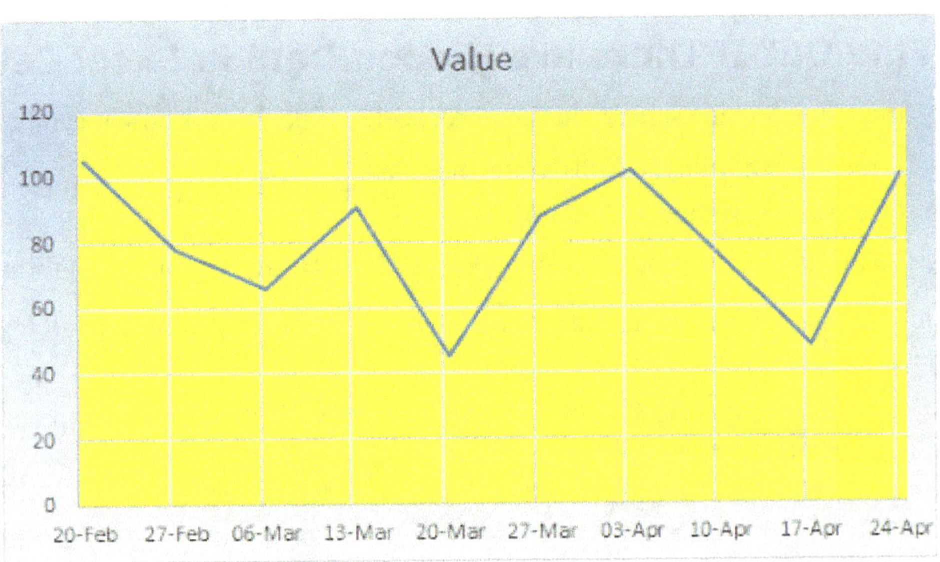

Now, when I create (or switch to) some different types of my chart, here's what I'm getting:

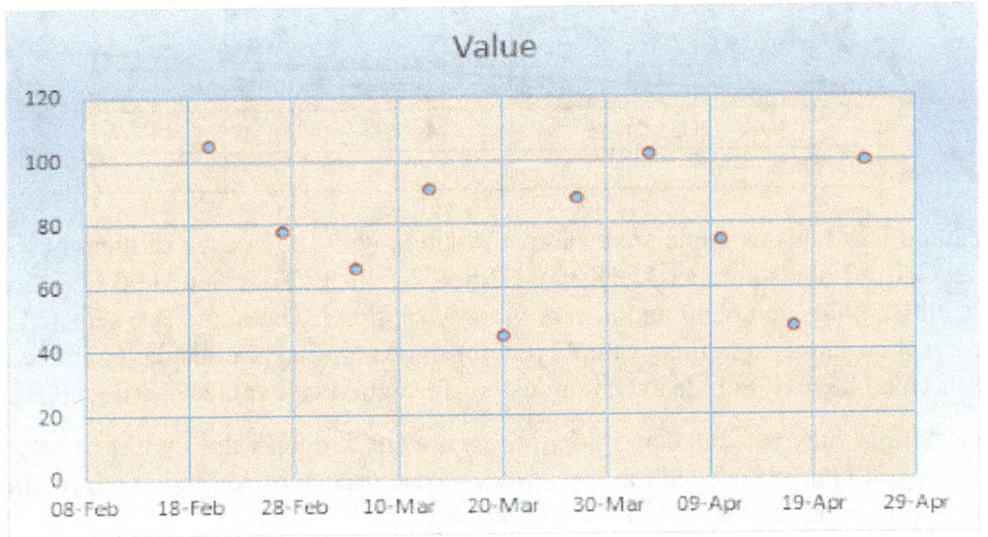

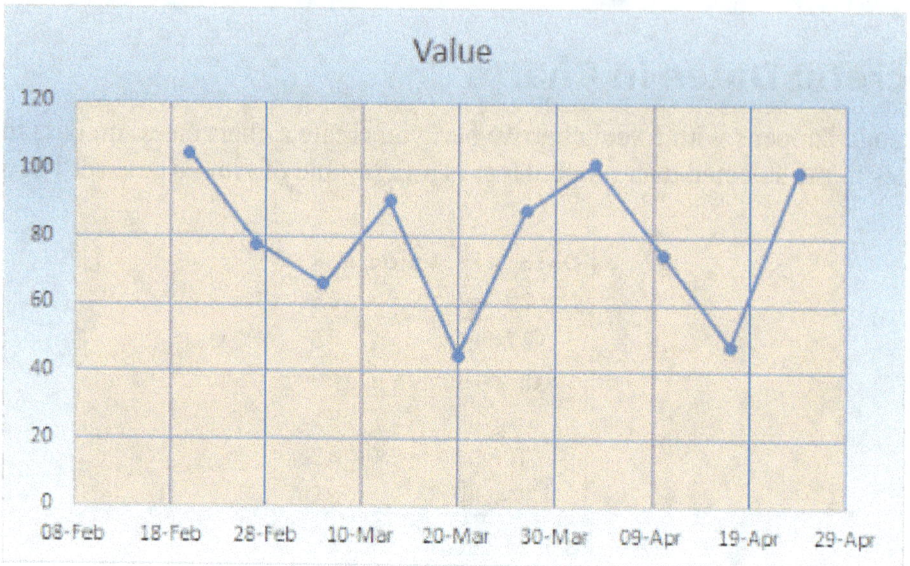

The X axis presents here completely different dates in different steps from those listed in my table. Why is this happening? Does anybody know? Is this one of Excel tricks?

For now, just be aware of this abnormality and examine your charts well before using/publishing them.

How to Find Out If There are Hidden Data in Excel Cells

You probably know how to hide some values in Excel cells. If not, this is how it can be done:

- select **Home > Format** in the Cells group, and then
- **Format Cells... > Number > Custom**, and then
- create the **;** or **;;** (single or double semicolon) and/or **;;;** (triple semicolon) formats

With **;** or **;;** format you will be able to hide numeric values, and with **;;;** format - all textual and numeric values.

The hiding of values can be enhanced with covering the cells with some graphics (pictures, icons, or shapes) as you can see in these examples:

	A	B	C	D	E	F
1	*Picture*		*Icon*		*Shape*	
2				5		
3	art		123		water	
4		ccc			drop	11.5
5						

Cells A2, C2 and E2 in this example are custom-formatted with ;;;, so each of them may hold a hidden value. Cell A2 holds number **32.58**, cell E2 holds value "**TEXT**" and cell C2 is left blank (no value). Cell B2 holds number **7** and is *not custom-formatted*. The range I've selected here is **A1:F5**. The graphics are used in this example just for masking; they are displayed in the top layer of the cells and may be used to hide even not custom-formatted cell value (like in cell B2).

Now, the question is, how you can determine if there are any hidden values within a selected range of cells. Even if you yourself created the spreadsheet some time ago, you may not remember if there are any hidden cell values and would like to check that.

You can use quite straightforward procedure to do that:

- select the range you want to check
- in the ribbon select **Home-Conditional formatting** (in Styles group) -**Highlight Cells Rules-Text that Contains...**
- under "**Format cells that contain the text:**" box enter * only and select highlighting option, e.g., **Green Fill...** , then click OK.

You'll see green-highlighted all cells that contain some values, including the hidden values.

	A	B	C	D	E	F
1	*Picture*		*Icon*		*Shape*	
2		☺	7		5	
3	art			123	water	
4		ccc			drop	11.5
5						

If any of the cells are 'masked' with graphics, you may need to check them individually by temporarily resizing/moving them to see underlying content (if any). This way you'll know that all the green-highlighted cells contain values (*doesn't matter if looking like blank or covered with graphics*). Cells A2 and E2 have also been highlighted with green. It means there are hidden values entered there. Clicking on green areas shows their content in the Formula Bar.

Later you can remove the highlighting, if no longer needed. In the meantime, by using some formulas, you can make some different checks on the cells in the selected range to confirm existence of cells with hidden values. E.g.:

- **=COUNT(A1:F5)** *Counts cells with numeric values in the selected range*
- **=COUNTA(A1:F5)** or **=COUNTIF(A1:F5,"<>")** or **=SUBTOTAL(103,A1:F5)** *Count cells with any value (not empty) in the selected range*
- **=SUM(A1:F5)** *Returns the sum of numeric values in the selected range*
- **=ISTEXT(E2)** *Returns TRUE if the cell contains text*
- **=COUNTIF(A1:F5,"")** or **=ROWS(A1:F5)*COLUMNS(A1:F5)-SUBTOTAL(103,A1:F5)** *Return count of blank cells in the selected range*
- **=IF(CELL("format",A2)="H","H","-")** *Returns "H" if the selected cell is custom-formatted to hide entered value*

The last formula can be used to check for hidden values within the whole range/table of data.

Find the Last FILLED Cell/Row/Column in a Worksheet

If you need to find the last <u>filled</u> cell (entry) located beyond your current view, one efficient way to do that is by using macros, like these three:

```vba
Sub FindLastCell()
'Search for any entry, by searching backwards by Rows, then by Columns.
Dim LastColumn As Integer
Dim LastRow As Long
Dim LastCell As Range
If WorksheetFunction.CountA(Cells) > 0 Then
```

```vba
        LastRow = Cells.Find(What:="*", After:=[A1], SearchOrder:=xlByRows, _
        SearchDirection:=xlPrevious).Row
        LastColumn = Cells.Find(What:="*", After:=[A1], SearchOrder:=xlByColumns, _
        SearchDirection:=xlPrevious).Column
        MsgBox Cells(LastRow, LastColumn).Address
        Range(Cells(LastRow, LastColumn).Address).Select
    End If
End Sub


Sub FindLastRow()
'Search for any entry, by searching backwards by Rows.
Dim LastRow As Long
If WorksheetFunction.CountA(Cells) > 0 Then
        LastRow = Cells.Find(What:="*", After:=[A1], SearchOrder:=xlByRows, _
        SearchDirection:=xlPrevious).Row
        MsgBox LastRow
        Range(Cells(LastRow, "A").Address).Select
    End If
End Sub

Sub FindLastColumn()
'Search for any entry, by searching backwards by Columns.
Dim LastColumn As Integer
Dim ColNum As Long
Dim ColLett As String
If WorksheetFunction.CountA(Cells) > 0 Then
        LastColumn = Cells.Find(What:="*", After:=[A1], SearchOrder:=xlByColumns, _
        SearchDirection:=xlPrevious).Column
        ColNum = LastColumn
        ColLett = Split(Cells(1, ColNum).Address, "$")(1)
        MsgBox "Col " & ColNum & "=Column " & ColLett
        Range(Cells("1", LastColumn).Address).Select
    End If
End Sub
```

You can assign each of the macros to a separate Control button. If you need help with that, see the **"Working with macros in Excel"** in this book.

To make things easier I've combined all three buttons into one, by moving and grouping them together like you see in this figure:

To find the position (address) of my last <u>filled</u> cell, row, or column in my worksheet I just click on appropriate line of text on the button.

Get DATES for the First 7 Days of Any Month of Any Year

What was the date of that first Wednesday of December, 1985? Was it the 3rd, or 4th of December? - you wonder.

Well, that kind of questions can be answered in Excel with a formula. It's not a short or simple one, but it works and can be used (with simple modification) to determine the date of **any first weekday** of any month of any year (from 1900 up). The figure below illustrates the result:

	A	B	C
1	**Date of the 1ˢᵗ … ↓**	**Dec-1985**	Enter month & year in "mmm-yyyy" format.
2	Monday in Dec 1985	02/12/1985	
3	Tuesday in Dec 1985	03/12/1985	
4	Wednesday in Dec 1985	04/12/1985	
5	Thursday in Dec 1985	05/12/1985	
6	Friday in Dec 1985	06/12/1985	
7	Saturday in Dec 1985	07/12/1985	
8	Sunday in Dec 1985	01/12/1985	

In order to produce this kind of table follow these steps:

- Enter "Date of the 1st …" in cell A1

- Enter the following formulas in cells A2 to A8:

  ="Monday in "&TEXT(B1,"mmm yyyy"

  ="Tuesday in "&TEXT(B2,"mmm yyyy")

  ="Wednesday in "&TEXT(B3,"mmm yyyy")

  ="Thursday in "&TEXT(B4,"mmm yyyy")

  ="Friday in "&TEXT(B5,"mmm yyyy")

  ="Saturday in "&TEXT(B6,"mmm yyyy")

  ="Sunday in "&TEXT(B7,"mmm yyyy")

- Enter the following formulas in cells B2 to B8:

=IF(DAY(DATE(YEAR($B$1),MONTH($B$1),1)-MOD(DATE(YEAR($B$1),MONTH($B$1),1)-2,7)+7)<>8,DATE(YEAR($B$1),MONTH($B$1),1)-MOD(DATE(YEAR($B$1),MONTH($B$1),1)-2,7)+7,DATE(YEAR($B$1),MONTH($B$1),1)-MOD(DATE(YEAR($B$1),MONTH($B$1),1)-2,7))

=IF(DAY(DATE(YEAR($B$1),MONTH($B$1),1)-MOD(DATE(YEAR($B$1),MONTH($B$1),1)-3,7)+7)<>8,DATE(YEAR($B$1),MONTH($B$1),1)-MOD(DATE(YEAR($B$1),MONTH($B$1),1)-3,7)+7,DATE(YEAR($B$1),MONTH($B$1),1)-MOD(DATE(YEAR($B$1),MONTH($B$1),1)-3,7))

=IF(DAY(DATE(YEAR($B$1),MONTH($B$1),1)-MOD(DATE(YEAR($B$1),MONTH($B$1),1)-4,7)+7)<>8,DATE(YEAR($B$1),MONTH($B$1),1)-MOD(DATE(YEAR($B$1),MONTH($B$1),1)-4,7)+7,DATE(YEAR($B$1),MONTH($B$1),1)-MOD(DATE(YEAR($B$1),MONTH($B$1),1)-4,7))

=IF(DAY(DATE(YEAR($B$1),MONTH($B$1),1)-MOD(DATE(YEAR($B$1),MONTH($B$1),1)+2,7)+7)<>8,DATE(YEAR($B$1),MONTH($B$1),1)-MOD(DATE(YEAR($B$1),MONTH($B$1),1)+2,7)+7,DATE(YEAR($B$1),MONTH($B$1),1)-MOD(DATE(YEAR($B$1),MONTH($B$1),1)+2,7))

=IF(DAY(DATE(YEAR($B$1),MONTH($B$1),1)-MOD(DATE(YEAR($B$1),MONTH($B$1),1)+1,7)+7)<>8,DATE(YEAR($B$1),MONTH($B$1),1)-MOD(DATE(YEAR($B$1),MONTH($B$1),1)+1,7)+7,DATE(YEAR($B$1),MONTH($B$1),1)-MOD(DATE(YEAR($B$1),MONTH($B$1),1)+1,7))

=IF(DAY(DATE(YEAR($B$1),MONTH($B$1),1)-MOD(DATE(YEAR($B$1),MONTH($B$1),1)+0,7)+7)<>8,DATE(YEAR($B$1),MONTH($B$1),1)-MOD(DATE(YEAR($B$1),MONTH($B$1),1)+0,7)+7,DATE(YEAR($B$1),MONTH($B$1),1)-MOD(DATE(YEAR($B$1),MONTH($B$1),1)+0,7))

=IF(DAY(DATE(YEAR($B$1),MONTH($B$1),1)-MOD(DATE(YEAR($B$1),MONTH($B$1),1)-1,7)+7)<>8,DATE(YEAR($B$1),MONTH($B$1),1)-MOD(DATE(YEAR($B$1),MONTH($B$1),1)-1,7)+7,DATE(YEAR($B$1),MONTH($B$1),1)-MOD(DATE(YEAR($B$1),MONTH($B$1),1)-1,7))

- Now, enter any month and year, as your need may be, in cell B1 (e.g., "Dec 2021").

Cells B2:B8 will display the dates you're looking for.

Outliers in Normally Distributed Datasets

I've already touched the subject of statistical analysis of data using Excel functions. Here I dive deeper into Excel statistical tools. It's about **outliers** in data sets, about numbers that can distort the state of reality and can lead to unsound findings and conclusions regarding specific areas of knowledge.

There are no strict statistical rules for indisputable ways of identifying outliers; we are dealing with probabilities. Nonetheless, there are guidelines and tests we can utilize to find outlying values, and they can significantly improve our intuition, *formally*.

Because of the importance of detecting outliers, I've prepared Excel workbook providing practical tools (tests) for identifying such deviating/departing values within any set of numerical data. The workbook includes basic guidelines for using some specific statistical tests; I'm showing here its fragment:

To run the outlier test, click the "Run Test for Outlier(s)" button on "Data" page and then select options provided. At first, you can select what do you want to do with outlying values: you can just mark them or remove them. Next, you make selection of test and any of the options related to the test of your choice. In addition to the test-specific statistics, a template for graphic representation of your data set is provided on "Data" page, i.e. a box plot, based on data quartiles. This can be helpul in overall examination of your data set and when deciding about removal of outlier(s). Note: vertical scales of the boxplot (left and right) have to be the same and need to be adjusted to the range of tested data set.

Test Name	Criteria for Determining Applicability of Test		
	Sample Size	Max. Number of Suspected Outliers	Options / Recommendations
User-Defined Boundaries	Any	Any	Anything beyond boundaries is considered an outlier.
Quartile Ranges	Any	Any	Values outside confidence interval (95% by default) are considered outliers.
Standard Error (z-Score): a) based on z-score b) based on modified z-score (MAD)	Any	Usually 1 or 2	Recommended for labelling suspected outliers, especially when used with MAD, the outlier resistant estimator.
Dixon's Test (Extreme Value Test)	3 to 25	Usually 1 or 2	Options available for: $n = 3$ to 7 $n = 8$ to 10 $n = 11$ to 13 $n => 14$ data points
Grubbs' Test (Extreme Studentized Deviate, ESD)	7 to 140	1 or 2	Allows checking for outliers in 3 different configurations (1 only, opposite pair, one-sided pair).
Rosner's Test (Generalized ESD)	25 to 500	Up to 10	Always identifies both low and high outliers (two-tailed).

The results of those statistical tests are presented in both descriptive and graphical way, as illustrated partially in this example:

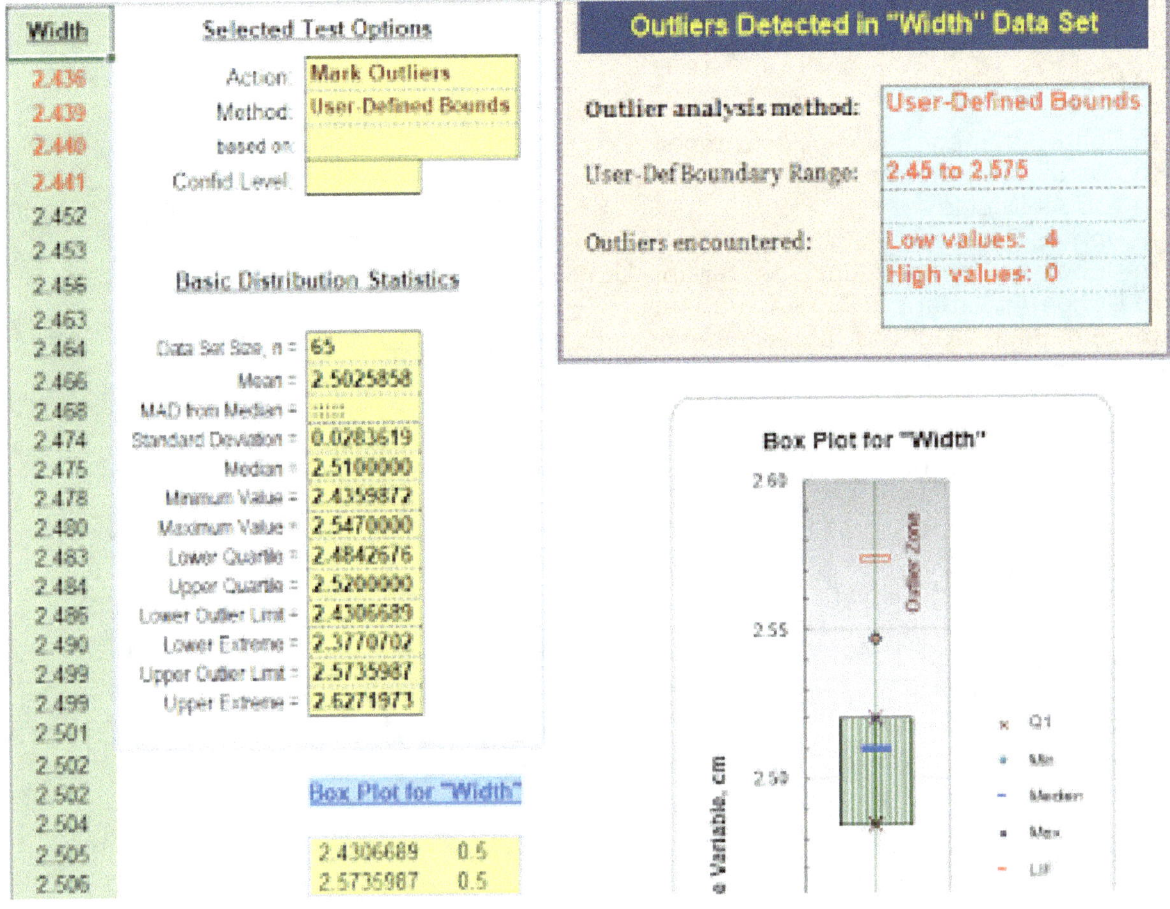

The outlying values can be either *marked* or *removed* from tested data set, in each of the tests.

If you're interested, I could share the workbook **("OutliersOut.xlsm" file)** with you upon your request.

Here's the macro included with the file and used to run the multi-choice show:

```
'GetOut macro, written by Ryszard (Richard) Raciborski, Last updated - May 2021
'This macro will allow you either mark or remove outliers for a specified variable (list of
values).
'You can select which method to find the outliers with - either by:
'User-def Bounds, Quartile Ranges, Means/StdError, or Dixon's/Grubbs'/Rosner's Test.
'Missing data is ignored.
Option Base 1
Option Explicit
Enum UCho1
        Mark = 1
        Remove = 2
End Enum
Sub GetOut()
    Dim DRange As Range
    Dim tf As Integer, bf As Integer, col As Integer
    Dim r As Double
    Dim LRow As Long
    Dim lambda As Single
    Dim check As Boolean
    Dim TabR As Range
    Dim Ops() As Variant, Opt() As Variant, Opm() As Variant
    Dim OpD() As Variant, OpC() As Variant
    Dim AbsDev() As Double, mmad As Double
    Dim xm() As Double, s() As Double, y() As Double
```

```vba
    Dim Mdn As Double, Q1 As Double, Q3 As Double, IQR As Double
    Dim RemoCnt As Integer
    Dim Coeff As String
    Dim RetVal
    Dim Ndata As Integer, Dpoint As Integer
    Dim i As Integer, j As Integer, k As Integer
    Dim LoB As Double
    Dim UpB As Double
    Dim UCho1 As Variant, UCho2 As Variant, UCho3 As Variant
    Dim UCho4 As Variant, UCho5 As Variant
    Dim RemoBoundaOuts As Integer, RemoQuartOuts As Integer
    Dim RemoStdErrOuts
    Dim x1, x2, x3, xn, xn_1, xn_2
    Dim Lqt, Hqt, CritVal
    Dim Variance As Double, variance2 As Double, variance3 As Double
    Dim sd As Double, Mean As Double, MeanL As Double, MeanH As Double
    Dim G11, G12, G2, G31, G32
'   Clear previous test output
    Worksheets("Data").Activate
    Worksheets("Data").Range("C2:D5").Select
    Selection.ClearContents
    Worksheets("Data").Range("K3").Select
    Selection.ClearContents
    Worksheets("Data").Range("H4:L10").Select
    Selection.ClearContents
    Columns("Z:Z").Select
    Selection.ClearContents
    Columns("A:A").Select
    Selection.Font.Bold = False
    Selection.Font.ColorIndex = 0
    LRow = Range("A:A").SpecialCells(xlCellTypeLastCell).Row - 1
    ActiveWorkbook.Worksheets("Data").Sort.SortFields.Clear
    ActiveWorkbook.Worksheets("Data").Sort.SortFields.Add2 Key:=Range("A2:A" & LRow), _
        SortOn:=xlSortOnValues, Order:=xlAscending, DataOption:=xlSortTextAsNumbers
    With ActiveWorkbook.Worksheets("Data").Sort
        .SetRange Range("A2:A" & LRow)
        .Orientation = xlTopToBottom
        .SortMethod = xlPinYin
        .Apply
    End With
    Worksheets("Data").Range("A1").Select
    Selection.Font.Bold = True
'=========================================
    On Error Resume Next
    With ActiveWindow
        .DisplayHeadings = False
        .DisplayVerticalScrollBar = False
        .DisplayWorkbookTabs = False
    End With
    Sheets("Bk").Visible = True
    Sheets("Bk").Select
    Ndata = Worksheets("Data").Range("C10").Value
    'If there are no valid observations then quit
    If Ndata = 0 Then
        Worksheets("Data").Range("H7").Value = "No valid observations. Check data."
        GoTo Out
    End If
'   Mark or Remove Option
    ReDim Ops(1 To 2)
```

```vba
        Ops(1) = "Mark Outliers"
        Ops(2) = "Remove Outliers"
        UCho1 = 0
        UCho1 = GetOption(Ops, 1, "Select Your Option")
        If UCho1 = False Then
            Worksheets("Data").Range("C2") = ""
            GoTo Out
        Else
            Worksheets("Data").Range("C2") = Ops(UCho1)
        End If
'Get which method of removal to perform
        ReDim Opt(1 To 6) As Variant
        Opt(1) = "User-Defined Bounds"
        Opt(2) = "Quartile Ranges"
        Opt(3) = "Means/Std.Error"
        Opt(4) = "Dixon's Test"
        Opt(5) = "Grubbs' Test"
        Opt(6) = "Rosner's Test"
        UCho2 = 0
        UCho2 = GetOption(Opt, 1, "Select Method of Outlier Removal")
        If UCho2 = False Then
            Worksheets("Data").Range("C3") = ""
            GoTo Out
        Else
            Worksheets("Data").Range("C3") = Opt(UCho2)
        End If
        Dim Mesg, Tit, Styl, Rsp
        Dim Deflt As String
'   Sort the data first to get a continuous range
        Worksheets("Data").Columns("A:A").Select
        Selection.Sort Key1:=Range("A2"), Order1:=xlAscending, Header:=xlGuess, _
            OrderCustom:=1, MatchCase:=False, Orientation:=xlTopToBottom
        Worksheets("Data").Range("A1").Select
        Select Case UCho2 'Evaluate Opt expression
            Case 1       'User-Defined Bounds
                Mesg = "Enter the lower boundary"
                Tit = "Lower Boundary"
                Deflt = "0"
                LoB = InputBox(Mesg, Tit, Deflt)
                Mesg = "Enter the upper boundary"
                Tit = "Upper Boundary"
                Deflt = "10"
                UpB = InputBox(Mesg, Tit, Deflt)
                Mesg = "Lower bound must be less than or equal to upper bound. Try again."
                Tit = "Your Entry Is Not Correct"
                Styl = vbExclamation
                If LoB > UpB Then
                    Rsp = MsgBox(Mesg, Styl, Tit)
                    GoTo Out
                End If
                GoSub RemoBoundaOuts
            Case 2     'Quartile Ranges
'               Dim LowQuart, UppQuart
                Mesg = "Please enter the IQ coefficient"
                Tit = "Coefficient"
                Deflt = "1.5"
                Coeff = InputBox(Mesg, Tit, Deflt)
                If Err.Number = 13 Then
                    Rsp = MsgBox("Coefficient must be numeric", vbExclamation)
```

```vba
            GoTo Out
        ElseIf Coeff <= 0 Then
            Rsp = MsgBox("Coefficient must be greater than zero", vbExclamation)
            GoTo Out
        End If
        GoSub RemoQuartOuts
    Case 3      'Means/Std.Error
'       Which method of Means/StdError option?
        ReDim Opm(1 To 2)
        Opm(1) = "Z-Score Mean"
        Opm(2) = "Z-Score MAD"
        UCho5 = 0
        UCho5 = GetOption(Opm, 1, "Select Your Method")
        If UCho5 = False Then
            GoTo Out
        Else
            Worksheets("Data").Range("C4") = Opm(UCho5)
        End If
        If UCho5 = 1 Then      'z-score Mean method
            Mesg = "Please enter the coefficient"
            Tit = "Coefficient"
            Deflt = "1.5"
            Coeff = InputBox(Mesg, Tit, Deflt)
            If Err.Number = 13 Then
                Rsp = MsgBox("Coefficient must be numeric", vbExclamation)
                GoTo Out
            ElseIf Coeff <= 0 Then
                Rsp = MsgBox("Coefficient must be greater than zero", vbExclamation)
                GoTo Out
            End If
            GoSub RemoStdErrOuts
        Else                'z-score MAD method
            Worksheets("Data").Range("K3").Value = "Means/StdError"
            Worksheets("Data").Range("K4").Value = " (z-score MAD)"
            'Calculate median and MAD
            ReDim AbsDev(Ndata)
            ' Median - output and sort in column P
            Mdn = Worksheets("Data").Range("C14").Value
            Worksheets("Data").Range("Z1").Value = "AbsDev"
            For i = 1 To Ndata
                Worksheets("Data").Range("Z" & (i + 1)).Value = _
Abs(Worksheets("Data").Range("A" & (i + 1)).Value - Mdn)
            Next i
            'Sort AbsDev values in column Z
            Worksheets("Data").Range("Z2:Z" & (Ndata + 1)).Select
            Selection.Sort Key1:=Range("Z2"), Order1:=xlAscending, Header:=xlGuess, _
OrderCustom:=1, MatchCase:=False, Orientation:=xlTopToBottom
            'MAD - here, the median of absolute deviation about the median
            mmad = Worksheets("Data").Range("C12").Value
'   With the coefficient of 1.4826, MAD - for normal population - is expected to approach
stdev
'   If z-score-3.5 then either mark or remove the data point
            k = 0
            For i = 1 To Ndata
                If Abs((Worksheets("Data").Range("A" & (i + 1)).Value - Mdn) / mmad) > 3.5 _
Then
                    Dpoint = i + 1
                    If Dpoint > (0.5 * Ndata) Then k = k + 1
                    GoSub MorR
```

```vba
                RemoCnt = RemoCnt + 1
            End If
        Next i
        'Write analysis of the variable
        With Worksheets("Data")
            .Range("H5").Value = "Outliers encountered:"
            .Range("K5").Value = "Low values:    " & (RemoCnt - k)
            .Range("K6").Value = "High values:   " & k
        End With
    End If
Case 4      'Dixon's Test
    ReDim OpD(1 To 4) As Variant
    OpD(1) = "3 to 7"
    OpD(2) = "8 to 10"
    OpD(3) = "11 to 13"
    OpD(4) = "14 to 30"
    UCho3 = 0
    UCho3 = GetOption(OpD, 1, "Select Sample Size Option")
    If UCho3 = False Then GoTo Out
    'At what confidence level do you want this test?
    ReDim OpC(1 To 6) As Variant
    OpC(1) = "80%"
    OpC(2) = "90%"
    OpC(3) = "95%"
    OpC(4) = "96%"
    OpC(5) = "98%"
    OpC(6) = "99%"
    UCho4 = 0
    UCho4 = GetOption(OpC, 1, "Select Confidence Level")
    If UCho4 = False Then
        Worksheets("Data").Range("C5") = ""
        GoTo Out
    Else
        Worksheets("Data").Range("C5") = OpC(UCho4)
    End If
    x1 = Worksheets("Data").Range("A2").Value
    x2 = Worksheets("Data").Range("A3").Value
    x3 = Worksheets("Data").Range("A4").Value
    xn = Worksheets("Data").Range("A" & (Ndata + 1)).Value
    xn_1 = Worksheets("Data").Range("A" & Ndata).Value
    xn_2 = Worksheets("Data").Range("A" & (Ndata - 1)).Value
    Select Case UCho3     'Evaluate OpD expression
        Case 1    'Sample 3 to 7
            CritVal = Worksheets("DixonCV").Range("J9").Value
            Lqt = (x2 - x1) / (xn - x1): Hqt = (xn - xn_1) / (xn - x1)
        Case 2    'Sample 8 to 10
            CritVal = Worksheets("DixonCV").Range("J42").Value
            Lqt = (x2 - x1) / (xn_1 - x1): Hqt = (xn - xn_1) / (xn - x2)
        Case 3    'Sample 11 to 13
            CritVal = Worksheets("DixonCV").Range("J176").Value
            Lqt = (x3 - x1) / (xn_1 - x1): Hqt = (xn - xn_2) / (xn - x2)
        Case 4    'Sample 14 to 30
            CritVal = Worksheets("DixonCV").Range("J207").Value
            Lqt = (x3 - x1) / (xn_2 - x1): Hqt = (xn - xn_2) / (xn - x3)
    End Select
    'Report
    With Worksheets("Data")
        .Range("K3").Value = "Dixon's Test"
        .Range("H5").Value = "Outliers encountered:"
```

```vba
            End With
        If Lqt < CritVal Then
            If Hqt < CritVal Then
                Worksheets("Data").Range("K5").Value = "NO OUTLIERS"
            Else
                Worksheets("Data").Range("H6").Value = "The highest (max) value..."
                Worksheets("Data").Range("K6").Value = "IS an outlier."
                Dpoint = Ndata + 1
                GoSub MorR
            End If
        Else
            If Hqt < CritVal Then
                Worksheets("Data").Range("H6").Value = "The lowest (min) value..."
                Worksheets("Data").Range("K6").Value = "IS an outlier."
                Dpoint = 2
                GoSub MorR
            Else
                With Worksheets("Data")
                    .Range("H6").Value = "The highest (max) value..."
                    .Range("H7").Value = "The lowest (min) value..."
                    .Range("K6").Value = "IS an outlier."
                    .Range("K7").Value = "IS an outlier."
                End With
                Dpoint = 2
                GoSub MorR
                Dpoint = Ndata + 1
                GoSub MorR
            End If
        End If
    Case 5       'Grubbs' Test
        'At what confidence level do you want this test?
        ReDim OpC(1 To 5) As Variant
        OpC(1) = "90%"
        OpC(2) = "92.5%"
        OpC(3) = "95%"
        OpC(4) = "97.5%"
        OpC(5) = "99%"
        UCho4 = 0
        UCho4 = GetOption(OpC, 1, "Select Confidence Level")
        If UCho4 = False Then
            Worksheets("Data").Range("C5") = ""
            GoTo Out
        Else
            Worksheets("Data").Range("C5") = OpC(UCho4)
        End If
        x1 = Worksheets("Data").Range("A2").Value
        x2 = Worksheets("Data").Range("A3").Value
        xn = Worksheets("Data").Range("A" & (Ndata + 1)).Value
        xn_1 = Worksheets("Data").Range("A" & Ndata).Value
        'Get mean, variance, std dev
        Mean = Worksheets("Data").Range("C11").Value
        sd = Worksheets("Data").Range("C13").Value
        Variance = sd * sd
        'Test for suspected single outlier
        G11 = Abs(Mean - x1) / sd
        G12 = Abs(Mean - xn) / sd
        'Test for pair of extreme values (masking each other)
        G2 = (xn - x1) / sd
        'Test for a pair of one-sided outliers
```

```vba
'Get variance for data without two highest values
Ndata = Ndata - 2
MeanL = WorksheetFunction.Average(Worksheets("Data").Range("A2:A" & (Ndata - 1)))
variance2 = WorksheetFunction.Var(Worksheets("Data").Range("A2:A" & (Ndata - 1)))
G31 = 1 - ((Ndata - 1) * variance2 / ((Ndata + 1) * Variance))
'Get variance for data without two smallest values
MeanH = WorksheetFunction.Average(Worksheets("Data").Range("A2:A" & (Ndata + 3)))
variance3 = WorksheetFunction.Var(Worksheets("Data").Range("A4:A" & (Ndata + 3)))
G32 = 1 - ((Ndata - 1) * variance3 / ((Ndata + 1) * Variance))
'Report
With Worksheets("Data")
    .Range("K3").Value = "Grubbs' Test"
    .Range("H5").Value = "Outliers encountered:"
    .Range("H6").Value = "The lowest (min.) value:"
    .Range("H7").Value = "The highest (max.) value:"
    .Range("H8").Value = "Next to the lowest value:"
    .Range("H9").Value = "Next to the highest value:"
End With
'Suspected single outliers
Ndata = Worksheets("Data").Range("C10").Value
If G11 > Worksheets("GrubbsCV").Range("N6").Value Then
    Worksheets("Data").Range("K6").Value = "Yes"
    Dpoint = 2
    GoSub MorR
Else
    Worksheets("Data").Range("K6").Value = "No"
End If
If G12 - Worksheets("GrubbsCV").Range("N6").Value Then
    Worksheets("Data").Range("K7").Value = "Yes"
    Dpoint = Ndata + 1
    GoSub MorR
Else
    Worksheets("Data").Range("K7").Value = "No"
End If
'Suspected pair of extreme values (masking each other at opposite ends)
If G2 > Worksheets("GrubbsCV").Range("N7").Value Then
Worksheets("Data").Range("K6").Value = Worksheets("Data").Range("K6").Value & "Yes"
Worksheets("Data").Range("K7").Value = Worksheets("Data").Range("K7").Value & "Yes"
    Dpoint = 2
    GoSub MorR
    Dpoint = Ndata + 1
    GoSub MorR
Else
Worksheets("Data").Range("K6").Value = Worksheets("Data").Range("K6").Value & "No"
Worksheets("Data").Range("K7").Value = Worksheets("Data").Range("K7").Value & "No"
End If
'Suspected pair of one-sided outliers
If G31 > Worksheets("GrubbsCV").Range("N8").Value Then
Worksheets("Data").Range("K6").Value = Worksheets("Data").Range("K6").Value & "Yes"
Worksheets("Data").Range("K8").Value = Worksheets("Data").Range("K8").Value & "Yes"
```

```vb
                Dpoint = 2
                GoSub MorR
                Dpoint = 3
                GoSub MorR
            Else
        Worksheets("Data").Range("K8").Value = Worksheets("Data").Range("K8").Value & _
    "No"
            End If
            If G32 > Worksheets("GrubbsCV").Range("N8").Value Then
        Worksheets("Data").Range("K7").Value = Worksheets("Data").Range("K7").Value & _
    "Yes"
                Worksheets("Data").Range("K9").Value = "Yes"
                Dpoint = Ndata
                GoSub MorR
                Dpoint = Ndata + 1
                GoSub MorR
            Else
                Worksheets("Data").Range("K9").Value = "No"
            End If
        Case 6      'Rosner's test
            'At what confidence level do you want this test?
            ReDim OpC(1 To 2) As Variant
            OpC(1) = "95%"
            OpC(2) = "99%"
            UCho4 = 0
            UCho4 = GetOption(OpC, 1, "Select Confidence Level")
            If UCho4 = False Then
                Worksheets("Data").Range("C5") = ""
                GoTo Out
            Else
                Worksheets("Data").Range("C5") = OpC(UCho4)
            End If
            x1 = Worksheets("Data").Range("A2").Value
            xn = Worksheets("Data").Range("A" & (Ndata + 1)).Value
            'After inspecting the probability plot, estimate the max # of outliers, r0
            ReDim OpD(1 To 6) As Variant
            OpD(1) = "one"
            OpD(2) = "two"
            OpD(3) = "three"
            OpD(4) = "four"
            OpD(5) = "five"
            OpD(6) = "ten"
            UCho3 = 0
            UCho3 = GetOption(OpD, 1, "Select Possible Max.# of Outliers")
            If UCho3 = False Then GoTo Out
            tf = 0: bf = 0
            Set DRange = Worksheets("Data").Range("A2:A" & (Ndata + 1))
            'Iterate through identification and removal of possible outliers
            ReDim xm(1 To 10) As Double
            ReDim s(1 To 10) As Double
            ReDim y(1 To 10) As Double
            For k = 1 To UCho3
                'Compute mean, stddev
                xm(k) = Application.WorksheetFunction.Average(DRange)
                s(k) = Application.WorksheetFunction.StDev(DRange)
                'Determine the farthest point from the mean
                If (xm(k) - Worksheets("Data").Range("A" & (2 + tf)).Value) > _
    (Worksheets("Data").Range("A" & (Ndata + 1 - bf)).Value - xm(k)) Then
                    tf = tf + 1
```

```vba
            y(k) = Worksheets("Data").Range("A" & (1 + tf)).Value
            Set DRange = Worksheets("Data").Range("A" & (2 + tf) & ":A" & (Ndata + 1 - bf))
        Else
            bf = bf + 1
            y(k) = Worksheets("Data").Range("A" & (Ndata + 2 - bf)).Value
            Set DRange = Worksheets("Data").Range("A" & (2 + tf) & ":A" & (Ndata + 1 - bf))
        End If
    Next k
    'Test for number of outliers (initial # of suspects =UCho3)
    RemoCnt = tf + bf
    check = True
    Set TabR = Worksheets("RosnerCV").Range("A6:M44")
    i = 0: j = 0
    Do
        r = Abs(y(RemoCnt) - xm(RemoCnt)) / s(RemoCnt)
        If UCho4 = 1 Then        'CL=95%
            col = RemoCnt + 1
            If RemoCnt = 10 Then col = 7
        Else                'CL=99%
            col = RemoCnt + 7
            If RemoCnt = 10 Then col = 13
        End If
        lambda = Application.WorksheetFunction.VLookup(Ndata, TabR, col)
        If r < lambda Then
            check = True
            If y(RemoCnt) < xm(RemoCnt) Then
                i = i + 1
            Else
                j = j + 1
            End If
        Else
            check = False
        End If
'        Ndata = Ndata + 1
        RemoCnt = RemoCnt - 1
        If RemoCnt = 0 Then check = False
    Loop Until check = False
    'Report comes here
    With Worksheets("Data")
        .Range("K3").Value = "Rosner's Test"
        .Range("H5").Value = "Outliers encountered:"
        .Range("K5").Value = "Low values:   " & (tf - i)
        .Range("K6").Value = "High values:  " & (bf - j)
    End With
    If UCho1 = Mark Then
        If tf > 0 Then
            For k = 1 To (tf - i)
                Dpoint = k + 1
                GoSub MorR
            Next k
        End If
        If bf > 0 Then
            For k = 1 To (bf - j)
                Dpoint = Ndata + 2 - k
                GoSub MorR
            Next k
        End If
    End If
```

```vba
            End If
        Case Else   'Anything else?
            '-----
    End Select
Mesg = "Please review the results"
Tit = "Outlier Report"
Styl = vbOKOnly
RetVal = MsgBox(Mesg, Styl, Tit)
GoTo Out
'

MorR:
'Mark or remove outliers
If UCho1 = Mark Then
    With Worksheets("Data").Range("A" & Dpoint).Font
        .Bold = True
        .ColorIndex = 3
    End With
Else
    Worksheets("Data").Range("A" & Dpoint).Value = ""
End If
Return
'

RemoBoundaOuts:
'Return the number of eliminated outliers
'Write analysis report while processing the outliers
Worksheets("Data").Range("K3").Value = "User-Defined Bounds"
Worksheets("Data").Range("H5").Value = "User-Def Boundary Range:"
Worksheets("Data").Range("K5").Value = LoB & " to " & UpB
RemoCnt = WorksheetFunction.CountIf(Worksheets("Data").Range("A2:A" & (Ndata + 1)), "<" _
& LoB)
If RemoCnt > 0 Then
    For j = 1 To RemoCnt
        Dpoint = j + 1
        GoSub MorR
    Next j
End If
k = RemoCnt
RemoCnt = RemoCnt + WorksheetFunction.CountIf(Worksheets("Data").Range("A2:A" & _
(Ndata + 1)), "-" & UpB)
If RemoCnt > k Then
    For j = 1 To (RemoCnt - k)
        Dpoint = Ndata + 2 - j
        GoSub MorR
    Next j
End If
Worksheets("Data").Range("H7").Value = "Outliers encountered:"
Worksheets("Data").Range("K7").Value = "Low values:    " & k
Worksheets("Data").Range("K8").Value = "High values:   " & (RemoCnt - k)
Return
'

RemoQuartOuts:
Worksheets("Data").Range("K3").Value = "Quartile Ranges"
Dim LoQuOut As Double
Dim UpQuOut As Double
Dim LoQuBound As Double
Dim UpQuBound As Double
Dim HiNonOut As Double
Dim LoNonOut As Double
Dim LoNonOutFound As Boolean
```

```vba
Dim HiNonOutFound As Boolean
'Lower and Upper quartiles
LoQuBound = Worksheets("Data").Range("C17").Value
UpQuBound = Worksheets("Data").Range("C18").Value
'Calculate the outlier value
LoQuOut = LoQuBound - (Coeff * (UpQuBound - LoQuBound))
UpQuOut = UpQuBound + (Coeff * (UpQuBound - LoQuBound))
RemoCnt = WorksheetFunction.CountIf(Worksheets("Data").Range("A2:A" & (Ndata + 1)), "<" _
& LoQuOut)
If RemoCnt > 0 Then
    For j = 1 To RemoCnt
        Dpoint = j + 1
        GoSub MorR
    Next j
End If
k = RemoCnt
RemoCnt = RemoCnt + WorksheetFunction.CountIf(Worksheets("Data").Range("A2:A" & _
(Ndata + 1)), "-" & UpQuOut)
If RemoCnt > k Then
    For j = 1 To (RemoCnt - k)
        Dpoint = Ndata + 2 - j
        GoSub MorR
    Next j
End If
'   Write analysis of the variable
With Worksheets("Data")
    .Range("H5").Value = "Outliers encountered:"
    .Range("K5").Value = "Low values:    " & k
    .Range("K6").Value = "High values:   " & (RemoCnt - k)
    .Range("H7").Value = "Calc non-outlier range:"
    .Range("K7").Value = LoQuOut & "  to  " & UpQuOut
    .Range("H8").Value = "Non-outliers range of data:"
    .Range("K8").Value = Worksheets("Data").Range("A" & (k + 2)).Value & "  to  " & _
Worksheets("Data").Range("A" & (Ndata + 1 - RemoCnt + k))
End With
Return
'

RemoStdErrOuts:
'Write analysis report while processing the outliers
Worksheets("Data").Range("H3").Value = "Outlier analysis method: "
Worksheets("Data").Range("K3").Value = "Means/StdError"
Worksheets("Data").Range("K4").Value = " (z-score Mean)"
Dim LoStdErrOut As Double
Dim HiStdErrOut As Double
Dim StdErr
'Get the variance and Ndata
Variance = WorksheetFunction.Var(Worksheets("Data").Range("A2:A" & (Ndata + 1)))
StdErr = (Variance / Ndata) ^ 0.5
Mean = Worksheets("Data").Range("C11").Value
LoStdErrOut = (Mean - StdErr) - (Coeff * ((Mean + StdErr) - (Mean - StdErr)))
HiStdErrOut = (Mean + StdErr) + (Coeff * ((Mean + StdErr) - (Mean - StdErr)))
RemoCnt = WorksheetFunction.CountIf(Worksheets("Data").Range("A2:A" & (Ndata + 1)), "<" _
& LoStdErrOut)
If RemoCnt > 0 Then
    For j = 1 To RemoCnt
        Dpoint = j + 1
        GoSub MorR
    Next j
End If
```

```vba
k = RemoCnt
RemoCnt = RemoCnt + WorksheetFunction.CountIf(Worksheets("Data").Range("A2:A" &
(Ndata + 1)), ">" & HiStdErrOut)
If RemoCnt > k Then
    For j = 1 To (RemoCnt - k)
        Dpoint = Ndata + 2 - j
        GoSub MorR
    Next j
End If
' Write analysis
With Worksheets("Data")
    .Range("H5").Value = "Outliers encountered:"
    .Range("K5").Value = "Low values: " & k
    .Range("K6").Value = "High values:  " & (RemoCnt - k)
    .Range("H7").Value = "Calc non-outlier range:"
    .Range("K7").Value = Round(LoStdErrOut, 4) & "  to  " & Round(HiStdErrOut, 4)
    .Range("H8").Value = "Non-outliers range of data:"
    .Range("K8").Value = Worksheets("Data").Range("A" & (k + 2)) & "  to  " &
Worksheets("Data").Range("A" & (Ndata + 1 - RemoCnt + k))
End With
Return
Out:
'-----
Sheets("Bk").Visible = False
With ActiveWindow
    .DisplayHeadings = True
    .DisplayVerticalScrollBar = True
    .DisplayWorkbookTabs = True
End With
Sheets("Data").Select
End Sub
```

Hope you'll find it useful.

Unique Advanced Filtering

Advanced filtering in Excel is in fact nothing new in recent years, but it is a very useful feature, worth revisiting and reminding its role in data analysis and presentation. In the following example I demonstrate how you can filter the selected data (a list in this case) to show the **unique names/IDs**, based on just one simple criteria. Not only that; at the same time, you can get an additional information - number of times each of the unique names/IDs appears in the list.

Here's the setup and the result.

	A	B	C	D
1	Names			
2	=*			
3				
4	Names		Filtered (Unique)	Count
5	Adam		Adam	2
6	Jane		Jane	4
7	Wanda		Wanda	1
8	Harold		Harold	1
9	Julie		Julie	2
10	Eric		Eric	1
11	Karol		Karol	2
12	Bart		Bart	1
13	Jane		Adam	2
14	Jane			
15	Julie			
16	Karol			
17	Jane			
18	Adam			

The list range is in column **A**. The criteria range - in the cell **A2** (it's * - the asterisk wildcard). For the filtered unique names, I've selected column **C**, and for the count of those unique names - column **D**. In cell **D5** I've entered this formula: **=COUNTIF($A$5:$A$18,C5)**, and extended it down the column to show the count.

To execute the filtering, first you need to select the **Data** menu tab, then the **Advanced** (in the **Sort & Filter** section). Next, you need to fill the **Advanced Filter** dialog box as shown here:

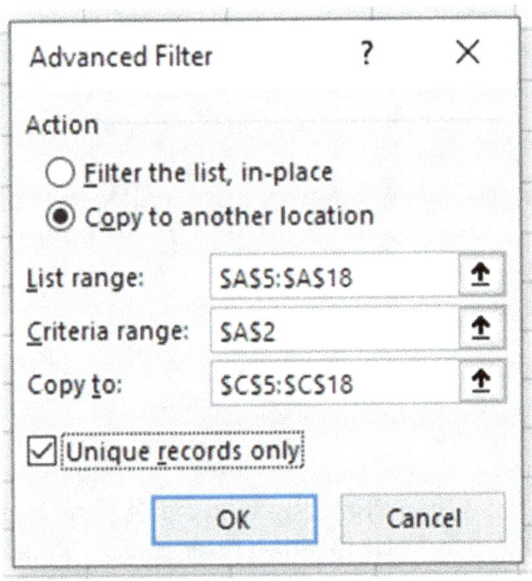

Obviously, you can use the Advanced Filter for any of your data lists or tables, with more complex multiple criteria, to extract your targeted records and complete desired additional operations on them.

Using Excel as Music Player

Do you like to listen in the background to your favourite music while working outside Excel, e.g., in Word, or on your emails? If so, you can use Excel as a music player. To prepare for that you need to create a music library, collection of your music files, located e.g., in **MyMusic** subdirectory, as in my example.

Having done that, next create in your Excel worksheet a list of **Hyperlinks** to those files (*by using* **CTRL+K** *shortcut for each of your music files*). The list can be arranged in any order and contain as many hyperlinks as needed. Here is a short example of my list:

	A	B	C	D	E	F	G	H
1	C:\MyMusic\The Road To Hell.mp3							
2	C:\MyMusic\Moby_Track3.mp3						**Play All**	
3	C:\MyMusic\ALLMYLUV.MID							
4	C:\MyMusic\DISTANCE.MID							
5	C:\MyMusic\ChopinHeroicPolonaise.mp3							
6	C:\MyMusic\Demarczyk - Tomaszow.mp3							
7	C:\MyMusic\HEY_JUDE.MID							
8	C:\MyMusic\SEEHEAVEN.MID							
9	C:\MyMusic\FlyingOnYourOwn.mp3							
10	C:\MyMusic\BelieveInAngels.mp3							
11	C:\MyMusic\BeachBoys - Kokomo.mp3							

To play your list, create the macro shown below. Just copy it to a module of your workbook's VBAProject (open it with **ALT+F11** shortcut).

```
Sub PlayAllMusic()
Dim i As Integer
Dim sFile As String
Application.DisplayAlerts = False   'Turns off alerts
sFile = Range("A1").Value
i = 1
Do While sFile <> ""
    Application.StatusBar = "Loading/playing " & sFile   'Displays message on Status Bar
    Worksheets(1).Range("A" & i).Select
    Selection.Hyperlinks(1).Follow NewWindow:=False, AddHistory:=True
    Application.Wait (Now + TimeValue("00:05:00"))     'Reserved time per one piece of music
    i = i + 1
    sFile = Range("A" & i).Value
Loop
Application.StatusBar = False
Application.DisplayAlerts = True   'Turns back on alerts
End Sub
```

The macro assumes that your list of hyperlinks starts in cell **A1** and contains no empty cells within the list. The **TimeValue** argument in **Wait** function reserves *five minutes* for playing each of the music files. These variables can be changed to fit your specific needs.

The last thing you may need to create is a **form Control button**, similar to that displayed above. After inserting on your worksheet, right-click the button, format it as you want to, right-click again and select "**Assign macro...**" option to assign the macro "PlayAllMusic" to it.

I'm using **Windows Media Player** for playing my music files, but some other players should work fine as well. If everything works as intended, click the button to play your list...

Using Camera Tool □

Although there are very versatile snipping tools available outside Excel, like e.g., "Snip and Sketch" in Windows, the Excel Camera tool (□) is still very useful in some situations when working on your workbook. This is due to a dynamic nature of the Camera snapshots. When you change something in the source of your worksheet, it'll be changed automatically in the pasted snapshot, too.

So, using the Camera tool is very helpful, especially in these areas:

- creating dashboards,
- watching particular areas/cells in a workbook,
- adding in-cell charts,
- printing multiple ranges of your workbook on a single page,
- pasting Excel ranges/objects in other applications.

If this tool is not included in your ribbon, it's worth to add it to the *Quick Access Toolbar* at the top of Excel screen. Adding it is a simple procedure, click on *File-Options-Quick Access Toolbar-All Commands*, find and select **Camera**, and add it to the Toolbar.

You can take snapshots of any cells/areas of your worksheets, including charts and other objects. However, remember that in the case of charts you must create shots from the range of cells covered by your chart, not from the chart itself! When you change chart position, the snapshot will be changed regarding to the cells data, not to the chart.

To take a screenshot:

1. Select your cells/area you want to take photo of
2. Click on Camera button
3. Select area where you want to paste your selection
4. Position the screenshot as you wish to

Pasted objects - while automatically updated - can be positioned and sized on a worksheet as needed. Because they are actually images, the Picture Format tab tools work with them, so you can do there anything you could do to a picture (e.g., cropping).

If you would like to use the Camera tool with some cells with Excel functions (like e.g., IF function), you should use Named Ranges instead of cell references in order to maintain the UPDATE connection.

Also, it's worth knowing that in many cases - instead of Camera tool - you can use **Copy** and **Paste - Linked Picture** option for pasting your snapshot.

And finally, when you paste your snapshot in other applications, the updating won't work in such a case, it will function just as a static image.

Goal Seek: Solving Cubic Equations

Let's say you know the desired result of some formula, but you need to find possible input value(s) to achieve that result. You may even know the approximate values of those parameters. However, it's probably nothing more than guessing, and you need exact values.

In such cases it's better to use Excel's **Goal Seek tool** which helps to arrive at exact solutions very efficiently.

I'm providing here an example of using the Goal Seek. The example shows how to setup your worksheet for solving a cubic equation, such as **Ac*x^3+Bc*x^2+Cc*x+Dc=0**, where I renamed the coefficients **a, b, c** and **d** to **Ac, Bc, Cc** and **Dc**.

In this case we want to find the roots for this specific equation:

2*x^3-15*x^2-195*x+990=0

So, you're looking for such values of **X** that turn the equation into correct equality.

You can try to begin with guessing some starting values for the roots, but in practice it's usually better to create a simple small table for a range of X values and get chart based on the table, like in this example:

X	Y
-10	-560
-8	566
-6	1188
-4	1402
-2	1304
0	990
2	556
4	98
6	-288
8	-506
10	-460
12	-54
14	808

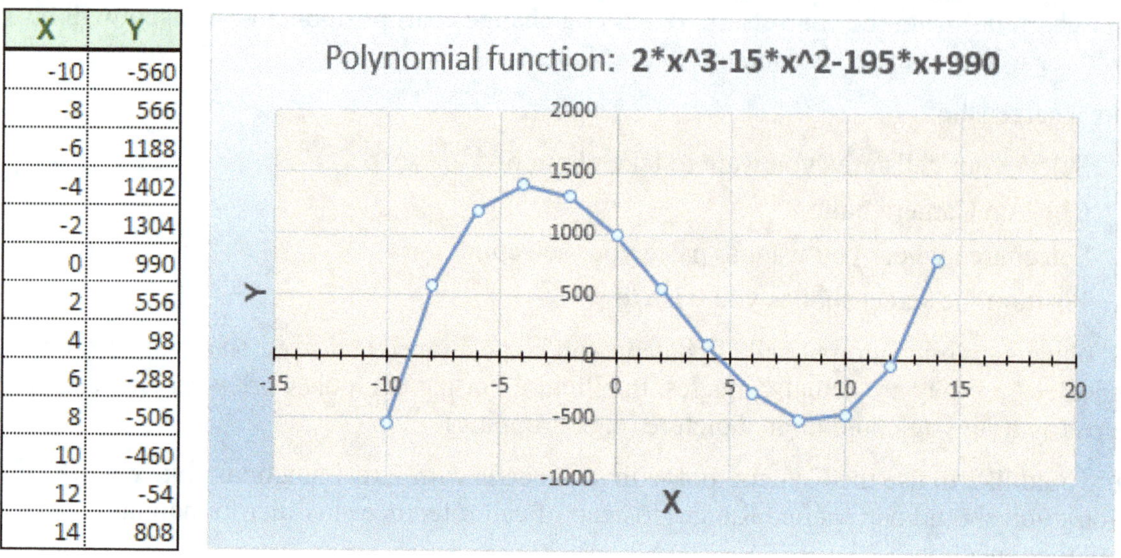

This way you can make quite good guesses for approximate values of the roots (=*crossings of X axis*) and use them as the starting values in calculations.

After this initial step you can now proceed as follows:

- Enter Ac, Bc, Cc, Dc into cells B5:B8
- Use **Formulas-Define Name**, and in the **New Name** box enter values as shown here:

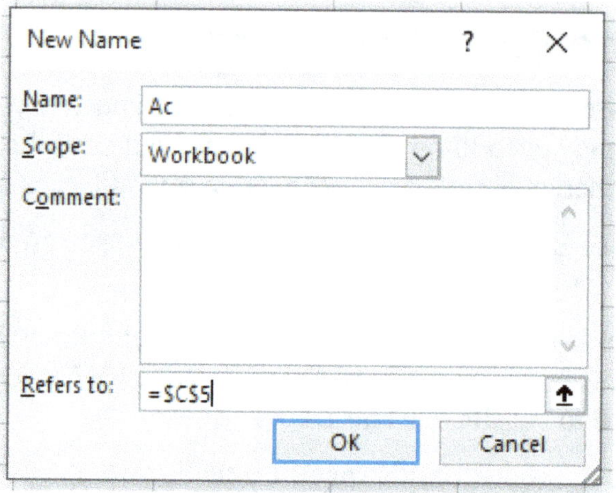

- Repeat the definition for Bc, Cc and Dc, referring them to $C$6, $C$7, $C$8.
- Enter the equation coefficients: 2, -15, -195, 990 into cells C5:C8.
- Enter the formula **=2*x^3-15*x^2-195*x+990** into cell D5 and copy it to cells D6 and D7.
- In cells E5:E7 enter the starting (guessed) X values that you can read from the chart created earlier, e.g., -10,5 and 12.
- Select cell D5 and use **Data-What-if Analysis-Goal Seek...**
- Fill the **Goal Seek** box as you see here:

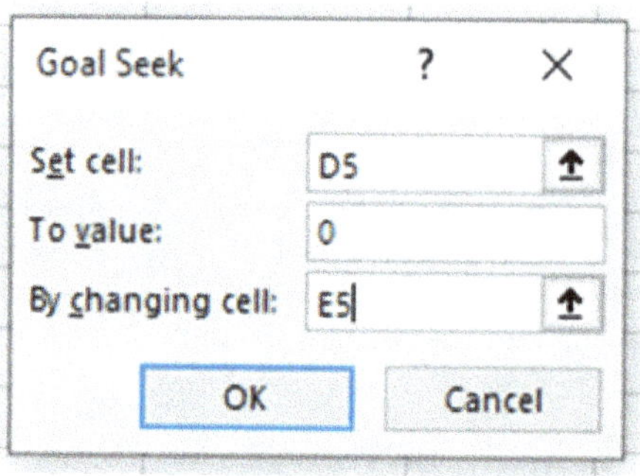

Repeat the step with the Goal Seek box for cell D6, entering **D6, 0, E6**, and for cell D7, entering **D7, 0, E7**.

Cells **E5:E7** should display the values of roots, the exact solutions you were looking for, as you can see in this table:

	Named Coefficients	Cubic Equation	Roots
5	Ac	2	0.00000	-9.126
6	Bc	-15	0.00054	4.457
7	Cc	-195	-0.00039	12.169
8	Dc	990		

Column C in this setup contains values we are certain of, they are given. **Column D** contains desired results (expected outcome of our equation). **Column E** shows the solutions, values of X that satisfy the equality of both sides of the equation.

The table can be used as a template for any of polynomial functions (cubic equations) you'd need to solve. All, you'd need to make use of it, would be:

1. 'guessing' and entering the starting values for the roots in cells E5:E7
2. entering coefficients of your equation into cells C5:C8
3. entering your equation into cells D5:D7, and then
4. running Goal Seek from cells D5, D6 and D7, consecutively.

Summarizing Large Data Sets with Pivot Tables

Are you working with large tables in Excel and preparing summary reports? If so, you need to use the **Pivot Tables tool.** All you need to do is just some mouse clicks to make interactive summary of your records quickly and efficiently.

Let's assume, you're creating a large table of data, several columns wide, thousands of rows. It's a good practice to organize the table in such a way that it:

- has unique and relevant headers,
- doesn't contain any blank cells and subtotals, and
- is named (by typing the name in the **Table Name box**, located under the **Table Design tab** in the ribbon, at the upper left corner of your worksheet)

Now your table is ready for converting (if not converted yet) into the **Excel Table**. It might look like in this small sample:

Date	Payment type	Details	Category	Expenses	Paid in
25-Jun-21)))		Moores	RG	£11.90	£0.00
29-Jun-21	VIS	Avi	IS	£17.47	£0.00
30-Jun-21	TFR	TFR-E	n/a	£0.00	£500.00
30-Jun-21)))		Acorn Nurse	HH	£10.80	£0.00
01-Jul-21	DD	AngW	HH	£32.40	£0.00
01-Jul-21	DD	BT gas	HH	£77.22	£0.00
01-Jul-21	DD	BT el	HH	£67.81	£0.00
02-Jul-21	DD	BT	HH	£83.43	£0.00
05-Jul-21	VIS	Amazon	RP	£4.99	£0.00
05-Jul-21	VIS	Amazon	ER	£10.99	£0.00
05-Jul-21	VIS	Amazon	ER	£25.55	£0.00
05-Jul-21)))		LIDL	RG	£30.15	£0.00

This will make it automatically expanding or contracting as you add new records or remove some old records from it.

At this point you're ready to use the **PivotTable tool**.

1. Click anywhere in the Excel table, and then
2. Click in the ribbon on **Insert tab > PivotChart & PivotTable**
3. In the displayed **Create PivotTable** window select your options (preferably a *New worksheet* for location) and click OK.
4. **PivotTable and PivotChart** place holders are created for you (at the same time), and the Fields with names of your Excel Table headers are listed in the **Fields** section at the right-hand part of your worksheet.

If the PivotChart is initially selected, the **PivotChart Fields** and the **Layout sections** are displayed there.

In the Fields section, select those check boxes for columns (fields) you want to add to the Layout section. By default, Excel adds dates and **non-numeric** fields (*dates, text, Boolean*) to the **Categories** axis. The **numeric** columns (fields) are added to the Values section.

You'll note that both the chart and table are automatically filled with relevant summaries of data and a plot. By default, again, Excel uses the **Sum function** for numeric data fields, and the **Count function** for non-numeric data fields. You can choose a different function by right-clicking on selected value field in the table and selecting one of the **Summarize Values By** option.

The rest belongs to your specific needs and creativity. Your choices. You can e.g.:

- rearrange the fields between the areas of the Layout sections
- choose different calculations (e.g., % or values) in Value fields
- experiment with layouts in order to get the best layout for your summary.

Better yet is this: *you can use the following clicks for your Pivot table and Pivot chart:*

With your selection anywhere in the Excel Table:

- Click on **Insert > Recommended PivotTables**, to see and select, if you like, any of several suggestions presented by Excel.

With your Chart selected:

- Click on **Insert > Recommended Charts**, to see and select, if you like, any of available options.

Here are some examples of my PivotTable and PivotChart I've created for my Excel Table shown above (*containing about 2000 records*).

Sum of Expenses	Column Labels												
Row Labels		CA	CM	ER	FT	HE	HH	IS	RG	RP	TR	TX	Grand Total
2017	0		100.95	87.16			38.43		498.71		64.35		789.6
2018	0	1120	1154.78	559.37	0.28	367.83	4003.96	402.82	6361.37		71.4	912	14953.81
2019	0	650	1395.12	804.21	0.54	137.71	4153.54	878.78	6871.64	331.08	117.54	2488.72	17828.88
2020	0	237	654.53	312.94	31.17	223.87	5033.45	855.36	5675.36	155.75		2552.06	15731.49
2021	0		389.85	592.94	19.5	178.28	2860.87	117.91	3398.13	4.99		1776.25	9338.72
Grand Total	0	2007	3695.23	2356.62	51.49	907.69	16090.25	2254.87	22805.21	491.82	253.29	7729.03	58642.5

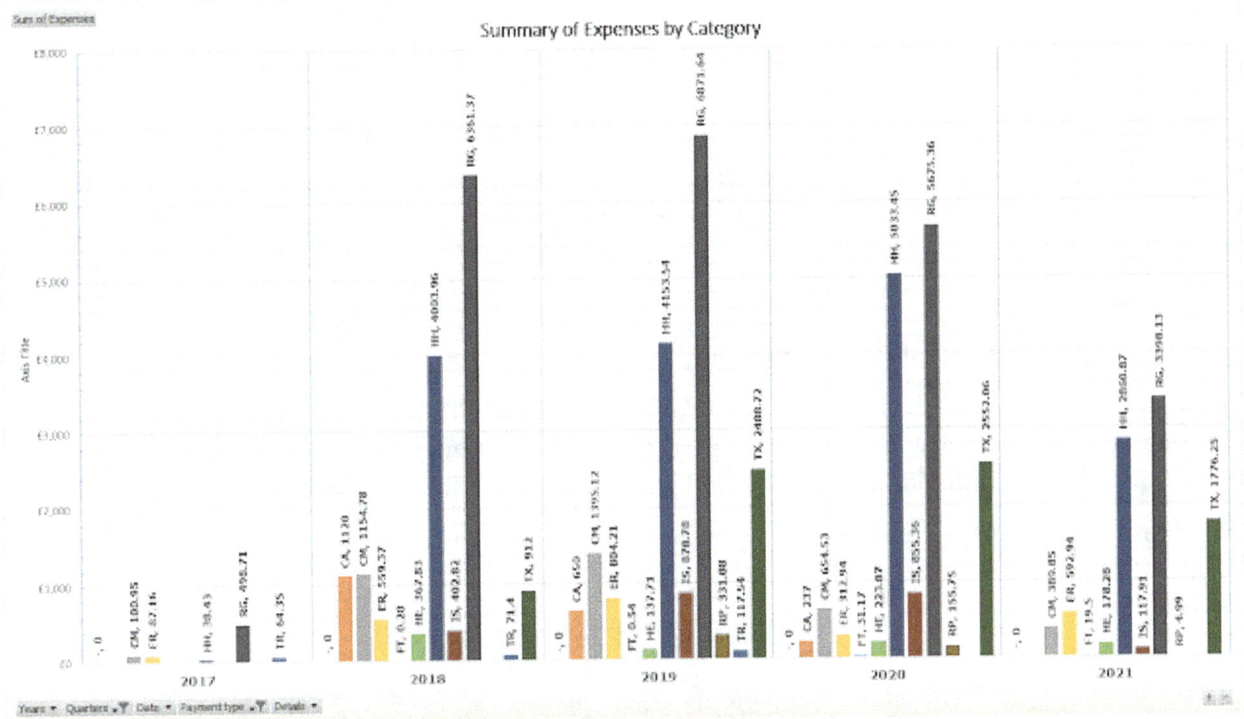

How to Create Mutually Dependent Cells

Mutual dependence of Excel cells means that some two cells in your workbook **refer** to each other. If the value of one of the two dependent cells changes it causes change of value in the other cell dependent on it. This normally leads to a problem called "*circular reference*". However, it is possible to set up mutually dependent cells by following steps shown in my example below.

First, enable **iterative calculation**. Go to **File** > **Options** > **Formulas** (in Excel Options window) and select options as you see in this image:

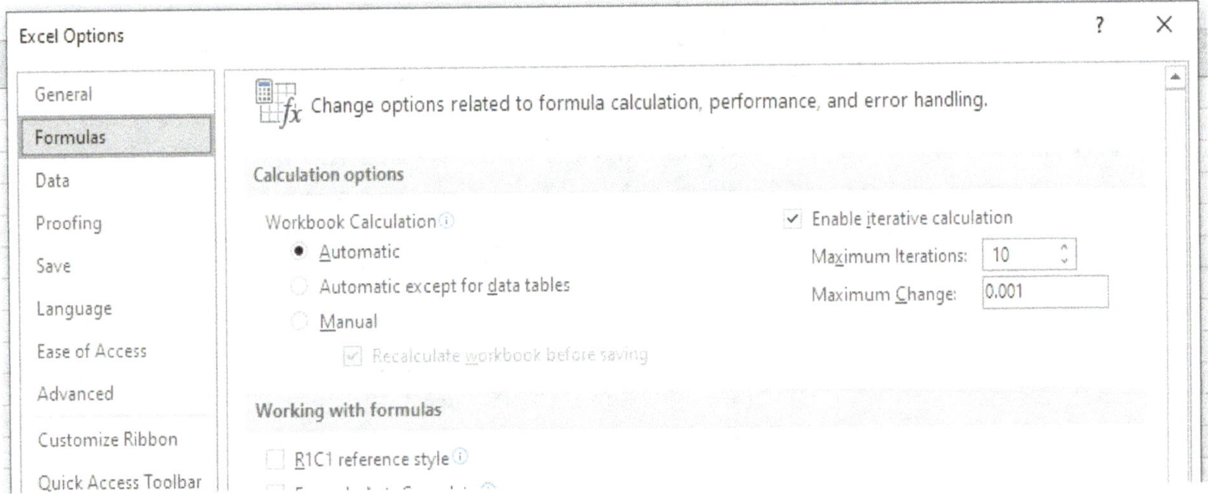

Next, make sure that, depending on your needs, either *Automatic* or *Manual* calculation option is selected (go to **Formulas** tab > **Calculation Options**).

Now, enter this kind of formulas in your workbook (*these are examples only*):

- in cell Sheet1!A1   =IFERROR(**SQRT(LOG(Sheet2!C3)+10**),"Error!")
- in cell Sheet2!C3   =IFERROR(**Sheet1!A1+20,1**)

Underlined expressions indicate parts *to be replaced* by the contents of your specific cells that you want to designate as mutually dependent ones.

As you'll see, the results displayed in each of the two cells are mutually dependent on each other and the circular reference issue is avoided. Make sure that the result of such dependence meets your expectations.

Keep in mind that each time you save/update your workbook or press F9 key, the dependent cells get updated, because if e.g., the value of cell A1 changes, the value of cell C3 also changes. This could go indefinitely... Would such mutual dependence make sense for you? This is the question you need to answer.

Using Excel Custom Lists

What are Custom Lists used for? They are used mainly for SORTING or FILLING any regular Excel lists and tables in a specific *user-defined* order. Using the lists may save you a lot of time when frequent sorting or filling your lists is needed when working with Excel data.

Excel provides couple of built-in lists by default, as you can see below:

How you can use them? Here is the way (*if you haven't used them never before*):

- in your selected cell type in any entry from the custom list, e.g., Jan, or Mon, etc.
- click on the small box at the bottom right corner and drag it any way you want to - down, up, right, left - to populate any number of cells, in rows or columns, with the list items.

There are also many "*hidden*" custom-like lists you can build and use easily as needed. Below are some examples of such lists that Excel accepts and readily auto fills for you:

List1	List2	List3	List4	List5	List6	List7	List8	List9	List10
Lesson 1	Element 1	Group a1	Item 01	1 tab	1 kit	Core 1.10	abc_a1	50	Qtr 1
Lesson 2	Element 2	Group a2	Item 02	2 tac	3 kit	Core 1.11	abc_a2	100	Qtr 2
Lesson 3	Element 3	Group a3	Item 03	3 tad	5 kit	Core 1.12	abc_a3	150	Qtr 3
Lesson 4	Element 4	Group a4	Item 04	2 tab	7 kit	Core 1.13	abc_a4	200	Qtr 4
Lesson 5	Element 5	Group a5	Item 05	3 tac	9 kit	Core 1.14	abc_a5	250	Qtr 1
Lesson 6	Element 6	Group a6	Item 06	4 tad	11 kit	Core 1.15	abc_a6	300	Qtr 2
Lesson 7	Element 7	Group a7	Item 07	3 tab	13 kit	Core 1.16	abc_a7	350	Qtr 3
Lesson 8	Element 8	Group a8	Item 08	4 tac	15 kit	Core 1.17	abc_a8	400	Qtr 4
Lesson 9	Element 9	Group a9	Item 09	5 tad	17 kit	Core 1.18	abc_a9	450	Qtr 1
Lesson 10	Element 10	Group a10	Item 10	4 tab	19 kit	Core 1.19	abc_a10	500	Qtr 2
Lesson 11	Element 11	Group a11	Item 11	5 tac	21 kit	Core 1.20	abc_a11	550	Qtr 3
...	...	...	...	...	...	...	...	...	...

In most cases you can use them by typing in just the first item, like e.g., "Lesson 1", "abc_a1", "Qtr 1", and dragging the cell's corner in any direction. But you can also use lists like the List5 or List6, typing in first two or three cells to initiate your custom list and then selecting them and dragging the lowest cell's corner in any direction.

Excel doesn't care about the case of items in the list, so if you type the first item e.g., in *Upper* case, all the following items will be displayed in the Upper case.

Keep in mind that if you'd like to build a list of numbers only, like e.g., <u>List9</u> above, the list must be formatted as *text* prior to including it as a Custom List.

Creating Your Own Custom Lists

To create and add your own **Custom lists** to those provided already in Excel you need to **Edit Custom Lists**. To do that follow these steps:

- type the values of the list you need to use quite frequently, like e.g., *currency codes of some countries*, in a column of your worksheet, as shown here
- select the cells with your entries
- go to **File** > **Options** > **Advanced** > **General**, find there the shaded **Edit Custom Lists** field and click on it
- in the box click **Import**, click **OK**; your list has been added to the Custom lists box and is ready to use.

Alternatively, you could also add your list by clicking **NEW LIST** in the **Custom lists** box, and entering your list in the **List entries** box, one by one (*pressing **Enter** key after each entry)*, and clicking **Add** when completed all entries.

USD - United States
EUR - The EU (19 states)
JPY - Japan
GBP - United Kingdom
AUD - Australia
CAD - Canada
CHF - Switzerland
CNY - China
SEK - Sweden
MXN - Mexico
NZD - New Zealand
PLN - Poland
SGD - Singapore
HKD - Hong Kong (China)
NOK - Norway
KRW - South Korea
TRY - Turkey
INR - India

Sorting by your Custom Lists

Now, you can use any of available custom lists for sorting your datasets. Click on one or more columns of your table, then click on **Sort & Filter** > **Custom sort...** > drop down the **Order menu** > **Custom List...** and find the list you'd like to sort by. Finish by clicking OK. Include as many columns as you need for sorting.

How to Create Nice Chart for Any Formula / Equation

Would you like to create impressive charts effortlessly, based just on a single formula? Would you like your charts look similarly to these examples? If so, follow the directions below.

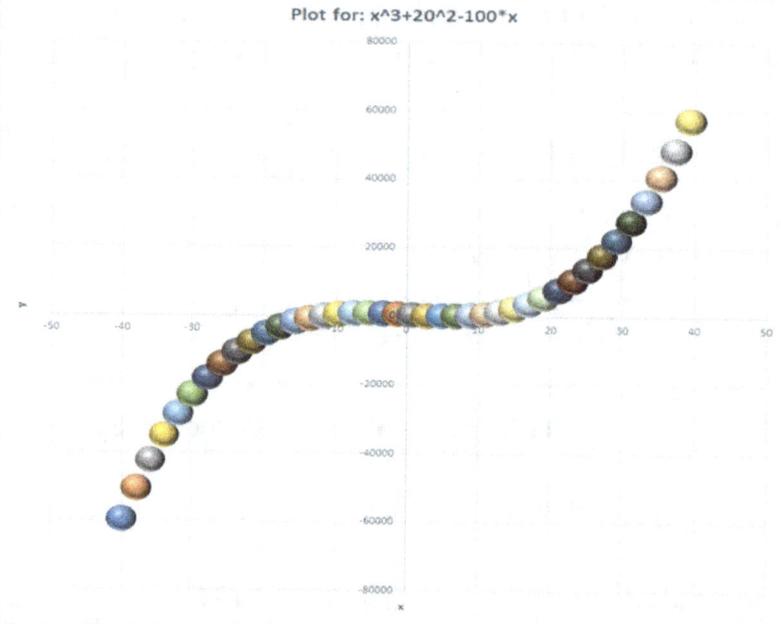

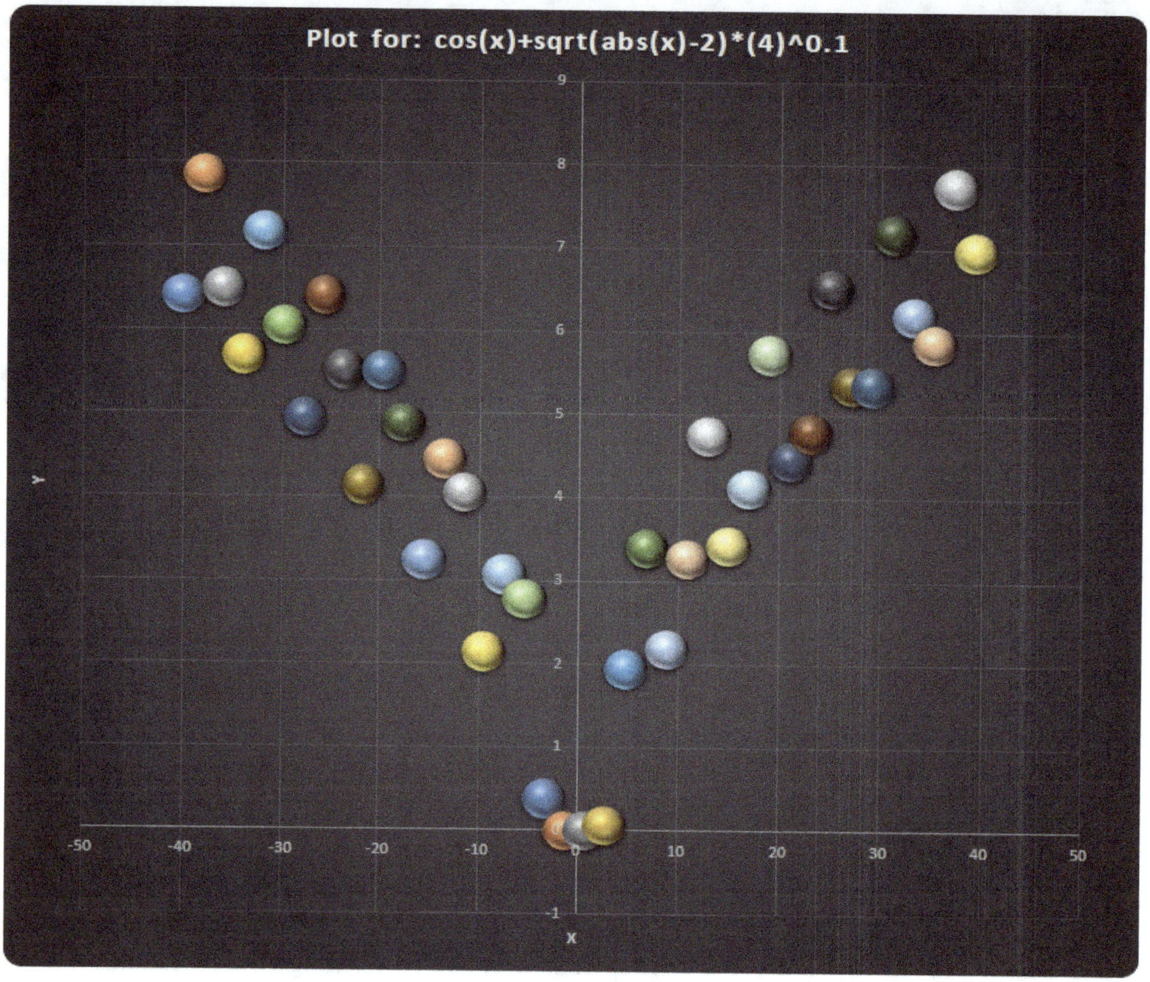

Plot for: cos(x)+sqrt(abs(x)-2)*(4)^0.1

One of interesting features related to charting in Excel allows you to plot charts based not on actual data ranges/tables but **based on formulas**.

Here are the basic steps to follow if you'd like to create such nice charts quickly. If you create just one of them, you can save the file as a template for future use.

The first thing to do is to enter/arrange all necessary information you'll need for your chart elements. So, enter the following in your worksheet:

Cell	Text entry	Cell	Data entry
A1	"Formula to plot"	**B1**	*Enter/paste your formula to be plotted*
A2	"xLeft"	**B2**	*Enter number for starting point of X axis*
A3	"xRight"	**B3**	*Enter number for ending point of X axis*
A4	"Number of points"	**B4**	*Enter number of points to be plotted*
A5	"Chart title"	**B5**	*Enter "**Plot for: "Sheet1!$B$1**"*
A7	**"List of formulas"**		
A8	Enter your first formula, e.g., **x^3+20^2-100*x**		
A9	and 2nd one, e.g.:		
A10	Etc….		

When you enter all the required information, your worksheet may look similarly to this one:

	A	B
1	Formula	sqrt(x-4)*2*x*3^2
2	xLeft	-80
3	xRight	80
4	xNoOfPoints	40
5	Chart Title	Plot for: sqrt(x-4)*2*x*3^2
6		
7	**Formulas for plotting**	
8	2*x^2-12*x+16	
9	18^3+30^2 -20*x+81	
10	(sqrt(cos(x))*cos(500*x)+sqrt(abs(x))-0.4)*(4-x*x)	
11	cos(x)+sqrt(abs(x)-2)*(4)^0.1	
12	sqrt(abs(x)-2)*(4)^0.1	
13	sqrt(x-4)*2*x*3^2	
14	0.5*(x-10)-0.9*sqrt(4-(x+1))^2+0.8*sqrt(20)	
15	x^3+20^2-100*x	

Remember that you must follow the format of the formulas exactly as shown here in the examples. *No free spaces are allowed within the equation*; they would create error message. Remember also that you can change the plot view by changing coordinates and number of points plotted (entries in cells B2:B4).

The second thing to do is to define some Names. On **Formulas** tab, in **"Define Names"** group, click **"Define Name"** and define the following Names, one by one:

Name	Refers To:
Formula	=Sheet1!$B$1
xLeft	=Sheet1!$B$2
xRight	=Sheet1!$B$3

xNoOfPoints	=Sheet1!$B$4
xRng	=xRight-xLeft
x	=xLeft+xRng/(xNoOfPoints-1)*(ROW(OFFSET(Sheet1!$A$1,0,0,xNoOfPoints,1))-1)
y	=EVALUATE(Sheet1!$B$1 & "+0*x"

Now, select any area in your worksheet and, in your **Menu Bar** select **Insert > Charts > Insert Scatter(X,Y)...** Select one of the **Scatter** charts. Place the chart conveniently in your worksheet and right-click on the chart area. In **Edit Series** window, click on **Edit** button and in **Edit Series** window enter:

- under **Series name:** select range B5 in the worksheet,
- under **Series X values:** enter "=Shee1!x"
- under **Series Y values:** enter "=Sheet1!y"

Now you can format your data points in the chart. Right-click in chart area and select **Change Chart Type**. Select **All Charts** and click on **3-D Bubble** icon. Click OK.

Next, right-click on data points (markers) and select **Format Data Series...** . Click on **Series Options** icon ( ) , set the **Scale bubble size to** e.g., *15* (Area of bubbles), then click on **Fill & Line** icon ( ), select **Fill > Automatic** and mark **Vary colours by point**.

If you need to edit/add chart title, right-click on the title box and either:

- select **Edit Text** and edit it, or
- in **Formula Bar** enter "=" and select cell B5.

Select the chart, click on **Chart Elements** icon ( ) and select those elements which you want to be displayed in the chart (titles, axes, gridlines, data labels, error bars, legend, trendline). Make any changes you want to those elements.

Select the chart and click on Chart Styles icon ( ) and select your favourite style and colour scheme for your chart.

Hyperlinks - Creating and Using

This function deserves special attention because it is very supportive and can be used in Excel in at least two essential ways, as:

- **searching** tool (looking for information on Internet), or
- **linking** tool (giving easy access to your documents)

The most useful SEARCHING tool is probably represented by this formula:

=HYPERLINK("http://www.google.com/search?q="&B1&"&safe=active","Search Google")

I've used to select two cells in one of the corners of my worksheet page for this function. E.g., cell A1 would contain the formula, and B1 would be used to enter my search text (anything you'd like to search for in Google), like shown here:

This is your Excel interface to the world of Internet or internal web (Intranet). While working on your workbook you have immediate access to any information you may need, without going back and forth to your browser.

I find also Hyperlink to be quite helpful in searching with Microsoft Bing engine. To use it, enter this kind of formula: **=HYPERLINK("https://bing.com/search?q=*Middleton*","Search Bing")** in any empty cell of your worksheet. Remember to enter your search term directly into the formula after the '=' sign (as given e.g., here: *Middleton*).

You can also use option like this: **=HYPERLINK("https://bing.com/search?q=","Search Bing")**. In this case the **www.bing.com** page will be opened, and you can search conveniently by voice, image, or simple text.

The second way of using Hyperlink function is as a LINKING tool. First, click on a cell in which you wish to place your link. Then just enter **CTRL+K** shortcut on your keyboard. This command shows "Insert Hyperlink" window, where you can choose appropriate option for your desired link. There are many of them.

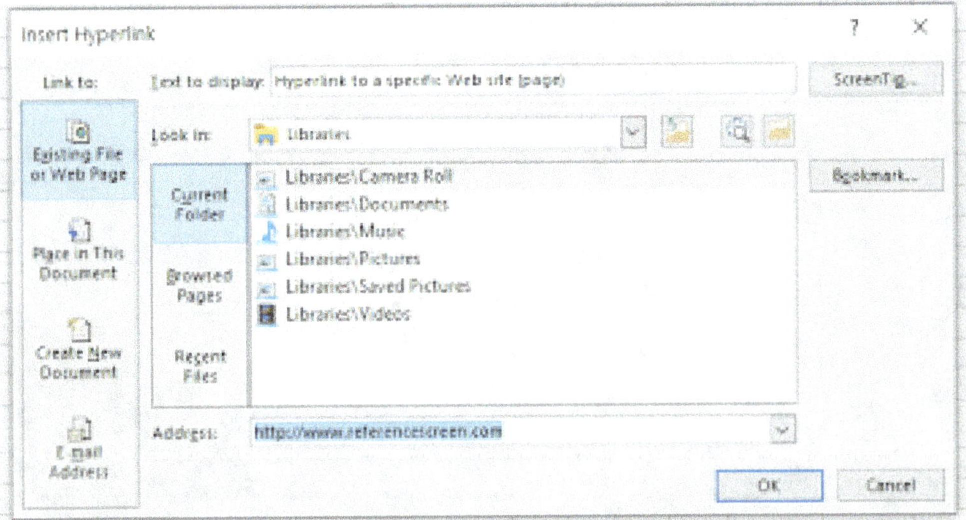

From here you can link to:
- current directory/folder
- any existing file on your computer
- currently used workbook
- recently used files/addresses
- specific places in workbooks
- browsed Internet pages
- specific places on web page/intranet
- email address

Always give meaningful names to your hyperlinks and, optionally, provide a "ScreenTip..." which will be displayed when your mouse is hovered over them.

Happy hyperlinking!

Presentations in Excel

If most of your work, you do for presentations, comes from Excel, there is no reason to use the PowerPoint instead of Excel itself for preparing your demonstration.

In fact, all your charts, tables, forms, textual info, background graphics, and even sounds, can be quite easily presented and put in order in Excel worksheets. All the hassle with extra work of copying and pasting into PowerPoint could not be necessary.

Let's say, you've carried out your data analysis and prepared workbook with 30 perfect worksheets ('slides') for your quarterly presentation. How would you proceed to get ready for reporting your work? Switching to PowerPoint? Not necessarily.

If you'd decide to stay with Excel, the following steps could probably be more efficient way to go.

First, put all your presentable worksheets in consecutive order in which they'll be presented.

Add a blank worksheet dedicated to a title page. Excel has all the tools needed to create an attractive design. Such a worksheet could show just the subject of your presentation or might be a bit more elaborated, as e.g., in this figure:

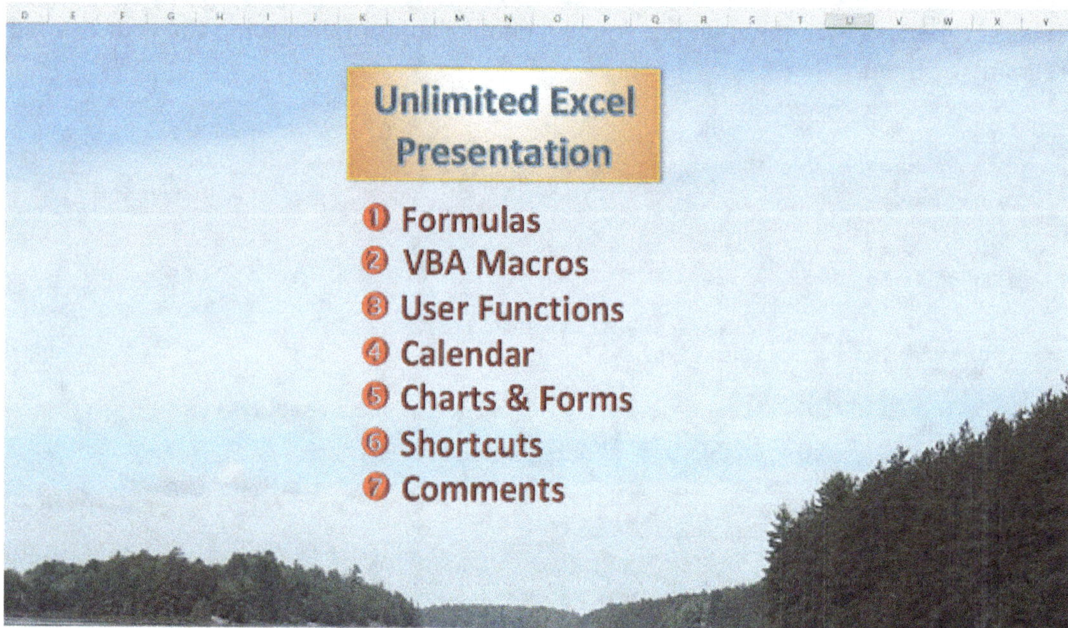

Similarly, you can add another worksheet for displaying "The end" page, if appropriate.

Plan for the time you'll need to properly present your content. If you want to stay in full control of time devoted to each of the worksheets, then you'd move from one sheet to the next one simply by using Excel shortcut **CTRL+PgDn** (or **CTRL+PgUp**) on your keyboard. But, if you'd prefer to switch from page to page automatically, then you could do it with the help of a simple macro, where you'd display each page for e.g., 90 seconds, as in this example:

```
Sub PresentInExcel()
Dim i as Integer
For i = 1 To Application.Worksheets.Count
        Application.Worksheets(i).Activate
        Application.Wait (Now + TimeValue("0:01:30"))
Next i
End Sub
```

Your presentation will look better if you use Full Screen option and turn off *Gridlines* and *Headings* on each worksheet (in *View > Show* menu). This step can be also included in the macro as shown here:

```
Sub PresentInExcel()
Dim i As Integer
'Hide Excel features (filename, bars, tabs, headings, ribbon)
    ActiveWindow.Caption = ""
```

```vba
    ActiveWindow.DisplayHorizontalScrollBar = False
    ActiveWindow.DisplayVerticalScrollBar = False
    ActiveWindow.DisplayHeadings = False
    ActiveWindow.DisplayWorkbookTabs = False
    ActiveWindow.DisplayGridlines = False
    Application.DisplayStatusBar = False
    Application.DisplayFormulaBar = False
For i = 1 To Application.Worksheets.Count
    Application.Worksheets(i).Activate
    ActiveWindow.DisplayHeadings = False
    ActiveWindow.DisplayGridlines = False
    Application.Wait (Now + TimeValue("0:01:30"))
Next i
'Show all Excel features (filename, bars, tabs, headings, ribbon)
    ActiveWindow.Caption = ThisWorkbook.Name
    ActiveWindow.DisplayHorizontalScrollBar = True
    ActiveWindow.DisplayVerticalScrollBar = True
    ActiveWindow.DisplayHeadings = True
    ActiveWindow.DisplayWorkbookTabs = True
    ActiveWindow.DisplayGridlines = True
    Application.DisplayStatusBar = True
    Application.DisplayFormulaBar = True
    Application.ExecuteExcel4Macro "show.toolbar(""Ribbon"",True)"
End Sub
```

Options such as ***Zoom In/Out*** can also be used during formatting of your worksheets for presentation to focus viewer's attention on some specific details.

If you decide on adding some sound/musical background while presenting your report you can do that in Excel as well. In such a case you would need to include some more VBA code to the Module holding your macro. You'd then be able to play any of **WAV** or **MIDI** files residing on your computer.

Overall, the following VBA procedures should be placed in your presentation **Project Module** of **Project Explorer** (accessible with ***CTRL+F11*** shortcut):

```vba
Private Declare Function mciExecute Lib "winmm.dll" _
    (ByVal lpstrCommand As String) As Long          'MIDI files
Private Declare Function PlaySound Lib "winmm.dll" Alias "PlaySoundA" _
    (ByVal lpszName As String, ByVal hModule As Long, ByVal dwFlags As Long) As Long
'WAV files
Const SND_SYNC = &H0              'WAV files
Const SND_ASYNC = &H1             'WAV files
Const SND_FILENAME = &H20000      'WAV files
Sub PlayWAV()
'The WAV file is played asynchronously, i.e. execution continues while the sound is playing
'To stop code execution while the sound is playing, use this statement instead:
'          Call PlaySound(WAVFile, 0&, SND_SYNC Or SND_FILENAME)
'Replace the path and WAV file name with your own
WAVFile = "C:\Users\Roman\MyMusic\02 - The Road To Hell (Part II).WAV"
Call PlaySound(WAVFile, 0&, SND_ASYNC Or SND_FILENAME)
End Sub


Sub PlayMIDI()
'Replace the path and MIDI file name with your own
        MIDIFile = "C:\Users\Roman\MyMusic\OCANADA.MID"
        mciExecute ("play " & MIDIFile)
```

End Sub

Sub StopMIDI()
'Replace the path and MIDI file name with your own
      MIDIFile = "C:\Users\Roman\MyMusic\OCANADA.MID"
      mciExecute ("stop " & MIDIFile)
End Sub

```vba
Sub PresentInExcel()
'Use this macro to set up and run your presentable worksheets
Dim i As Integer
'Hide Excel features (filename, bars, tabs, headings, ribbon)
    ActiveWindow.Caption = ""
    ActiveWindow.DisplayHorizontalScrollBar = False
    ActiveWindow.DisplayVerticalScrollBar = False
    ActiveWindow.DisplayHeadings = False
    ActiveWindow.DisplayWorkbookTabs = False
    ActiveWindow.DisplayGridlines = False
    Application.DisplayStatusBar = False
    Application.DisplayFormulaBar = False
    Application.ExecuteExcel4Macro "show.toolbar(""Ribbon"",False)"
Call PlayWAV
For i = 1 To Application.Worksheets.Count
    Application.Worksheets(i).Activate
    ActiveWindow.DisplayHeadings = False
    ActiveWindow.DisplayGridlines = False
    Application.Wait (Now + TimeValue("0:01:30"))
Next i
'Show all Excel features (filename, bars, tabs, headings, ribbon)
    ActiveWindow.Caption = ThisWorkbook.Name
    ActiveWindow.DisplayHorizontalScrollBar = True
    ActiveWindow.DisplayVerticalScrollBar = True
    ActiveWindow.DisplayHeadings = True
    ActiveWindow.DisplayWorkbookTabs = True
    ActiveWindow.DisplayGridlines = True
    Application.DisplayStatusBar = True
    Application.DisplayFormulaBar = True
    Application.ExecuteExcel4Macro "show.toolbar(""Ribbon"",True)"
End Sub
```

This is just an example to be adapted for your specific project.
Happy presenting!

Solve Quadratic Equations, Fast

Have lots of equations to solve? It's easy and can be done at lightning speed.

First, add a Command button on your worksheet: on the **Developer** tab, in the **Controls** group, click **Insert**, and then under **ActiveX Controls**, click **Command Button.** Next, click the worksheet location at which you want the upper-left corner of the command button to appear and adjust its size and properties, so it looks similarly to this presented here:

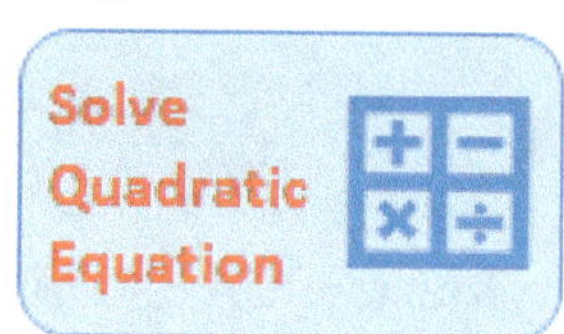

Click **View Code** in the **Controls** group. This will launch the Visual Basic Editor. Add the following VBA macro code in the window:

```vba
Sub SolveQuadraticEquation()
'Quadratic Equation Solver
Dim a, b, c, det, root1, root2 As Single
On Error GoTo ErrHandler
coef = InputBox("Enter a b c coefficients separated by slash(/)", "Quadratic Equation Solver", "1.5/-2/3")
a = Left(coef, Application.WorksheetFunction.Search("/", coef, 1) - 1)
b = Left(Right(coef, Len(coef) - Application.WorksheetFunction.Search("/", coef, 1)), Application.WorksheetFunction.Search("/", Right(coef, Len(coef) - Application.WorksheetFunction.Search("/", coef, 1)), 1) - 1)
c = Right(coef, Len(coef) - Len(a) - Len(b) - 2)
det = (b ^ 2) - (4 * a * c)
If det > 0 Then
        root1 = (-b + Sqr(det)) / (2 * a)
        root2 = (-b - Sqr(det)) / (2 * a)
        outp = MsgBox("Root1: " & root1 & "  Root2: " & root2, , "Roots of the equation")
ElseIf det = 0 Then
        root1 = (-b) / 2 * a
        outp = MsgBox("Root1: " & root1 & "  Root2: " & root1, , "Roots of the equation")
Else
        outp = MsgBox("NO ROOT", , "Roots of the equation")
End If
ErrHandler:
End Sub
```

Close the Visual Basic Editor, and click **Design Mode** to ensure design mode is off. When you click the button, the macro will run and show the following window:

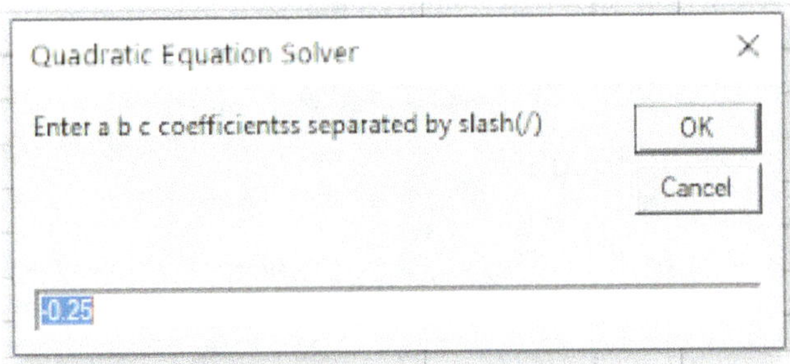

Enter the three coefficients of your equation, separated by slash, and click OK button. The result will be displayed immediately.

How to Insert and Store All of Your Images in Excel File(s)

This is probably one of the best, most efficient ways to organize all your images in Excel workbooks. Easy to insert, easy to find and easy to access/display them at any size, any scale. You can arrange them in any way you want to. You can store thousands of them in just a single worksheet, available at click of a button. No, you **don't need** even to click. They show up when you are hovering over your cell of choice with your mouse. This is about keeping your images (photos and all kinds of graphics) hidden in cell Comments.

Personally, I keep almost all of my images in .jpg and .png formats, but this is not the limitation here. Other formats can be stored this way as well.

Here is an example how to start with inserting your images and how your worksheet could initially look like:

	A	B	C	D	E	F	G
1	Galactic	NewtFract	NovaFract	CoronaVi	Pangolin	TaZyt2010	
2							
3							
4							
5							
6							
7							
8							
9							
10							

Insert Picture

How to proceed
First, select a cell for your Image location, then run the macro "Insert Picture".

To start, open a new workbook. First, you'll need to add some VBA code to your workbook, so press **ALT+F11** on your keyboard and add a module. Just right-click within VBA Project Explorer and select **Insert**, and then choose **Module** from the menu.

Next, copy the code (the macro and the related function) I'm providing below, and paste it into the Module window:

```vba
Option Explicit
Sub InsertImgInComment()
'This macro will insert your picked image into the active cell's Comment
'and scale it, as required, at locked aspect ratio
'Using UDF GetImgDim
Dim pPath As String
Dim cBox As Comment
Dim iScale As Single
Dim iTitle As String
iScale = Application.InputBox("Enter scale value for your image, e.g. 0.5 or 2 or 2.5")
With Application.FileDialog(msoFileDialogFilePicker)
    .AllowMultiSelect = True
    .ButtonName = "Insert image"
    .Filters.Clear
    .Filters.Add "Images", "*.png; *.jpg"
    .Title = "Select image"
    .Show
    On Error GoTo Err
    pPath = .SelectedItems(1)
End With
Application.ActiveCell.ClearComments
Set cBox = Application.ActiveCell.AddComment
cBox.Text Text:=""  'remove any default Comment text
'Insert the image and resize
cBox.Shape.LockAspectRatio = False
cBox.Shape.Fill.UserPicture (pPath)
cBox.Shape.Width = Trim(Left(GetImgDim(pPath), 6)) * iScale
cBox.Shape.Height = Trim(Right(GetImgDim(pPath), 6)) * iScale
'Set Comment to Hidden; switch to True if you want it visible
cBox.Visible = False
iTitle = Application.InputBox("Enter name for your image, e.g., TeaTime")
ActiveCell.Value = iTitle
'Exit Sub
Err:
End Sub


Function GetImgDim(imgPath As String) As Variant
'Returns image width and height in pixels
```

```vba
'Refers to MS Windows Image Acquisition Library v2.0
Dim imgSize(1) As Integer    'array
Dim fot As Object
'Create the ImageFile object; check if it exists
On Error Resume Next
Set fot = CreateObject("WIA.ImageFile")
If fot Is Nothing Then Exit Function
On Error GoTo 0
'Load the ImageFile object with the specified File
fot.LoadFile imgPath
'Get the width and height
imgSize(0) = fot.Width
imgSize(1) = fot.Height
Set fot = Nothing
GetImgDim = imgSize(0) & "    x    " & imgSize(1)
End Function
```

Now switch back to Excel worksheet (by pressing ALT+F11 again) and add a button. I've added a rectangular shape (from ***Insert > Shapes > Rectangles***) with rounded corners. Place it conveniently on your worksheet, right-click on it and select **Assign Macro...** from the menu. In displayed window select **InsertImgInComment** macro. Select **Edit Text** to enter name of the button, like e.g., **"Insert Picture"**. Format the button to your liking.

You're ready to test your creation and insert your first image into cell's Comment. Select e.g., cell A2 and click on the button you've just created. If everything works correctly you should see input box allowing you to define *scale* of your image. Depending on its original size you may need to reduce it by entering value below 1.0, or increase it by entering value above 1.0. The macro will process the image accordingly, and after that you'll be asked to enter some *name* for your image. That's it.

After that, hovering over the cell with your mouse, you should see the image scaled to your specified size. By right-clicking on the cell you can play with various options available in the menu.

Insert more images the same way as the first one, and organize them your way. Enjoy!

Returning the Downmost Value from a Specific Column

=INDEX(C:C,MATCH(MAX(C:C),C:C,1))   *'in column C*

It works also with some empty cells in the column.

Filtering to a Standard Deviation

Let's say, you have a data set in column B (range B2:B1000). To filter that data so that only those values that are within one standard deviation of the mean are visible, follow these steps:

- Enter the two formulas into cells e.g., C1 and D1 (*MIN* & *MAX* values limiting the Filter)

    =AVERAGE(B2:B1000) - STDEV(B2:B1000) 'MIN value
    =AVERAGE(B2:B1000) + STDEV(B2:B1000) 'MAX value

- Click on B1 (column header) and select **Data** tab > **Filter** (in Sort & Filter group)
- Click the arrow ▼ in the column header to clear all check boxes in the displayed list
- Click on "**Number Filters**" option and select "**Between...**" option
- In **Custom AutoFilter** window enter the MIN and MAX numbers from cells C1 and D1, as illustrated in this example:

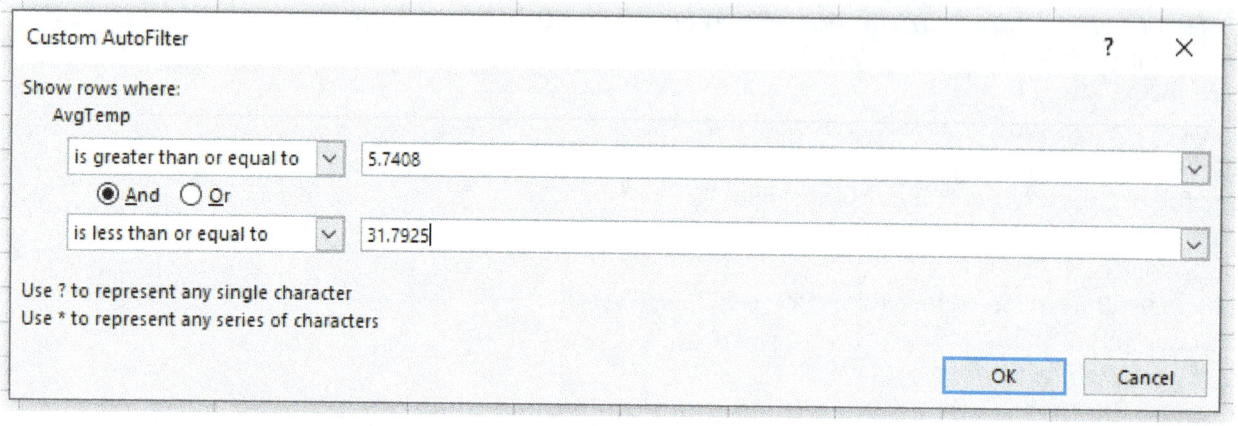

Click **OK**. Filtering accomplished.

FORMATTING / PRINTING

Conditional Formatting in Excel: All You Need to Know

This is about **visual identification and/or formatting** (differentiation) of our data sets based on our questions (conditions), in order to:

- mark/reveal some data of interest, present them
- take some action (e.g., find errors, correct, sort, delete, evaluate), or
- find out some trends and patterns, compare.

Here is the **Conditional Formatting** main menu (on the left) + **More Rules** dialog:

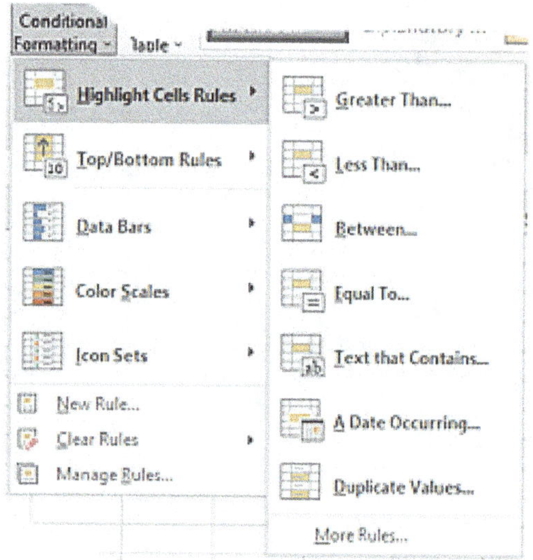
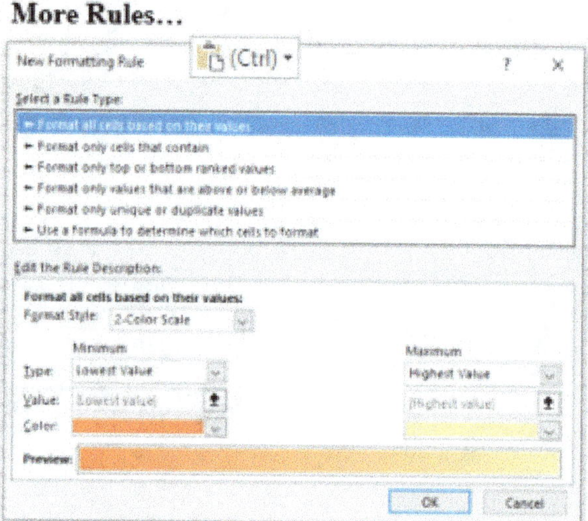

And here is the account of **what we can find out** in our dataset, using all those options available to a user.

Identify and format cells/ranges containing:

- values (numbers or text) which are **=, >, <, <....>** any values or limits (boundaries)
- some text (strings, phrases)
- dates occurring within some time frames
- duplicates or unique values
- blanks
- errors
- top or bottom ranked values (one or many)
- top or bottom ranked values, within some percentage (e.g., 10%)
- average value in a range
- values below or above statistical parameters (some average value or 1,2,3 standard deviations, etc.)

Identify and format cells based on evaluation of their content by any applied Excel **formula** resulting to TRUE.

Some examples of such formulas (**rules**):

=ISFORMULA(B2), used to highlight cells with formulas in a selected range

=ISEVEN(ROW()), used to shade alternative rows of data

=B3 >= $B$2

=A2=A1, used to hide duplicate values

=AND(cond1,cond2)

=IF(AND(cond1,cond2),TRUE,IF(AND(cond1,cond2),TRUE),FALSE)

=OR(AND(cond1,cond2),cond3)
=MIN(range)
=MOD(ROW(),2) <> 0

In most cases we can format (enhance visually) the identified cells with all kinds of *COLOURS, COLOUR SCALES, DATA BARS or ICON SETS* (directional, shapes, indicators, or ratings).

Here is e.g., **Icon Sets** menu available for formatting:

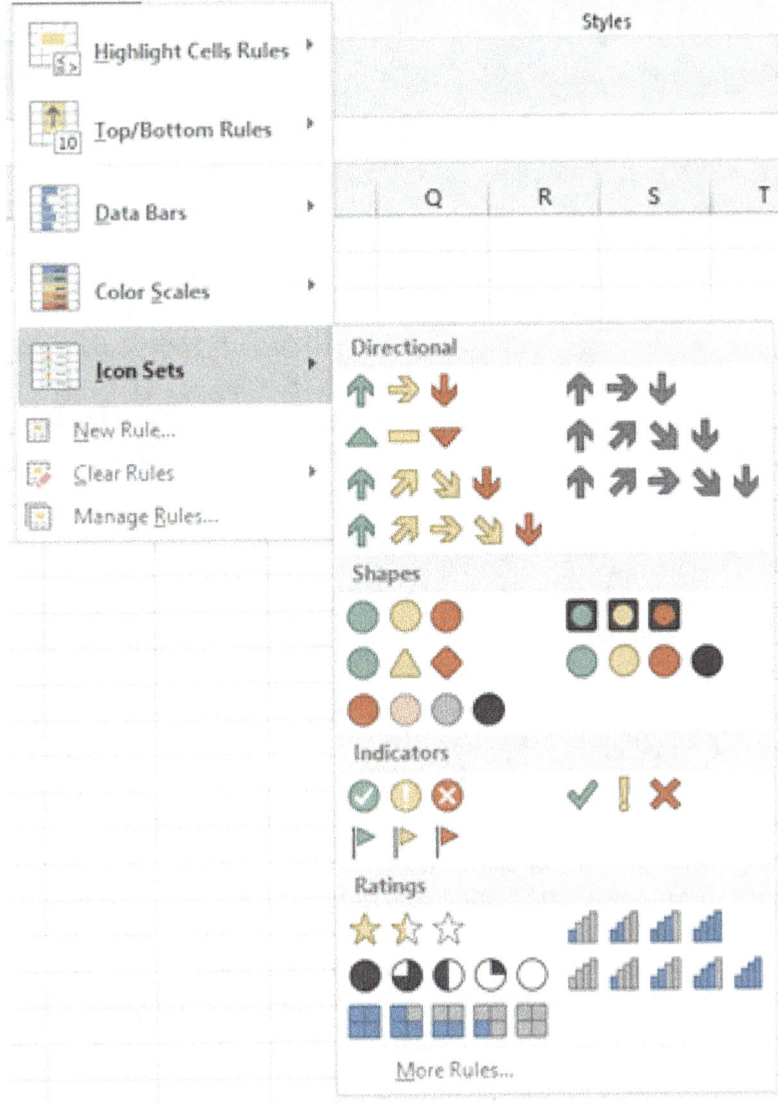

Any of the **rules** applied in identifying and formatting of cells/ranges (or even of the whole worksheet) can be managed, i.e., edited, prioritized, deleted, or added, using **Manage Rules...** options.

How to Design Colourful Cell Contents in Excel

If you need to design a colourful title or banner or something similar, so that every character or group of characters or digits has a distinct colour, then you can find this help useful. Here are just two simple examples of effects, you can achieve:

A 5.280439167

You can easily produce such effects *quickly* by entering your text (including also digits) in any cell of your worksheet, selecting the cell, and running the macro listed below. Just remember that if your cell contains just a number it must be formatted as text for this purpose.

The macro can be entered/copied into any VBA module of your workbook. Obviously, it can be modified as needed for your specific needs. Enjoy the colouring!

```vba
Sub clrFonts()
'Colours every character within a string of selected cell
Dim cnt As String
Dim rng As Range
Dim n As Long
Set rng = ActiveCell
For n = 1 To Len(rng.Value)
    cnt = Mid(rng.Value, n, 1)
     If cnt = "a" Then rng.Characters(n, 1).Font.Color = RGB(0, 0, 255): GoTo cont    'blue
     If cnt = "b" Then rng.Characters(n, 1).Font.Color = RGB(0, 255, 0): GoTo cont    'green
     If cnt = "c" Then rng.Characters(n, 1).Font.Color = RGB(255, 0, 0): GoTo cont    'red
     If cnt = "d" Then rng.Characters(n, 1).Font.Color = RGB(0, 0, 255): GoTo cont    'blue
     If cnt = "e" Then rng.Characters(n, 1).Font.Color = RGB(153, 51, 0): GoTo cont    'brownish
     If cnt = "f" Then rng.Characters(n, 1).Font.Color = RGB(255, 0, 255): GoTo cont    'd red
     If cnt = "g" Then rng.Characters(n, 1).Font.Color = RGB(0, 255, 255): GoTo cont    'green blue
     If cnt = "h" Then rng.Characters(n, 1).Font.Color = RGB(128, 0, 0): GoTo cont    'brown
     If cnt = "i" Then rng.Characters(n, 1).Font.Color = RGB(0, 128, 0): GoTo cont    'vd green
     If cnt = "j" Then rng.Characters(n, 1).Font.Color = RGB(0, 0, 128): GoTo cont    'd blue
     If cnt = "k" Then rng.Characters(n, 1).Font.Color = RGB(128, 128, 0): GoTo cont    'd grey
     If cnt = "l" Then rng.Characters(n, 1).Font.Color = RGB(128, 0, 128): GoTo cont    'vd brown
     If cnt = "m" Then rng.Characters(n, 1).Font.Color = RGB(192, 192, 192): GoTo cont    'l grey
     If cnt = "n" Then rng.Characters(n, 1).Font.Color = RGB(128, 128, 128): GoTo cont    'l green
     If cnt = "o" Then rng.Characters(n, 1).Font.Color = RGB(153, 153, 255): GoTo cont    'l blue
     If cnt = "p" Then rng.Characters(n, 1).Font.Color = RGB(153, 51, 102): GoTo cont    'vvd brown
     If cnt = "q" Then rng.Characters(n, 1).Font.Color = RGB(255, 255, 204): GoTo cont    'vl yellow
     If cnt = "r" Then rng.Characters(n, 1).Font.Color = RGB(51, 153, 102): GoTo cont    'green blue
     If cnt = "s" Then rng.Characters(n, 1).Font.Color = RGB(102, 0, 102): GoTo cont    'vvvd brown
     If cnt = "t" Then rng.Characters(n, 1).Font.Color = RGB(255, 128, 128): GoTo cont    'd orange
     If cnt = "u" Then rng.Characters(n, 1).Font.Color = RGB(0, 102, 204): GoTo cont    'vdd green
     If cnt = "v" Then rng.Characters(n, 1).Font.Color = RGB(204, 204, 255): GoTo cont    'dd grey
     If cnt = "w" Then rng.Characters(n, 1).Font.Color = RGB(0, 0, 128): GoTo cont    'vvd blue
     If cnt = "x" Then rng.Characters(n, 1).Font.Color = RGB(204, 153, 255): GoTo cont    'violet
     If cnt = "y" Then rng.Characters(n, 1).Font.Color = RGB(51, 102, 255): GoTo cont    'md blue
     If cnt = "z" Then rng.Characters(n, 1).Font.Color = RGB(102, 102, 153): GoTo cont    'greenish
     If cnt = "0" Then rng.Characters(n, 1).Font.Color = RGB(0, 0, 0): GoTo cont    'black
     If cnt = "1" Then rng.Characters(n, 1).Font.Color = RGB(0, 255, 0): GoTo cont    'green
     If cnt = "2" Then rng.Characters(n, 1).Font.Color = RGB(255, 0, 0): GoTo cont    'red
     If cnt = "3" Then rng.Characters(n, 1).Font.Color = RGB(0, 0, 255): GoTo cont    'blue
     If cnt = "4" Then rng.Characters(n, 1).Font.Color = RGB(0, 255, 255): GoTo cont    'l blue
     If cnt = "5" Then rng.Characters(n, 1).Font.Color = RGB(102, 0, 150): GoTo cont    '???
     If cnt = "6" Then rng.Characters(n, 1).Font.Color = RGB(128, 128, 0): GoTo cont    'greenish
     If cnt = "7" Then rng.Characters(n, 1).Font.Color = RGB(128, 0, 128): GoTo cont    'd brown
     If cnt = "8" Then rng.Characters(n, 1).Font.Color = RGB(0, 128, 128): GoTo cont    'd green
     If cnt = "9" Then rng.Characters(n, 1).Font.Color = RGB(255, 153, 204): GoTo cont    'rouge
    If cnt Like "[A-Z]" Then
        rng.Characters(n, 1).Font.Color = RGB(255, 0, 255)    'dark red
```

```vba
    ElseIf cnt <> " " Then
        rng.Characters(n, 1).Font.Color = RGB(0, 0, 0)     'black
    End If
cont:
Next n
End Sub
```

COLOURS in Cells: How to Get, Set and Use Them

It's really easy to colour Excel cells, their background, content or borders. We can do it either directly (using **Format Cells...** or some **Font** options) or indirectly - using **Conditional Formatting** in a variety of available ways in the Excel menu.

When it comes to determining (getting) exact codes/names of colours being already used in a worksheet, it can be a bit complicated. And it may happen that you need to know what colours were originally used for background filling of some cells. Well, we can't find it out by using any Excel function or formula. So, practically, we must use macros (VBA codes) to solve such puzzles. E.g., the following code will determine Colour Index for background colour of cell e.g., **A2**.

Press ALT+F11 keys to display the VBA editing window and enter there this code:

```vba
Sub getCellBG()
Dim getC as Integer
getC=Range("A2").Interior.ColorIndex
End Sub
```

When you run this code line by line (pressing F8 key) in VBA window, then you'll see the *getC* value of the ColorIndex displayed in the **Immediate** field beneath the code area. You can take note of it and use it later, if needed. This is OK for just sporadic determination of the background fill colour. If you need to get the colour many times and for many cells then much better solution is to use a UDF (<u>U</u>ser <u>D</u>efined <u>F</u>unction), like the following one (also to be entered in VBA window):

```vba
Function getCellRGB(myCell As Range) As String
    Dim bgColor As Long
    Dim R As Long, G As Long, B As Long
    bgColor = myCell.Interior.Color
    R = bgColor Mod 256
    G = (bgColor \ 256) Mod 256
    B = (bgColor \ 65536) Mod 256
    getCellRGB = "R:G:B = " & R & ":" & G & ":" & B
End Function
```

To get the RGB **decimal** colour code for cell **A2**, select any blank cell and type this formula:
=getCellRGB(A2)

Note that by using this UDF function we get the Colour Index expressed in a very versatile **Red:Green:Blue** format and recorded in a selected cell, while the proceeding macro provides the result from **VBA Colour Palette** (number from 1 to 56) and for temporary viewing only.

<u>Setting</u> **cell colours** by using VBA code is much simpler than **getting** them. Here are some examples of settings by including the lines of code in a macro.

```vba
Range("A2").Interior.ColorIndex = 4   'Sets background colour of A2 to green
Range("A2").Font.ColorIndex = 5       'Sets font colour in A2 to blue
Range("A2").Borders.ColorIndex = 3    'Sets borders colour of A2 to red
```

Range("B2").Interior.ColorIndex = Range("A2").Interior.ColorIndex   *'Sets background colour of cell B2 to the colour of cell A2*

If we need to use a much broader range of colours, we can also use RGB colours instead, e.g.:

Range("A2").Font.Color =RGB(120,45,205)   *'Sets font colour in A2 to kind of magenta*

The easiest way of setting some colours is by using the **VB *named*** colours, but in this case our options are limited in Excel to just **8** colours, namely:

vbBlack, vbWhite, vbCyan, vbBlue, vbYellow, vbRed, vbMagenta and vbGreen,

so, e.g., this line of code sets cell A2 background colour to yellow:

Range("A2").Interior. Color = vbYellow

Cell colours are not used just for colouring or formatting. They are very useful in summarizing and analysing of data lists and tables. Let's consider just two cases here - **counting cells** by their background colour *and* **summing up numbers** by the background colour of cells.

Here's an example:

	A Values1	B Values2	
2	2	23	
3	8	31	
4	23	2	
5	32	45	
6	38	4	
7	47	18	
8	5	34	
9	11	41	
10	14	9	
11	17	67	
12	20	45	
13			
14	3	4	**Count** *blue cells*
15	72	126	**Sum** *blue cells*

- Formula used in the row 14 is: **= cntBCC()**
- Formula used in the row 15 is: **= sumBCC()**

Both formulas refer to the following user defined functions (**UDFs**) that you need to copy (or enter) into one of VBA modules of your project in order to use them:

Function cntBCC() As Double
'Counts specifically coloured cells in specified column range
Dim rng As Variant
Dim clr As Integer
rng = InputBox("Enter the range (in a single column) of specifically coloured cells you want to sum up:")
clr = InputBox("Enter ColorIndex number (from 1 to 56) of cells you want to sum up:")
For Each cell In Range(rng)
   If cell.Interior.ColorIndex = clr Then
      cntBCC = cntBCC + 1
   End If

Next cell
End Function

Function sumBCC() As Double
'Sums values of specifically coloured cells
Dim rng As Variant
Dim clr As Integer
rng = InputBox("Enter the range (in a single column) of specifically coloured cells you want to sum up:")
clr = InputBox("Enter ColorIndex number (from 1 to 56) of cells you want to sum up:")
For Each cell In Range(rng)
    If cell.Interior.ColorIndex = clr Then
        sumBCC = sumBCC + cell.Value
    End If
Next cell
End Function

<u>**Note**</u> that the functions require your input: ***the range*** of your column data and the ***ColorIndex*** that you need to determine before using the functions.

Formatting / Editing / Moving Around in a Workbook

Excel is equipped with hundreds of formatting and editing tools, key codes and alternative handling of data. Some of them are more useful than others. The following list presents some of the most helpful and time saving tips for frequent users.

Format Painter - If you ***double-click*** the Painter in the ribbon, you can copy formatting of your selection (cell, range) repeatedly or singularly into multiple disparate cells or ranges. Click Format Painter once to quit it, if necessary.

Multiple lines in a cell - Two or more lines can be inserted into a cell by pressing **ALT+ENTER** after entering some value in the original line. It's just another way of wrapping text in a cell.

Borders - If you select (in the Home tab) **Borders > More Borders...**, you can select and add *diagonal lines* in active cell or range of cells to divide them e.g., in two parts. Then, you can add some value/text into the cell and press **ALT+ENTER** to type another value/text in the second line. Alignment of the entries can be fixed using *spacebar*, if needed. Example:

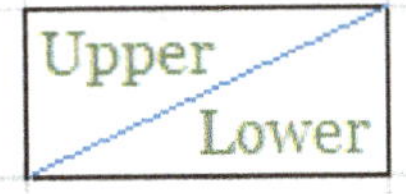

The diagonal lines can be entered also into a range of cells as shown here:

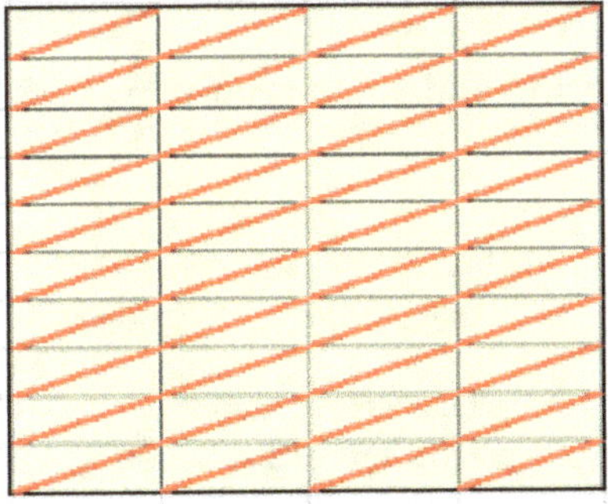

Shortcut menu for any selection - to display the menu use **Right-click** with your mouse or press **SHIFT+F10**.

Moving around in a workbook - ALT key is the most essential for this purpose. You can get to every command on the ribbon by using _Key Tips_ (the little black boxes with letters or digits) available by pressing the **ALT** key or **F10** key first. To access a menu of additional options, use the following combinations:

- **ALT+F** - to open the **File** page options
- **ALT+H** - to open the **Home** tab options
- **ALT+N** - to open the **Insert** tab options
- **ALT+A** - to open the **Data** tab options
- **ALT+R** - to open the **Review** tab options
- **ALT+W** - to open the **View** tab options

Use again the **ALT** key and appropriate **Key Tips** to select desired option in the available menu. You can go directly to your option if you remember the key sequence. E.g., you can use **ALT+E+B** to display Office _clipboard_, or **ALT+'** (apostrophe) to display _Style > Format_ menu for your selection.

Selected shortcuts using CTRL and SHIFT keys - These are quite handy, too:

- **CTRL+1**   - to **display Format Cells** dialog box
- **CTRL+T or CTRL+L** - to **display Create Table** dialog box
- **CTRL+Arrow keys**   - to **move up/down/right/left** on the worksheet
- **CTRL+SHIFT+=**   - to **display Insert dialog box** (for inserting cells, rows, columns)
- **CTRL+#**   - to **apply the Date format** with the _day-month-year_
- **CTRL+SHIFT+!**   - to **apply the Number format** with 2 decimals, 1000 separator
- **CTRL+SHIFT+&**   - to **apply outline border** to a cell or selected range
- **SHIFT+F2**   - to **add (or edit) Comment** to a selected cell
- **CTRL+`** (quotation mark)- to **toggle formula view** (alternate between value and formula)

There are, obviously, many more shortcuts available for moving around in Excel and elsewhere. One of them, namely **ALT+TAB** is worth mentioning here, because it can be used (without engaging the mouse) to switch between windows; sometimes called as '_task switcher_'. You can use it to alternate between the two opened workbooks or between a full-scale window and the desktop, or between several application-level windows.

Traps of Custom Formatting

Numbers can coexist in Excel cells with text strings. What may surprise you is that the contents of such cells can be treated and used as _numbers_. It means that they can be used as ordinary numbers in mathematical calculations, functions, and formulas. This happens when you apply some kinds of **custom formatting** for cells.

Here is such **example** of cell formatting and some confusing results of using it in formulas involving text strings.

A4			f_x	0.432027024598925

	A	B	C	D
1				
2	.525 Out		0.898	=A3*A6
3	.911 In		0.329	=SQRT(A5)
4	.432 Out		0.973	=A6^2
5	.108 Out		0.33	=SUBTOTAL(7,A2:A5)
6	.986 In		17	=LEN(A6)
7	.953 In		66801	=RIGHT(A7,5)

I've used the following **custom format** for cells in column **A**:

[Blue][>0.9]#.### "In";[Red][<=0.9]#.### "Out";General

so that values higher than **0.9** are coloured **in blue** and have added (*in the same cell*) custom text "**In**" indicating that they meet my requirements. The values equal or below **0.9** are coloured **in red** and have added custom text "**Out**" indicating that they do not meet my requirements.

Cells in column **C** have the General or Number format and contain the underlying formulas (shown in column **D**), resulting in displayed values. As you can see, the formulas ignore the added text strings in column **A** cells and work fine, on numbers only.

However, the results shown in cells **C6** and **C7** look somewhat strange. What's wrong with them? Have a look at the value shown in the *Formula Bar*; it displays the full length of the number displayed in the cell **A4**. The same format applies to all cells in Column **A**, so cell **C6** shows also the full length of the value, i.e., **17**. And cell **C7** displays the right five digits of the number displayed in cell **A7** (where only first three digits are displayed).

Conclusion: *custom formatting of cells in Excel can be very useful in most cases, but not always. Caution is advised, when applying complex custom formatting, because unreliable / unintended results can be obtained unexpectedly in some cases.*

Header/Footer: What Can Be Entered There?

Excel offers the following built-in headers and footers. They can be added to your worksheet easily, with a single mouse click.

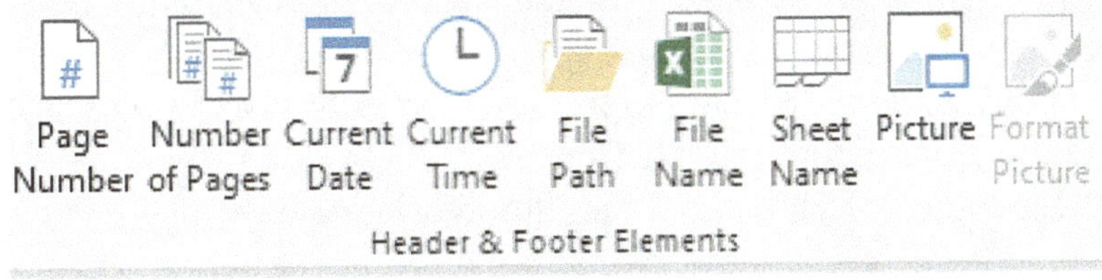

However, we're not limited to those options. In fact, you can enter **any text/string** into your worksheet **cell** and add it to any part of the header or footer with just one line of VBA code of a macro. E.g., this line of code will add contents of cell B2 to the left part of a header:

ActiveSheet.PageSetup.LeftHeader=Range("B2").Value

Such a line can be included in the VBA code (see the example in one of the macros below).

The built-in header/footer options allow us to create e.g., such a footer (at the bottom of the snippet):

		Math and trigonometry:	
25	ATAN2 function	Math and trigonometry:	Returns the arctangent from x- and y-coordinates
26	ATANH function	Math and trigonometry:	Returns the inverse hyperbolic tangent of a number

Type and description

The **Left** section contains edited cell value with red one-liner text. The **Center** section contains a properly sized picture (it could be e.g., a company logo). And the **Right** section contains another edited cell value, but in multi-line format and using different font type. The height of the footer/header can be easily changed in the page setup, as required, to fit the text length and the picture size.

In order to show the whole length of text string you may need to divide it into couple of lines by pressing ENTER at the end of each part of the text. And, if text includes ampersand (&) you must add another one (&&) to display one in the header/footer.

That's fine, but what if we need to add some specific *different values* to headers or/and footers in each of the pages to be printed? Well, it **is** possible, with the help of a macro like in this example:

```
Private Workbook_BeforePrint (Cancel As Boolean)
'This event-driven macro will enter different header/footer (as encoded
'below by the user), based on selected relevant worksheet/workbook cells,
'on each printed worksheet page.
Dim pgs As Integer
Dim topLeft As String
Dim PgArea As String
Dim i As Integer
Dim pgRows As Integer
pgs = ActiveSheet.HPageBreaks.Count
topLeft = "$A$1" 'Change this setting, if needed
pgRows = 50      'Page break set every 50 rows; change as needed
For i = 1 To pgs
    If i > 1 Then topLeft = "$A$" & pgRows * (i - 1) + 1
    PgArea = topLeft & ":$I$" & pgRows * I     'Change col. "I" to whatever is needed
    ActiveSheet.PageSetup.PrintArea = PgArea
'   Cell from 1st row in col. A of the printed page is selected in the following line
    ActiveSheet.PageSetup.RightFooter = Cells(pgRows *( i-1)+1, 1)
    ActiveSheet.PrintOut copies:=1, collate:=True, ignoreprintareas:=False
Next i
End Sub
```

As commented above, the macro places specified cell value from column A on each printed sheet whenever the user initiates worksheet printing. Obviously, it must be modified to fit user's needs, but it's not that difficult.

And in a simple case, like e.g., to add the date and time to the left footer just before your workbook is printed, you could use the macro like this one:

```
Private Sub Workbook_BeforePrint(Cancel As Boolean)
'This macro will insert current date and time on every printed page
Dim wsh As Worksheet
For Each wsh In ThisWorkbook.Worksheets
        wsh.PageSetup.LeftFooter = "Printed on: " & Format(Now, "dd-mmm-yyyy hh:mm")
Next wsh
End Sub
```

Possibilities are unlimited...

Printing Multiple Workbook Ranges on One Page

Sometimes we may need to print couple of areas located in separate ranges of our worksheet or on different worksheets in our workbook. This way we could simply save couple of paper sheets. Also, such combining of separate ranges on one page might be useful, or even necessary, for comparison / presentation purposes, etc.

So, how could we do that?
The easiest way is to employ the Excel Camera tool. The tool might not be available by default on your **Quick Access Excel toolbar** (top-left corner). If so, you can add it there by choosing the **Toolbar > Customize > More Commands...** Scroll through the list of **Commands** to find **Camera** and drag it to the toolbar. From now on it'll be always ready for you to use.

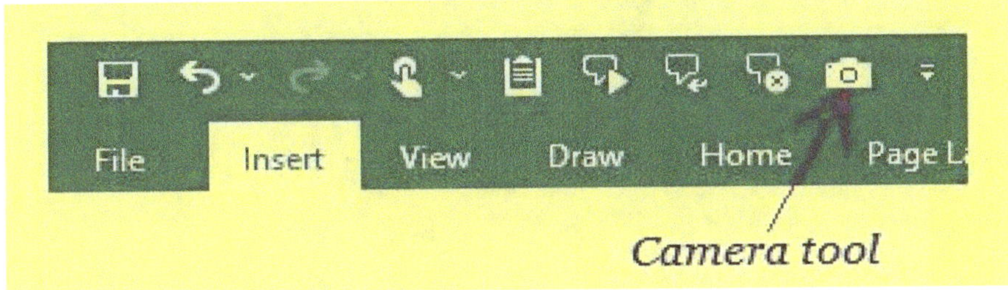

Here's how to use it, e.g., for printing:

- open a blank worksheet in your workbook, where you'll insert your "pictures" for printing
- select the first range, you need to take picture of, and click on the Camera tool
- switch to the blank worksheet and click where you want the picture to appear; move and resize it as needed
- select, one by one, any other ranges on your worksheet(s) you want to print, click the Camera each time, and insert them the same way as the first one
- arrange all of them to fit for printing on a single page (or on more than one, if necessary)

The "pictures" remain dynamic, i.e., if you make changes to the contents of the original worksheet ranges, they'll be reflected in the pictures you've taken. This is pretty cool and convenient in many situations.

5

FUNCTIONS / FORMULAS / MACROS

RAND() Function: Distribution of the Ratios of TWO Rand() Functions

Excel **Rand()** function generates a random real number in a standard continuous UNIFORM distribution of less than 1 and equal/greater than 0. It means that in this distribution every value between 0 and 1 is equally likely to be chosen. The mean of the distribution is 0.5. The variance is equal to 1/12 (=0.083333).

The Rand() function is used mainly as a random number generator. Its distribution is pretty simple and straightforward. Much more interesting are distributions of quotient (ratio), product, difference or sum of two independently run Rand() functions. Their usefulness in practical applications is not yet well defined.

I've looked closer at the distribution function of the quotient, denoted here as F(z), where z=X2/X1. The result of distribution, based on the sample of 2000 outcomes (*vertical axis*) is presented on the following chart (**z** *on horizontal axis*):

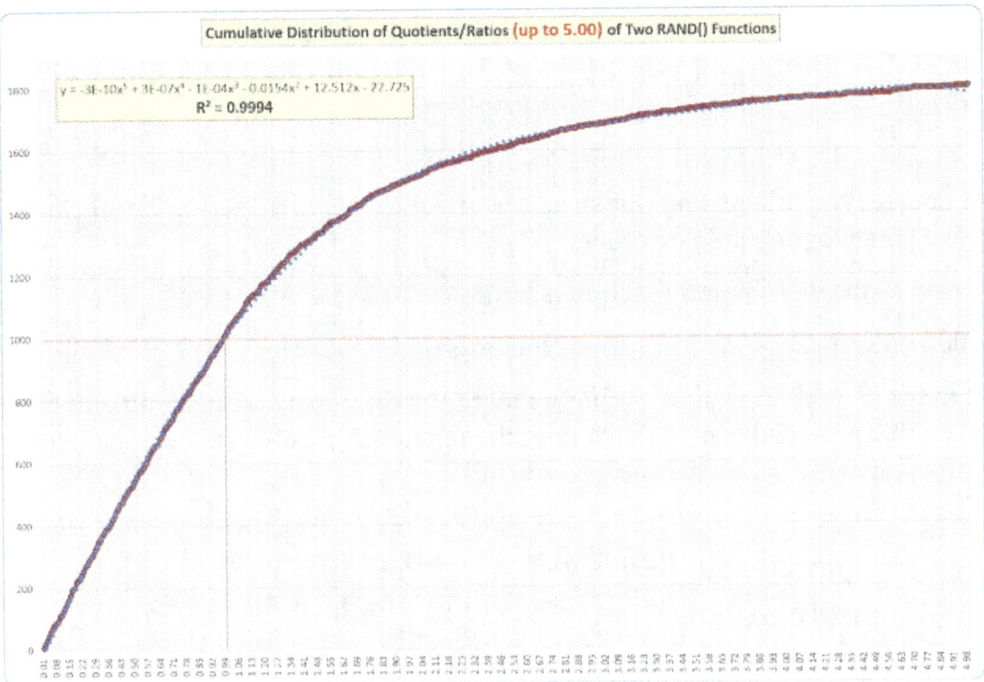

As you can see, there are two distinct intervals of **z** values: 0<z<1 and z-1, as illustrated below:

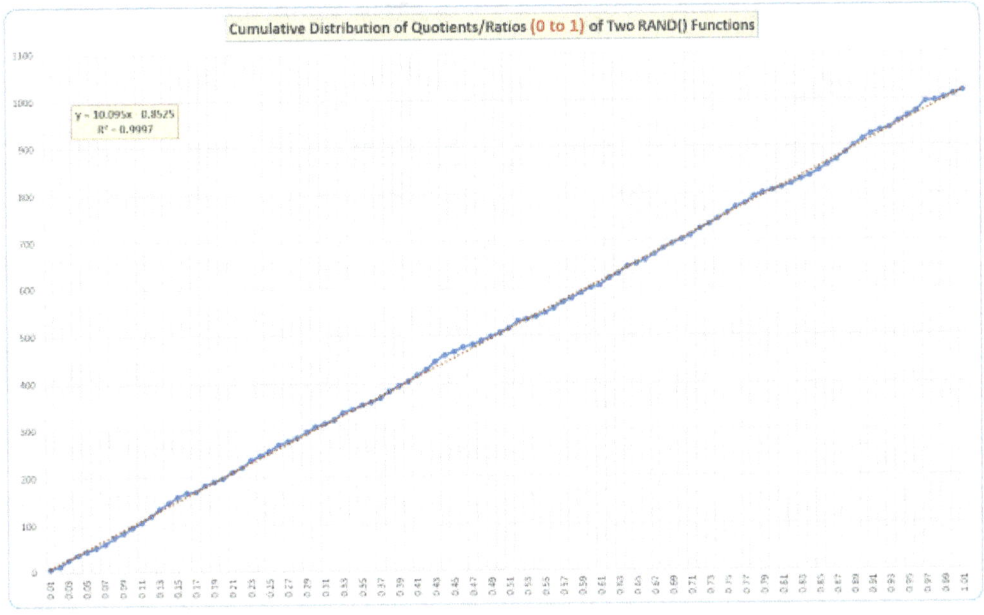

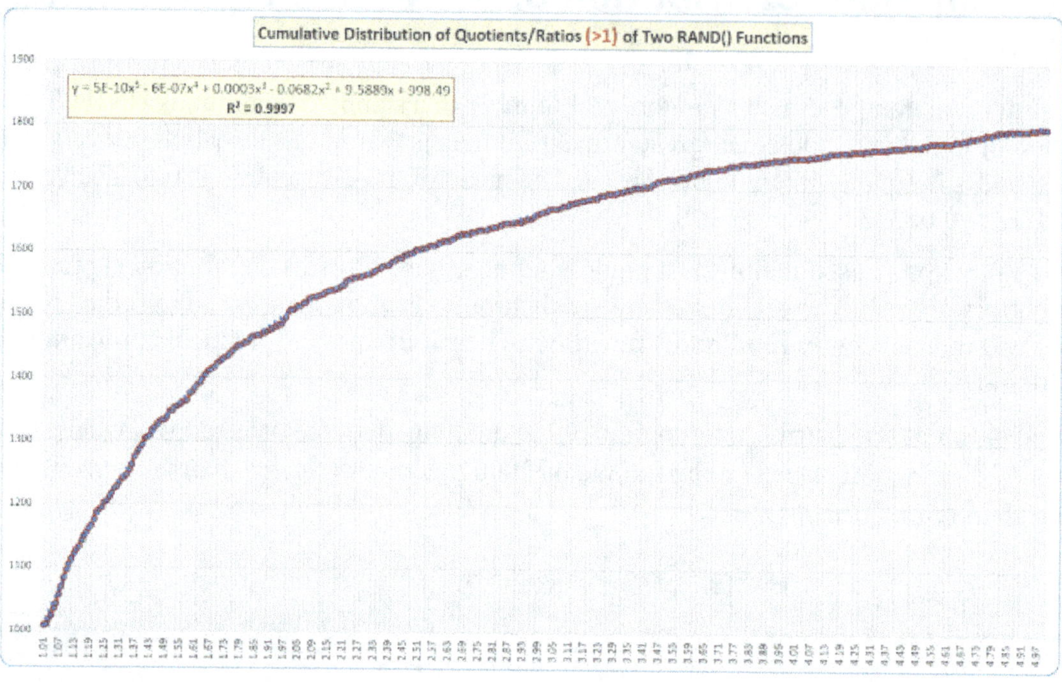

This is quite unique, very interesting statistical feature of the quotient series. From chaotic randomness we come to probabilistic order...

In the first interval, the distribution function is LINEAR: $P(X2<=z*X1) = 0.5*z$.

P value at 1000 outcomes (50% results in my analysis) = **1**.

The **P** value in the second interval (z-1) follows a POLYNOMIAL pattern, according to this formula: **1-1/(2*z)**. The table provided beneath illustrates the relationship between the **z** quotient and the probability of its outcome below the specific **z** value:

Quotient outcome value (z)	Probability (P) of the quatient outcome below z value	No. of outcomes (from series of 2000) below z	% of outcomes (from series of 2000) below z
1.0	0.5000	1000	50.0
1.5	0.6667	1333	66.7
2.0	0.7500	1500	75.0
2.5	0.8000	1600	80.0
3.0	0.8333	1666	83.3
3.5	0.8571	1714	85.7
4.0	0.8750	1750	87.5
4.5	0.8889	1778	88.9
5.0	0.9000	1800	90.0
10.0	0.9500	1900	95.0
20.0	0.9750	1952	97.6

And, finally, the chart presented below illustrates just exemplary distribution (sample) of two Rand() function series, in red and blue colours, respectively.

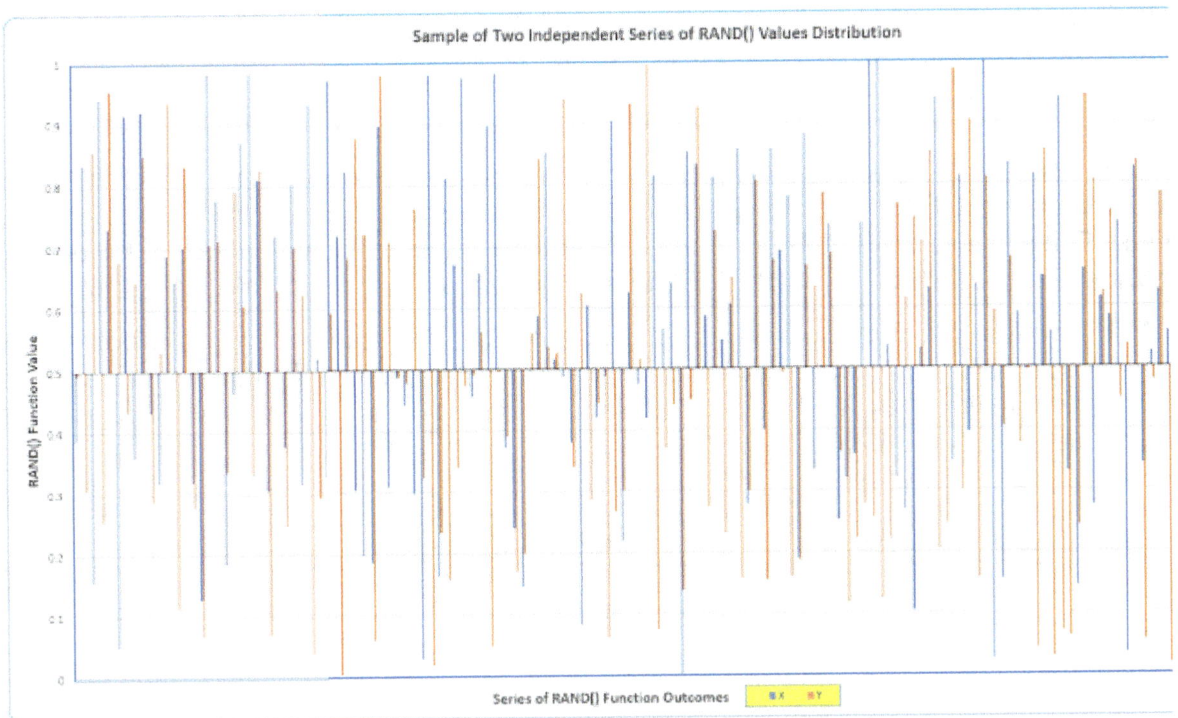

Working with Functions and Formulas

Excel **FUNCTIONS** = Predefined formulas used for specific values in a specific order. They operate usually on data entered in a range of cells. Total number of the functions available in Excel is close to **700**.

Some of the most important of them (most frequently used) are: SUM, IF, MIN, MAX, AND, OR, AVERAGE, COUNT, DAYS, VLOOKUP, DATE, ... etc. and some of the functions working with text: UPPER, LOWER, PROPER,... etc.

Excel **FORMULAS** = Expressions operating on values in a range of cells and operators. Can utilize several Excel functions and work with both numeric and textual data. ARRAY formulas are a special type of formulas, and can be very complex.

Here is the list and description of some of the most useful shortcuts used in conjunction with Functions and Formulas. I hope you'll find them helpful.

ALT+= - Inserts Auto Sum below the selected range of cells and displays small **Quick Analysis** icon. Clicking on the icon displays dialog box with data analysis tools (like *charts, colour-coding, formulas, tables, sparklines*).

CTRL+` - Alternates between displaying *cell values* and *formulas* (if there are any) in the worksheet.

CTRL+' - Copies a formula from the cell above the active cell.

CTRL+K - Displays the **Insert Hyperlink** dialog box for you to enter a new hyperlink, or **Edit Hyperlink** for editing an existing hyperlink.

SHIFT+F3 - Displays the **Insert Function** dialog box and subsequently all the Help on the selected function. Exceptionally practical and beneficial.

CTRL+A - After you type "=" and a valid <u>function name</u> in your formula, displays the **Function Arguments** (kind of *formula palette*) dialog box. If you do not actually enter anything, but your worksheet contains some data, the shortcut selects the *current region*, otherwise selects the entire worksheet. Pressing the shortcut for a second time (in the case of already selected current region) it selects also the entire worksheet.

CTRL+SHIFT+A - After you type = (equal sign) and a valid <u>function name</u> in your formula, it inserts the argument names and parenthesis for the function.

ALT+T+U+F - Displays the **Evaluate Formula** dialog box for a selected cell with a formula.

CTRL+SHIFT+ENTER - This shortcut must be used to enter a formula as an array formula. This specific requirement differentiates an *array formula* from a *regular Excel formula*. To enter array formula, first you must select the output range, enter the formula in the top-left cell of the output range, and then pressing CTRL+SHIFT+ENTER to confirm it.

ARRAY formulas can also be considered as great shortcuts. They can be used to perform multiple calculations on items in an array (which is a range of cell values). Array formulas can return a single result or multiple result. The example below illustrates how array formulas can be used to output values in cells B2:B7 and in cell C3.

	A	B	C
1	**Strings**	**Length**	**Formulas**
2	Let's talk	11	
3	about growing	14	86
4	tomatoes	9	86
5	in grow bags	13	
6	specifically made	18	
7	for growing tomatoes.	21	
8			Let's talk about growing tomatoes in grow bags specifically made for growing tomatoes.

Here, just one *array formula* - using the **LEN** function - returns the length of each text string in each of the cells in A2:A7 range. The **SUM** function in combination with **LEN** function is used in another *array formula* to calculate the total length of the combined text string (shown in cell C8). For better clarity, the following image shows the above range of cells with applied formulas displayed.

B2		f_x	{=LEN(A2:A7)}

	A	B	C
1	**Strings**	**Length**	**Formulas**
2	Let's talk	=LEN(A2:A7)	
3	about growing	=LEN(A2:A7)	=SUM(LEN(A2:A7))
4	tomatoes	=LEN(A2:A7)	=SUM(B2:B7)
5	in grow bags	=LEN(A2:A7)	
6	specifically made	=LEN(A2:A7)	
7	for growing tomatoes.	=LEN(A2:A7)	
8			=CONCAT(A2:A7)

Array formula shown above in the Formula Bar was entered in cell B2, while the range B2:B7 was selected. Another array formula was entered in cell C3. Formulas in C4 and C8 are regular formulas.

Pie chart: Wheel of VBA Colours

If you use Excel VBA and need to set colour or get colour for cell, shape or chart, you may need the VBA colour code list for reference purposes. The ColorIndex offers 56 basic colours and it's hard to remember VB codes for all of them. The following chart can be helpful, if you don't recall the colour code for your specific task:

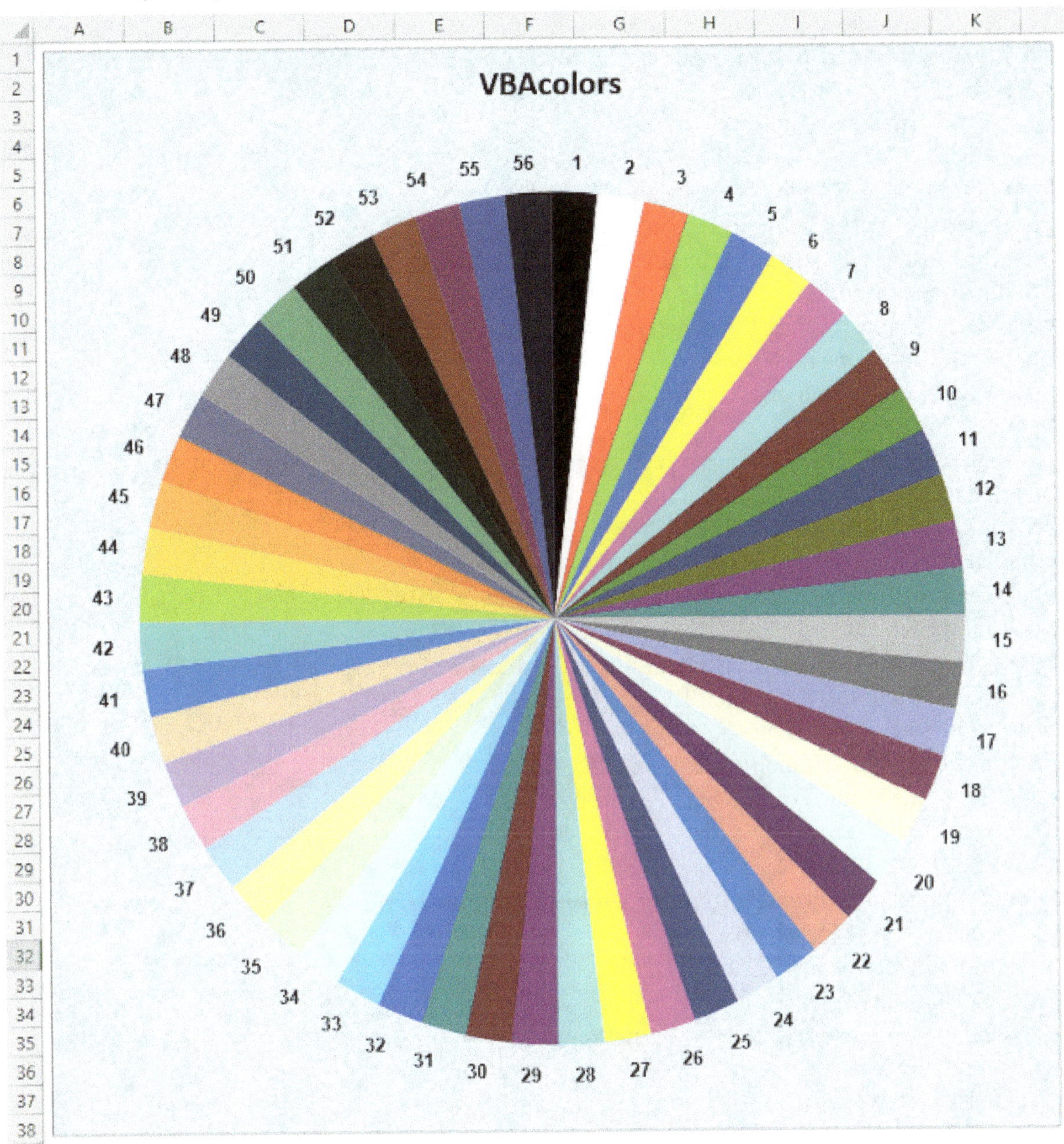

In case you'd need to recreate the chart on your own computer, here's my macro created just for this purpose. Open a new workbook, paste the code into its Module and run the macro. Modify the created chart if you need a different format.

```vba
Sub ColorPies()
'Creates wheel of VBA colours
Dim i As Integer
Range("Y1").Value = "VBAcolors"
Range("Z1").Value = "Labels"
Range("Y1:Z1").Select
Selection.Font.Bold = True
Range("Y2:Y57").Value = 0.017857143
```

```vba
For i = 1 To 56
    Range("Z" & (i + 1)).Value = i
Next i
Range("Y1:Z57").Select
ActiveSheet.Shapes.AddChart2(1, xlPie).Select
ActiveChart.SetSourceData Source:=Range("Sheet1!$Y$1:$Z$57")
ActiveSheet.ChartObjects("Chart 1").Activate
With ActiveChart.SeriesCollection(1)
For i = 1 To 56
    .Points(i).Interior.ColorIndex = i
Next i
    ActiveSheet.Shapes("Chart 1").IncrementLeft -500
    ActiveSheet.Shapes("Chart 1").IncrementTop -175
    ActiveSheet.Shapes("Chart 1").ScaleWidth 1.5, msoFalse, _
        msoScaleFromTopLeft
    ActiveSheet.Shapes("Chart 1").ScaleHeight 2.6, msoFalse, _
        msoScaleFromTopLeft
    ActiveChart.Legend.Select
    Selection.Delete
    ActiveSheet.ChartObjects("Chart 1").Activate
    ActiveChart.FullSeriesCollection(1).Select
    ActiveChart.FullSeriesCollection(1).ApplyDataLabels
    ActiveChart.FullSeriesCollection(1).DataLabels.Select
    ActiveChart.FullSeriesCollection(1).HasLeaderLines = False
    Selection.ShowValue = False
    ActiveChart.SeriesCollection(1).DataLabels.Format.TextFrame2.TextRange. _
        InsertChartField msoChartFieldRange, "=Sheet1!$Z$2:$Z$57", 0
    Selection.ShowRange = True
    Selection.Position = xlLabelPositionOutsideEnd
    With Selection.Format.TextFrame2.TextRange.Font
        .Name = "Arial"
    End With
    Selection.Format.TextFrame2.TextRange.Font.Bold = msoTrue
    ActiveChart.ChartArea.Select
    With ActiveSheet.Shapes("Chart 1").Fill
        .Visible = msoTrue
        .PresetTextured msoTextureBlueTissuePaper
        .TextureTile = msoTrue
        .TextureOffsetX = 0
        .TextureOffsetY = 0
        .TextureHorizontalScale = 1
        .TextureVerticalScale = 1
        .TextureAlignment = msoTextureTopLeft
    End With
End With
End Sub
```

PhotoShow: Looping Through Images in a Folder

There are occasions when you'd like to demonstrate your photos or other images on your computer screen, in a continuous display, each one for predetermined number of seconds, or whatever time span you choose.

This can be quite easily accomplished (automated) with the following VBA macro:

```vba
Sub ImageShow()
'Displays images located in a folder on your computer for predetermined times
Dim myFolder As String, myFile As String
Dim imgPath As String
ActiveWindow.DisplayHeadings = False
Application.DisplayScrollBars = False
ActiveWindow.DisplayGridlines = False
ActiveWindow.DisplayWorkbookTabs = False
Application.DisplayFullScreen = True
Application.DisplayStatusBar = False
Range("A1").Select
'Select your folder (with photos/images only)
MsgBox "Please select your folder with photos/images"
With Application.FileDialog(msoFileDialogFolderPicker)
    .AllowMultiSelect = False
    .Show
    myFolder = .SelectedItems(1)
End With
myFile = Dir(myFolder & "\", vbReadOnly)
Do
    imgPath = myFolder & "\" & myFile
    'Open consecutively each image in the selected folder
    ActiveSheet.Shapes.AddPicture Filename:=imgPath, LinkToFile:=msoFalse, _
        SaveWithDocument:=msoTrue, Left:=ActiveCell.Left, Top:=ActiveCell.Top, Width:=-1,
Height:=-1
    ActiveSheet.Pictures.Select     'Resize the image to fit screen size
        With Selection
            .ShapeRange.LockAspectRatio = msoTrue
            .ShapeRange.Height = 725   'Change the height to fit your screen size
        End With
    Application.Wait (Now + TimeValue("00:00:05"))
    Range("AA5").Value = myFile    'Change the range if needed for visibility
    DoEvents
    Selection.Delete    'Delete displayed image
    myFile = Dir
    If myFile = "" Then Application.Wait (Now + TimeValue("00:00:05")): Exit Do
Loop While myFile <> ""
Application.DisplayStatusBar = True
ActiveWindow.DisplayHeadings = True
Application.DisplayScrollBars = True
ActiveWindow.DisplayGridlines = True
ActiveWindow.DisplayWorkbookTabs = True
Application.DisplayFullScreen = False
Range("AA5").Value = "" 'Change the range to match the location set above
End Sub
```

The macro allows you to select folder with your images you want to display, and then displays the images, one by one, every 5 seconds (or whatever you set) and, additionally, shows the filename of the displayed image.

To make use of the macro, copy and paste it into a Module of your VBA Project (go to **Developer > Visual Basic > View > Project Explorer > Insert > Module**). After pasting you can change couple of parameters in the macro, like **Height** of images (set at 725 there), **TimeValue** (set at 00:00:05 = 5sec there), and the **Range** (cell) where you want to show the filename of the image being displayed (set for AA5 cell there).

Next, go back to your worksheet and add a **Form Control Button** (**Developer > Insert** [in the Controls menu]). Place it on the right side of the worksheet window, format it as needed and assign the **ImageShow** macro to it.

That's it. You're ready to run the show. Just make sure that the macro works the way you've expected.

How to Generate Random Strings of Characters

To generate any random string of characters, including letters, digits and symbols, enter all the characters you want to use, into any cell of your worksheet. E.g., enter this sequence in cell A1:

abcdefghijklmnopqrstuvwxyzABCDEFGHIJKLMNOPQRSTUVWXYZ0123456789

and then use the following formula in any other cells to get your random strings:

=MID($A$1,RANDBETWEEN(1,62),1)&MID($A$1,RANDBETWEEN(1,62),1)&MID($A$1,
RANDBETWEEN(1,62),1)&MID($A$1,RANDBETWEEN(1,62),1)&MID($A$1,RANDBET
WEEN(1,62),1)&MID($A$1,RANDBETWEEN(1,62),1)&MID($A$1,RANDBETWEEN(1,62),
1)&MID($A$1,RANDBETWEEN(1,62),1)&MID($A$1,RANDBETWEEN(1,62),1)&MID(A
1,RANDBETWEEN(1,62),1)

This specific formula produces 10-character string, but you can change the number of segments (*MID($A$1,RANDBETWEEN(1,62),1)*) in it, to generate string of any length, from 1 to 100 characters, and even more.

The above sequence is 62 characters long. If you want to use a different one then the number **62** in the formula must be replaced to reflect the length of your new sequence.

Font Colour Change with Cell Formula (no conditional formatting)

Formulas in Excel usually don't care about the font colour in displaying their results in a cell. However, you may need sometimes to distinguish between some results of your calculations by using specific font colours.

It is possible to assign a specific font colour to a cell value, without any conditional formatting.

E.g., let's say, you want to compare two numbers (located in cells A1 and B1) and assign font colour to the result of the formula like this one: **=IF(A1>B1,22,33)**. Depending on the outcome of comparison, if A1>B1 then you want to display *22 in green* colour; otherwise, you want to display *33 in red*.

To do that with a formula, you need to amend the formula with this kind of UDF (User Defined Function):

```
Function fColor(num1 As Double, num2 As Double) As Boolean
    If num1 <= num2 Then
```

```vba
        Application.Caller.Font.ColorIndex = 3    'red
    Else
        Application.Caller.Font.ColorIndex = 10   'green
    End If
End Function
```

so that your formula looks like this: **=IF(A1>B1,22,33)+fColor(A1,B1)**.

To make use of the function, you must copy and paste it first into a *Module* of your *VBAProject* (your workbook) or of your Personal workbook.

The function can be quite easily modified for use with other Excel formulas and colours.

VLOOKUP Function Without Limits (case-sensitive)
That is: Using IF+ INDIRECT+MATCH+EXACT+INDEX Functions

Here is a small data table, as an *example* of Excel table, created for the purpose of this exercise:

	A	B	C
1	Item	Price	Comment
2	038Rvc4t	£155.00	Out of stock
3	038Rvc4T	??	Price not set yet
4	038Rvci3u	£90.00	No comment
5	038Rvci3U	£54.00	Ships in 3 days
6	038Rvc5v	£159.00	""
7	038Rvc5V	£28.00	The lowest price

What if you are working with a real very big table, let's say - 20 columns and 20000 rows, and want to retrieve quickly some specific information from such table, from any row and any column. The following table provides some examples of lookups (based on my small table) you'd might want to do:

Reference to match	Lookup for what?	Result of the lookup	
038Rvc4T	Price for Item **038Rvc4T**	??	1
038Rvc4T	Comment for Item **038Rvc4T**	Price not set yet	2
038Rvci3u	Price for Item **038Rvci3u**	£90.00	3
038Rvci3u	Comment for Item **038Rvci3u**	No comment	4
The lowest price	Item with Comment 'The lowest price'	038Rvc5V	5
Out of stock	Price with Comment 'Out of stock'	£155.00	6
The lowest price	Price with Comment 'The lowest price'	£28.00	7

It's somewhat self-explanatory. The first column says what our lookup is about (*reference*) and the third column displays information (*result* that we're looking for) about that reference. But how exactly do we get the result we want to?

The answer is in formulas sitting in the background of the 'Result' column. All of them are the **array formulas**, so REMEMBER to enter them using the keyboard keys **CTRL+SHIFT+ENTER,** after you type them in.

Here they are, case by case:

1. This formula looks for the price of **038Rvc4T** product in col. B of the data table:

=IF(INDIRECT("A"&(1+MATCH(TRUE, EXACT(A$2:A$7, $E2), 0)))<>"", INDEX(B$2:B$7, MATCH(TRUE, EXACT(A$2:A$7, $E2), 0)), "")

Surprisingly, in response we get question marks only...

2. So, I'm using another formula to check the Comment column in the data table:

=IF(INDIRECT("A"&(1+MATCH(TRUE, EXACT(A$2:A$7,$E2), 0)))<>"", INDEX(C$2:C$7, MATCH(TRUE, EXACT(A$2:A$7, $E2), 0)), "")

This time I get info saying that '*Price not set yet*', so it does clarify the question marks.

3. Now I want to get price of **038Rvci3u** item, so I'm using this formula:

=IF(INDIRECT("A"&(1+MATCH(TRUE, EXACT(A$2:A$7, $E4), 0)))<>"", INDEX(B$2:B$7, MATCH(TRUE, EXACT(A$2:A$7, $E4), 0)), "")

This time I get the result = £90.00 .

4. And I wonder now if there is any Comment for the same Item:

=IF(INDIRECT("A"&(1+MATCH(TRUE, EXACT(A$2:A$7,$E4), 0)))<>"", INDEX(C$2:C$7, MATCH(TRUE, EXACT(A$2:A$7, $E4), 0)), "")

The result is '*No comment*'. That's fine.

5. Next I want to know which of the products (Items) has **the lowest price**, so I'm using this formula:

=IF(INDIRECT("C"&(1+MATCH(TRUE, EXACT(C$2:C$7, $E6), 0)))<>"", INDEX(A$2:A$7, MATCH(TRUE, EXACT(C$2:C$7, $E6), 0)), "")

and getting this result: **038Rvc5V** (cell B7).

6. How about the **price** of the product *038Rvc4t*, that temporarily is *out of stock?* Well, the following formula allows me to find it out:

=IF(INDIRECT("C"&(1+MATCH(TRUE, EXACT(C$2:C$7, $E7), 0)))<>"", INDEX(B$2:B$7, MATCH(TRUE, EXACT(C$2:C$7, $E7), 0)), "")

The *price* is **£155.00** (cell B2).

7. And what's the **price** of the product with the Comment saying '*The lowest price*'. To find out I'm using this formula:

=IF(INDIRECT("C"&(1+MATCH(TRUE, EXACT(C$2:C$7, $E8), 0)))<>"", INDEX(B$2:B$7, MATCH(TRUE, EXACT(C$2:C$7, $E8), 0)), "")

£28.00 (cell B7) is the answer.

As you can see, using this type of formula structure, we can get all kinds of answers, without limitations related to the VLOOKUP function.

Although the formulas look a bit complex, in fact they contain only two main parts. The first one checks if our table contains the string (or other value) we are referring to, then - if that's **true** - the second part finds the value (*result*) we are looking for.

Reminder: all presented formulas are **array formulas**! (use CTRL+SHIFT+ENTER to enter them).

****

For better understanding of the formula structure, here is some **basic** information about all the functions involved above:

IF function can have two results. E.g., **IF(A2=”Y”,1,0)** returns 1 if 'Y' is True, otherwise returns 0.

INDIRECT function returns **reference** specified by a text string. We use it to change reference to a cell without changing the formula itself.

Syntax: **INDIRECT(ref_text,[a1])**.

E.g., if ref_text is 'A3' and cell A3 contains *Reference* to the cell B3, then INDIRECT(A3) returns the value sitting in cell B3.

MATCH function returns the **position** of the item in a range. We use it to provide e.g., a value for row_num of the INDEX function.

Syntax: **MATCH(lookup_value,lookup_array,[match_type])**.

E.g., if the range C2:C4 contains 10,20 and 30, the formula MATCH(20,C2:C4,0) returns **2**, because 20 is the *2nd* item in the range.

EXACT function returns TRUE if two compared strings are exactly the same; FALSE otherwise. It's case-sensitive!

Syntax: **EXACT(text1, text2)**

INDEX function returns a cell reference from a given range/array. We combine it usually with the MATCH function (which provides the position of data point in a range) to get the resulting value from a table/range.

There are two versions of the function available:

Array form syntax is: **INDEX(array, row_num, [column_num])**, e.g.: *INDEX(A2:A30,8,2)* returns the value of 8th row and 2nd column, i.e., of cell B8.

Reference form syntax is: **INDEX(reference, row_num, [column_num],[area_num])**, e.g.: INDEX(A2:C30,F2:M30),5,8,2) returns the value of cell M6 in the second area. If *area_num* is omitted, the function returns result for the first area listed.

The array form of INDEX function is used in the examples above.

Remember, this is just **basic** information about the functions. There are more detailed descriptions available from the Excel Help, and many other sources.

Complex Array Formulas

An array is a row or column of values, or a combination of them. Array formulas can be very useful in many applications where normal Excel formulas don't work. An array formula is a formula that can perform multiple calculations on one or more items in an array.

Array formulas can return either multiple results, or a single result. We can use array formulas to perform complex tasks, such as:

- create quickly sample datasets
- count some values contained in a range of cells
- sum numbers that meet certain conditions, such as the lowest values in a range
- sum every N^{th} value in a range of cells
- find specific values in a cell or a range of cells
- etc.

Returning the Rightmost Value from a Specific Row

The following example shows you how the single-cell array formula can find the last filled cell in a given row and show its value. Here is the formula:

=CELL("contents",INDIRECT(SUBSTITUTE(ADDRESS(1,VALUE(MAX(COLUMN(C:MZ)*(C2:MZ2<>"")))),4),1,"")&ROW(B2)))

And here's its application. I've entered it in cell **A2** as array formula (pressing **Ctrl+Shift+Enter** at the same time) and copied it down the column A in order to automatically see values of the last filled cell in each of the rows, as illustrated below.

	A	B	C	D	E	F	G	H	I
1	Last Test Result	Student	Run1	Run2	Run3	Run4	Run5	Run6	Run7	Run8
2	7.9	Rian	10.4		9.7	8.2		8.8	7.9	
3	5.9	Richard	6.0		6.0	6.3	6.5	5.9		
4	21.8	Mason	20.8	19.0	19.1	17.9		20.0		21.8
5	15.1	Brian	15.0	16.0	18.2	17.5	15.1			
6	160.2	Jason	110.0	98.6	110.8	160.2				

The range used in the example formula (C:MZ) can, obviously, be changed to fit a specific data set you're working on. This is just one example of using array formulas where regular formulas cannot provide desired results.

Find ADDRESSES of Specific CELL CONTENTS in Excel Workbook

Let's say we are dealing with Excel table several columns wide and hundreds and hundreds, or even thousands of rows long. Just for illustration, I'm providing here a small fragment of such a large table:

	A	B	C	D	E	F
1	Snum	Description	Name	Year	Fair	Adjusted
2	300	Melcor	Browns	07/07/1965	6978	8495
3	200	Western	Johns	08/07/1920	12066	12326
4	400	Alterra	Browns	02/07/1905	1881	2107
5	600	Yamana	Smith	18/06/2021	135718	34744
6	1100	Western	Davis	10/04/2022	24090	21125
7	1000	Medical	Johnsons	15/09/2021	3020	2890
8	500	Cenovus	Davis	15/04/2022	6250	18193
9	1500	Melcor	Browns	06/07/1947	54465	48565
10	650	Western	Johns	06/07/1995	15275	15600
11	97	Wheaton	Johns	04/07/1955	3	53
12	15	Medical	Davis	09/07/1947	295	785
13	600	Alterra	Smith	09/07/1941	29742	30048
14	300	Yamana	Johnsons	06/07/1947	6519	7500
15	10000	Graphite	Davis	06/07/1938	450	1857
16	800	Western	Browns	08/07/2011	18200	18560
17		Western	Browns	08/07/1947	2148	2552
18	1000	Melcor	Browns	05/07/2000	8920	8380
19	4500	Medical	Smith	05/07/1947	67500	91358
20	0	Wheaton	Smith	08/07/19841	3570	2994
21	40	Wheaton	Johns	03/07/1947	21376	32679
22	800	Western	Davis	09/07/1999	9808	10806
23	4500	Yamana	Smith	07/07/1947	15075	16738

Working on such a large table we may need to find addresses of cells containing some specific values, name, date, number, etc., and we need to look for them quickly.

Here are some examples how we can find - using array formulas - addresses of the first occurrences of the LOWEST value in a column and the HIGHEST value.

A	B	C	D	E	F
Full cell addresses, but for the first occurrence of the value only					
$A$17	Lowest value *(1st occurrence)*		$D$4	$E$11	$F$11
$A$12	Lowest value *(1st occurrence)*, excluding 0s & empty cells		$D$4	$E$11	$F$11
$A$15	Highest value *(1st occurrence)*		$D$8	$E$5	$F$19

The **array formulas** used for the three cases presented above are:

=ADDRESS(MIN(IF(A2:A23=MIN(A2:A23),ROW(A2:A23),"")),COLUMN(A2:A23))

=ADDRESS(MIN(IF(A2:A23=MIN(IF(A2:A23<>0,A2:A23)),ROW(A2:A23),"")),COLUMN(A2:A23))

=ADDRESS(MIN(IF(A2:A23=MAX(A2:A23),ROW(A2:A23),"")),COLUMN(A2:A23))

We enter them in column A and then copy to other relevant columns, here col. D, E and F. As commented, the addresses point to the first occurrences of the values, we are looking for, in specified single columns.

A	B	C	D	E	F
Longest string *(1st occurrence). Works with strings & integers only.*					
$A$15	$B$15	$C$7	$D$20	$E$5	$F$3

Now we are looking for address of the first occurrence of the longest string in each of the columns, entering this array formula and copying it to the remaining columns:

=ADDRESS(MIN(IF(LEN(A2:A23)=MAX(LEN(A2:A23)),ROW(A2:A23),"")),COLUMN(A2:A23))

A	B	C	D	E	F
ROW #s only, but for all occurences of the value (shown in the arrays)					
7		5	6		7
18		14	8		
		23	12		
			15		
			22		

As indicated above, we are presented here with arrays showing only ROW numbers (not full addresses), but of **all occurrences** of specific numbers or strings in each of the columns. The following array formulas are used:

Col. A: =SMALL(IF(1000=$A$2:$A$23, ROW($A$2:$A$23)-ROW($A$2)+2), ROW(1:1))

Col. B: =SMALL(IF("Yamana"=$B$2:$B$23, ROW($B$2:$B$23) - ROW($B$2)+2),ROW(1:1))

Col. C: =SMALL(IF("Davis"=$C$2:$C$23, ROW($C$2:$C$23)-ROW($C$2)+2), ROW(1:1))

Col. F: =SMALL(IF(2890=$F$2:$F$23, ROW($F$2:$F$23)-ROW($F$2)+2), ROW(1:1))

These **array formulas** were expanded down the rows until the #**NUM!** error showed up, indicating the end of array (i.e., no more addresses found).

The row numbers found with array formulas are easily transformed into **full cell addresses** using standard (not array) formulas (shown below), based on the row numbers found with the array formulas above:

A	B	C	D	E	F
Full cell addresses for all occurrences of the value (shown in the arrays)					
$A$7	$B$5	$C$6			$F$7
$A$18	$B$14	$C$8			
	$B$23	$C$12			
		$C$15			
		$C$22			

Col. A: =ADDRESS(A33,COLUMN(A33))

Col. B: =ADDRESS(B33,COLUMN(B33))

Col. C: =ADDRESS(C33,COLUMN(C33))

Col. F: =ADDRESS(F33,COLUMN(F33))

<u>Two important notes</u>:

1. All ARRAY formulas must be entered using **CTRL+SHIFT+ENTER** keyboard keys.

2. **Dates** - with exception of string length case - are treated in comparisons of their values as **serial numbers**.

How to REPLACE Any Substrings or COUNT Them in a String

Let's say we are dealing with the following string entered in cell A1:

"Examples of replacing or counting any string elements in a cell"

To **replace** e.g., the **3rd letter 'a'** with **'A'** in the string, we would use this formula:

=SUBSTITUTE($A$1,"a","A",3)

To **count** e.g., the **number of SPACES** in the string, the following formula can be used:

=LEN($A$1) -LEN(SUBSTITUTE($A$1," ",""))   *(result = 10)*

To **count** the **number of substrings**, such as e.g., "e", "in", "le" or "**count**" in the string, the following formulas can be used:

- =(LEN($A$1) -LEN(SUBSTITUTE($A$1,"e","")))/LEN("e")   *(result = 6)*

- =(LEN($A$1) -LEN(SUBSTITUTE($A$1,"in","")))/LEN("in")   *(result = 4)*

- =(LEN($A$1) -LEN(SUBSTITUTE($A$1,"le","")))/LEN("le")   *(result = 2)*

  - =(LEN($A$1) -LEN(SUBSTITUTE($A$1,"count","")))/LEN("count")   *(result = 1)*

Summing Up a Variable Number of the Largest or Smallest Values in a Range

Here is a range of numbers provided as an example. It could be any unsorted range/list of numbers you're working on:

	A	B	C	D	E	F	G	H	I	J
2	22	89	89	40	27	21	85	97	44	19
3	11	56	92	31	17	17	77	85	90	40
4	30	100	15	35	15	54	44	41	27	7
5	8	21	35	79	23	81	90	20	49	40
6	50	40	7	73	19	67	1	4	74	66

Your data set is large and for some specific analytical reason you'd like to track the **sum of several** largest and smallest numbers in your set. The ARRAY formulas come to help and are very efficient in such cases.

Based on the range of data presented above, the following table is an example of output you can obtain with array formulas:

	L	M	N	O	P	Q	R	S	T	U	V
2	No. of Values →	1	2	3	4	5	6	7	8	9	10
3	Σ of the Largest	100	197	289	379	469	558	647	732	817	898
4	Σ of the Smallest	1	5	12	19	27	38	53	68	85	102

The following formulas have been used in cells Q3 and Q4 to get the sum of <u>**five**</u> largest and smallest values; both formulas reference cell **Q2** (where number **5** was entered into the cell):

=SUM(LARGE($A$2:$J$6,ROW(INDIRECT("1:"&Q$2))))

=SUM(SMALL($A$2:$J$6,ROW(INDIRECT("1:"&Q$2))))

To obtain sums for any other number of the largest and smallest values you just enter the numbers, like 1 to 10 in the row 2 in this example, and refer to them (cells M2 to V2) in the formulas copied to the remaining columns in row 2 and 3.

*Remember that these are ARRAY formulas, so - after typing them in - they must be entered using **CTRL+SHIFT+ENTER** keyboard sequence.*

In reference to cell M2 (=**1**) you get, obviously, the *Maximum* and *Minimum* value from your data set.

Further, the sums of the largest and smallest values can be presented graphically, if needed, like in these examples (**Funnel** chart and **Clustered column** chart):

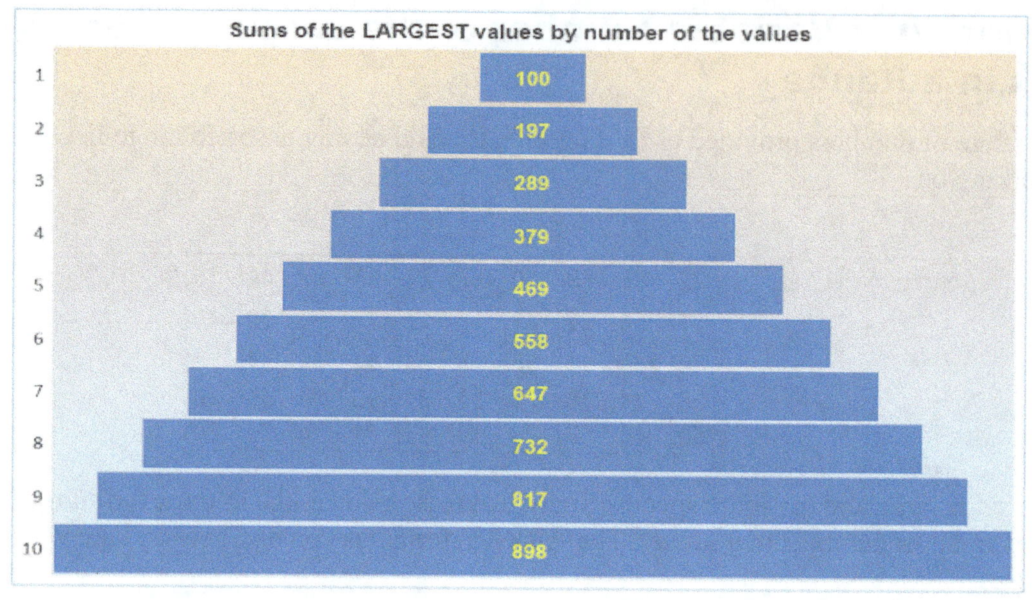

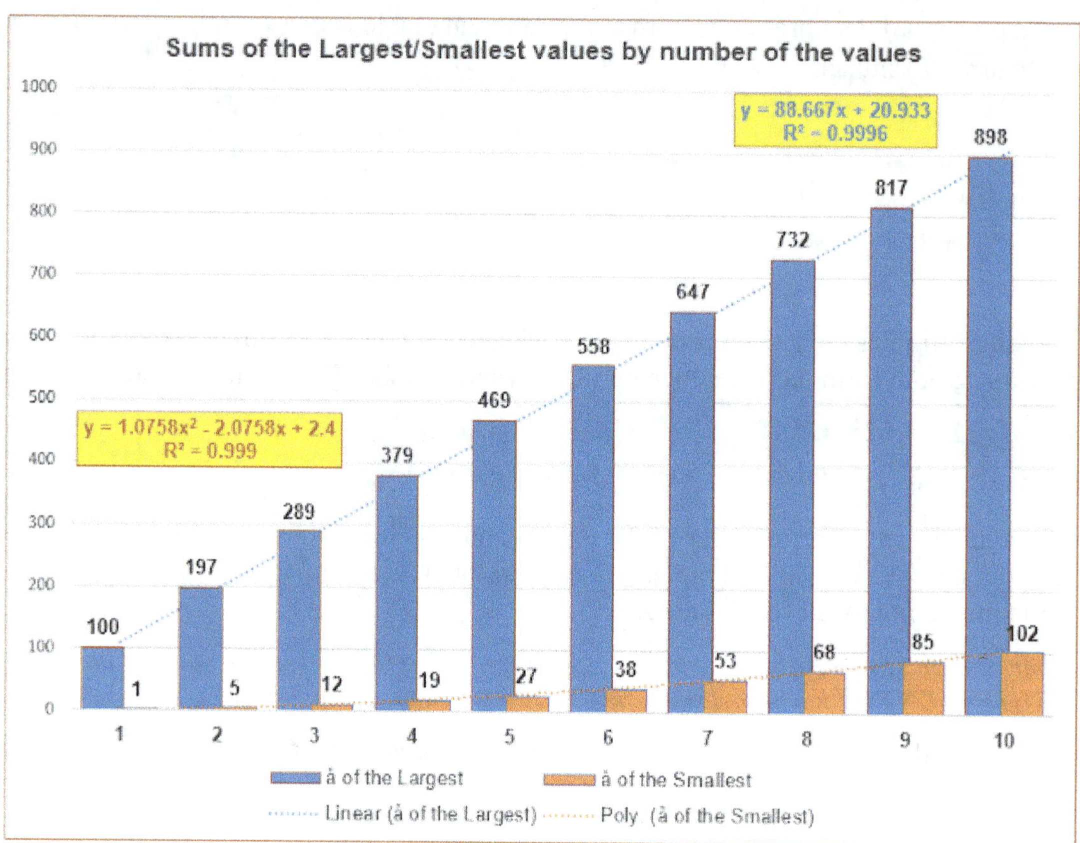

SUMMING UP Selectively Based on References - Using ARRAY FORMULAS

Some business sells some products, e.g., vegetables, to various countries/ merchants. Records of sales are kept in Excel table, like in this example:

	Product ⏷	Country ⏷	March ⏷	June ⏷	October ⏷
2	Broccoli	NL	402	786	536
3	Carrot	PL	257	569	260
4	Onion	LV	472	329	628
5	Tomato	CH	384	941	497
6	Radish	UK	996	951	113
7	Onion	DK	362	678	658
8	Tomato	SK	296	915	752
9	Carrot	CZ	222	250	555
10	Broccoli	RO	331	888	643
11	Tomato	IS	156	120	930

The business owner needs to keep his eye on total sales of individual vegetables over some periods. He could do necessary calculations by e.g., filtering the specific column and summing up individual rows. However, much more efficient way of doing it - in such a case - is using ARRAY formulas, as you can see below.

The totals of sales by the product, over the three months (cols. C, D and E), are calculated by formulas underlying the values presented in col. H and presented on the right side of that column:

Product	Sold	
Broccoli	3586	=SUM((C$2:C$11+D$2:D$11+E$2:E$11)*(--(A$2:A$11=G2)))
Carrot	2113	=SUM((C$2:C$11+D$2:D$11+E$2:E$11)*(--(A$2:A$11=G3)))
Onion	3127	=SUM((C$2:C$11+D$2:D$11+E$2:E$11)*(--(A$2:A$11=G4)))
Radish	2060	=SUM((C$2:C$11+D$2:D$11+E$2:E$11)*(--(A$2:A$11=G5)))
Tomato	4991	=SUM((C$2:C$11+D$2:D$11+E$2:E$11)*(--(A$2:A$11=G6)))

If needed, similar formulas could be used to sum up the sales by the country (col. B) or other references to the table entries.

Reminder: ARRAY formulas, after typing them in, must be entered using the keyboard sequence CTRL+SHIFT+ENTER. Note also the double-dash operator used in the formulas.

How to Retrieve Some of the LONGEST/SHORTEST Text Entries from Excel List

Suppose you want to find the longest or shortest entry from a long list of text strings. Or, maybe you need to retrieve the 2nd, or 3rd or 4th longest/shortest entry from the list. How to do it?

Let's start with this small fragment of a big table, for example:

LIST of Strings	String LENGTH	Sorted Z-A Length	Nth Longest strings	N	Sorted A-Z Length	Nth Shortest strings
tamarisk	8	11	composition	1	3	nob
composition	11	11	composition	2	4	part
part	4	10	production	3	4	part
Marta	5	9	let it be	4	4	part
aromat	6	8	tamarisk	5	6	Marta
Barbara	7	7	Barbara	6	5	Marta
production	10	7	Barbara	7	5	Marta
burst	5	6	aromat	8	5	Marta
ambaras	7	5	Marta	9	5	Marta
rama	4	5	Marta	10	5	aromat
let it be	9	5	Marta	11	7	Barbara
mart	4	5	Marta	12	8	Barbara
drone	5	5	Marta	13	7	tamarisk
nob	3	4	part	14	9	let it be
store	5	4	part	15	10	production
12345	5	4	part	16	11	composition
participant	11	3	nob	17	11	composition

The first column of this table contains the subject **list** of arbitrary textual entries. All other columns are provided for explanatory purpose only.

If all, what you need, is just finding the longest or shortest entry in the list, then you can use the following ARRAY formulas to find both the longest and the shortest entry:

=INDEX($A$2:$A$18,MATCH(MAX(LEN($A$2:$A$18)),LEN($A$2:$A$18),0))

Result: **composition**

=INDEX($A$2:$A$18,MATCH(MIN(LEN($A$2:$A$18)),LEN($A$2:$A$18),0))

Result: **nob**

As you can see, the list contains *two* entries (composition, participant) of the maximum length (11 characters), but the formula finds the **first** matching value equal exactly to the lookup value, because the strings are not sorted in any way and the formula uses **0** match-type (the strings are and can be in any order).

In the second case (smallest strings) there is only one 3-character entry (nob), so it is the first matching value by default.

That was relatively easy task. But what if you'd like to retrieve the 2nd, 3rd, 4th, etc. longest or shortest textual entries?

Well, in such cases you'd need to use slightly modified ARRAY formulas that are shown below, first three for the longest strings and the last three for the shortest strings:

=INDEX($A$2:$A$18,MATCH(LARGE(LEN($A$2:$A$18),2),LEN($A$2:$A$18),1))

Result: **participant** (the **2nd** longest string; **1** requires ascending sort order of entries, and composition, participant are, in fact, in ascending order in the list)

=INDEX($A$2:$A$18,MATCH(LARGE(LEN($A$2:$A$18),3),LEN($A$2:$A$18),0))

Result: **production** (the **3rd** longest string)

=INDEX($A$2:$A$18,MATCH(LARGE(LEN($A$2:$A$18),4),LEN($A$2:$A$18),0))

Result: **let it be** (the **4th** longest string)

=INDEX($A$2:$A$18,MATCH(SMALL(LEN($A$2:$A$18),2),LEN($A$2:$A$18),0))

Result: **part** (the **2nd** shortest string)

=INDEX($A$2:$A$18,MATCH(SMALL(LEN($A$2:$A$18),3),LEN($A$2:$A$18),0))

Result: **part** (the **3rd** shortest string)

=INDEX($A$2:$A$18,MATCH(SMALL(LEN($A$2:$A$18),4),LEN($A$2:$A$18),0))

Result: **part** (the **4th** shortest string)

In all three cases of the shortest strings, only *the first occurrence* of 4-character strings is shown, because the strings (part, rama, mart) are not sorted in any way in the list.

Similarly, **Barbara** and **Marta** strings are repeated as the results of subsequent formulas, for the same reason (unsorted order in the list).

When using this type of formulas, you must **remember** that:

1. The formulas are of ARRAY type so, after typing in, you must enter them using **CTRL+SHIFT+ENTER** keyboard sequence.

2. Any **spaces** included in the entries are _counted_ with LEN function, so pay attention to that.

3. If there are multiple longest or shortest entries in the list, the formulas will find just the first one. To find out, if there are more than one Max/Min length entries, you'd need to use **Find** feature provided in Excel ribbon.

4. The formulas do not work with multiple columns.

How to Find Some LARGEST or SMALLEST Numbers In a Range

There are situations when you need to find out what is the highest or the lowest value in your table or any array of numbers. And sometimes you may need to determine what is the second or third highest or lowest value in a given range. In all such cases ARRAY formulas are very helpful, so I'm providing some examples of using them.

Let's look first at finding the highest/lowest values in an array/table of numbers. Here is a small sample range of numbers:

A	B	C	D	E	F	G	H	I	J
2	12	8	-3	31	21	20	16	50	47
3	17	40	-5	26	17	-2	26	45	-7
4	9	-9	-8	25	30	24	-5	39	45
5	3	-2	43	16	28	18	53	21	29

To extract the maximum and minimum values from this range we use this kind of array formulas:

=MAX(IF(ISERROR($B$2:$J$5),"",$B$2:$J$5)) Answer: **53**

=MIN(IF(ISERROR($B$2:$J$5),"",$B$2:$J$5))   Answer: **-9**

If we want to find out also what are the second, third, etc... largest/smallest values within the range, we need to use different array formulas as shown in the following examples.

For 2nd largest: =LARGE(IF(ISERROR($B$2:$J$5),"",$B$2:$J$5),2)   Answer: **50**

For 3rd largest: =LARGE(IF(ISERROR($B$2:$J$5),"",$B$2:$J$5),3)   Answer: **47,** and so on.

For 2nd smallest: =SMALL(IF(ISERROR($B$2:$J$5),"",$B$2:$J$5),2)   Answer: **-8**

For 3rd smallest: =SMALL(IF(ISERROR($B$2:$J$5),"",$B$2:$J$5),3)   Answer: **-7,**

and so on.

To make the formulas much more flexible we can use cell references instead of **2, 3** (marked by pink colour in the formulas above).

Couple **important** notes related to those formulas:

1. The formulas are of ARRAY type so, after typing in, you must enter them using **CTRL+SHIFT+ENTER** keyboard sequence.

2. Even if there are some *strings* included in the tested range the formulas will provide correct results.

3. If there is any empty cell within the range of *positive* values only, you will get **0** result as the *minimum* value, so be careful.

4. If there are multiple largest or smallest numbers in the range, the formulas will find just the first one. To find out, if there are more than one max/min values, you'd need to use **Find** feature provided in Excel ribbon.

Using Array Formulas to Summarize Tables with Multiple Conditions

Let's assume that you are using Excel table for recording sales of some products by several agents. From time to time, you need to check how your business is doing.

The table is getting larger and larger. I set its size arbitrarily to 1000 rows, but this is up to the user needs. Here is just its small fragment:

	A	B	C	D	E	F
1	Description	Name	Snum	Fair	Adjusted	Result
2	Melcor	Browns	300	6978	8495	-1516.98
3	Western	Johns	200	12066	12326	-259.98
4	Alterra	Browns	400	1881	2107	-225.23
5	Yamana	Smith	600	135718	34744	974.01
6	Western	Davis	1100	24090	21125	2964.62
7	Medical	Johnsons	1000	3020	2890	130.00
8	Cenovus	Davis	500	6250	18193	-11943.13
9	Melcor	Browns	1500	54465	48565	5900.19
10	Western	Johns	650	15275	15600	-283.98
11	Wheaton	Johns	97	68	53	-50.44
12	Medical	Davis	15	295	785	-489.95
13	Alterra	Smith	600	29742	30048	-306.00
14	Yamana	Johnsons	300	6519	7500	-981.00
15	Graphite	Davis	1950	450	1857	-1406.95
16	Western	Browns	800	18200	18560	-360.00
17	Western	Browns	320	2148	2552	-403.54
18	Melcor	Browns	1000	8920	8380	540.12
19	Medical	Davis	4500	67500	91358	-23857.60
20	Wheaton	Smith	0	3570	2994	575.69
21	Wheaton	Johns	40	21376	32679	-11303.00
22	Western	Davis	800	9808	10806	-998.26
23	Yamana	Smith	4500	15075	16738	-1662.68

One day you may need to know, e.g., the **total value** of *Western* items sold by *Davis*. What kind of formula would you use to obtain the value quickly and automatically? Well, in such a case I'd recommend an array formula like this one:

=SUM((Sheet3!A2:A1000="Western")*(Sheet3!B2:B1000="Davis")*(Sheet3!C2:C1000))

The answer you'd get is **1900**.

Similar formula could be used, e.g., to **count** the number of all sales in the table, **except for those** in which *Davis* sold the *Medical*. Here's the example:

=SUM(IF((Sheet3!A2:A1000="Medical")+(Sheet3!B2:B1000="Davis")<>2,1,0))-COUNTIF(Sheet3!A2:A1000,"")

The answer would be equal to **20**.

Based on these examples, a number of similar formulas can be created to make summing and counting immediate and effortless, for many real needs and situations.

<u>**Remember**</u>: these are array formulas, so - after typing them in – each one must be entered using simultaneously **CTRL+SHIFT+ENTER** keystrokes; otherwise, you may get an error or wrong result.

UNIQUE Random Strings of Letters

	A	B	C	D	E	F	G
1	LIST	UNIQUE STRING:	IDOVEHLMUBFNXJWSGQPAYCK TZR				
2	I	ITS LENGTH:	26				
3	D						
4	O						
5	V						
6	E						

This is about creating strings of up to 26 letters with **no repeats** of any letter, using an array formula. Here's the setup.

<u>**Steps to follow**</u>

Copy this array formula into cell **A2**:

=IFERROR(CHAR(IFERROR(LARGE(ROW(INDIRECT("65:90"))*NOT(COUNTIF_($A$1:A1,CHAR(ROW(INDIRECT("65:90"))))),RANDBETWEEN(1,26)),""),""),"")

To enter it correctly, hold **CTRL+SHIFT** and press **ENTER** key on your keyboard. Next, select the cell **A2** and using its **fill handle** (small square at the lower right corner of the cell), hold and drag the handle down the column over the cells until you reach **row 101** (in this setup). The formula will be expanded into the cells.

Now, enter into cell **C1** this standard formula: =CONCAT(A2:A101). It will display the unique string of letters (in most cases 26 letters, but occasionally a bit less). Each time - whenever you select e.g., cell A1 and click in the **formula bar**, or when you change any other cell contents - it will be a different string.

You can also enter this formula =COUNTA(A2:A101)-COUNTBLANK(A2:A101) in cell **C2** to get **count of letters** in the created string.

Unique Macro Buttons - Unlimited

If you use macros (*VBA code*) in Excel you probably use macro buttons as well. There are many ways to create them, but the one I like the most is to utilize just the Excel cells. Yes, nothing else but the cells. Cells are '*pictures*'. Obviously, if you'd like to "decorate" them in any way, you could; and at least you'd probably like to mark them somehow in order to recognize that they refer to your macro code.

So, you'd start with selecting a cell and entering some (centred) text into it, e.g., 'Run abc...'. Next, to create the button, you'd:

- **copy** the cell (using **CTRL+C** shortcut) and **paste** it to the same cell (*or another - it's your choice*) **as a Picture** (using **ALT+H+V+U** shortcut)

- **right-click** in the cell and select **Size & Properties - Properties** and select **Move & size with cells** option (*this way the 'picture' will always fit and stay in the same cell*)

- **right-click** again, select **Assign Macro...** from the menu and select your macro from the list you'd see in **Assign Macro** dialog.

The **cell** is now your macro button. Click it to run your assigned macro.

If you'd like to make the button more distinct (visible) you'd add some *shape* or *photo* or *icon* and/or *format the cell* at your will (*prior to pasting it (!) as a Picture*). Here is a couple of ideas, if you want to make the button unique:

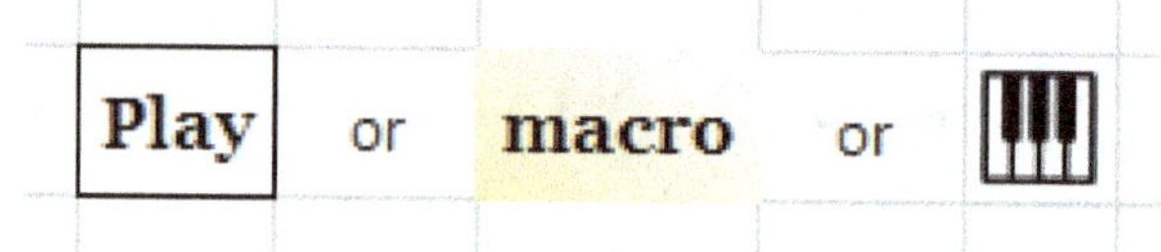

How to Count Any Characters and Digits in a Text String Using ARRAY Formula

Let's say you need to find out how many characters, like e.g., **a**, or **b**, or **w**, or any **other** alphabetic character, or even **digits**, are there in a text string subject to your analysis.

Here is an example of a string located in cell A2:

"Security guards at the hotel make sure guests remain in isolation, while police outside ensure no one enters the premises".

I want to count all characters (i.e., determine their frequency), from **a** to **z** (and **A** to **Z**) present within that string. This snip shows how easily it can be done using the ARRAY formula presented here:

Character	Count of characters
a	5
b	0
c	2
d	2
e	18
f	0
g	2
h	4
i	9
j	0
k	1
l	4
m	3
n	7
o	7
p	2
q	0
r	7
s	11
t	9
u	6
v	0
w	1
x	0
y	1
z	0

```
=LEN(CONCAT(IF(MID(A$2,ABS(ROW(INDIRECT(LEN(A$2)&":1"))-LEN(A$2)-1),1)=A5,A5,"")))
=LEN(CONCAT(IF(MID(A$2,ABS(ROW(INDIRECT(LEN(A$2)&":1"))-LEN(A$2)-1),1)=A6,A6,"")))
=LEN(CONCAT(IF(MID(A$2,ABS(ROW(INDIRECT(LEN(A$2)&":1"))-LEN(A$2)-1),1)=A7,A7,"")))
=LEN(CONCAT(IF(MID(A$2,ABS(ROW(INDIRECT(LEN(A$2)&":1"))-LEN(A$2)-1),1)=A8,A8,"")))
=LEN(CONCAT(IF(MID(A$2,ABS(ROW(INDIRECT(LEN(A$2)&":1"))-LEN(A$2)-1),1)=A9,A9,"")))
=LEN(CONCAT(IF(MID(A$2,ABS(ROW(INDIRECT(LEN(A$2)&":1"))-LEN(A$2)-1),1)=A10,A10,"")))
```

etc....

The array formulas shown on the right side above are underlying the results shown in column B. If there are any digits in your string, they can be counted too, if entered and formatted in column A as **text**(!).

The formula used here is not case-sensitive, so counting includes both lower- and upper-case characters (like **s** and **S** in the example above).

Reminder: the ARRAY formulas must be entered - after typing them in - using the keyboard sequence ***CTRL+SHIFT+ENTER***.

In Reverse: Going Backwards with ARRAY Formulas

Do you need to type or use expressions or numbers in reverse?

Trivial or not, in fact we need sometimes to display or read some numbers or text/expressions in reverse. There are several options available in Excel to do just that. You can do it in a macro way or using some known Excel formulas. E.g., you may use the following ARRAY **formula** for reversing digits in a number:

=SUM(VALUE(MID(B2,ROW(INDIRECT("1:"&LEN(B2))),1))*10^(ROW(INDIRECT("1:"&LEN(B2)))-1))

However, at a closer look, the formula works fine with **digits only**. If you enter *12481632* into cell B2, it returns 23618421, but after entering 2.35 it returns error **#VALUE!** . In addition, it doesn't return trailing zeroes.

So, after some experimenting, I've created my own dynamic ARRAY formula. Here is its exemplary application:

	V	W	X	Y	Z	AA	AB
1							
2	**Reverse the string**	*String*		12481632450	*Number of digits*		
3	gnirts eht esreveR	*Reversed string*		05423618421	*Reversed number of digits*		
4							
5	=CONCAT(MID(V2,ABS(ROW(INDIRECT(LEN(V2)&":1"))-LEN(V2)-1),1))						

The formula reverses whatever string, number or a mix of letters and digits you'd like to reverse. Just remember: this is an ARRAY formula, so - after typing it in - you need to simultaneously hold down the **CTRL** and the **SHIFT** keys as you press **ENTER** on your keyboard.

Counting Cells Containing Numbers Meeting Specific Criteria

Most of the time we organize our data in orderly Excel tables making their analysis quite easy and well arranged. Sometimes, however, we may have to deal with chaotic sets of numbers located all over different ranges/worksheets, like in this somewhat bloated example:

	A	B	C	D	E	F
2		7.50	26/06/2021	9	12/09/2021	
3		22.00	15/01/2021	10	13	read
4		0.25	2	11	trend	
5		3.00		20	8	70.222
6		4.00	11	21	7	
7		50.50	5	1		Julia
8		6.00	form	23	7	
9		7.00	Monday	24		
10		25.00	10	8	0.25	

How to count and analyse them? Couple of examples follow.

Example 1

> For **basic counting** of all cells containing numbers within a selected range(s) we can use a simple formula, e.g.: **=COUNT(B2:F10)**

What if we want to get some idea about e.g., distribution of those numbers, or we'd like to find out if there are any outliers in the set of data, etc. Among many possible solutions, I'd recommend using just one amazing ARRAY formula, in many available formats. Here are some of them.

Example 2

> Having counted all cells containing numbers, now you want to know how many of those numbers are <u>higher than 50</u>:
>
> **=INDEX(FREQUENCY((B2:F10),50),2)**
>
> or <u>equal to and lower than 50</u>:
>
> **=INDEX(FREQUENCY((B2:F10),50),1)**

Example 3

> Your data are located in three different ranges and you'd like to know how many of the numbers exceed 22:

=INDEX(FREQUENCY((A4:A10,B3:C21,R8:R25),22),2)

Those three array formulas shown above are SINGLE-CELL arrays. After typing them in, you must press **CTRL+SHIFT+ENTER** keys to enter them.

Example 4

You want to know distribution of the numbers within selected range in these **three** intervals, e.g.: <=5, >5 and <=20, >20:

=INDEX(FREQUENCY((B2:F10),{5,20}),{1;2;3})

This is **MULTI-CELL** array formula. To enter this array - first select **three** cells in a column, and then type the formula in and press CTRL+SHIFT+ENTER keys.

Example 5

You want to know distribution of the numbers within selected range in these **four** intervals, e.g.: <=4, >4 and <=9, >9 and <=22, >22:

=INDEX(FREQUENCY((B2:F10),{4,9,22}),{1;2;3;4})

This is also **MULTI-CELL** array formula. To enter this array - first select **four** cells in a column, and then type the formula in and press CTRL+SHIFT+ENTER keys.

Here are the results of all those formulas:

Example 1	Count of all numbers within the range	31
Example 2	Count of numbers >50	5
	Count of numbers <=50	26
Example 3	Count of numbers >22 from 3 different ranges	3

Example 4	Count of numbers falling into three set boundaries, e.g.:		
		<=5	7
		>5 and <=20	14
		>20	10

Example 5	Count of numbers falling into four set boundaries, e.g.:		
		<=4	6
		>4 and <=9	9
		>9 and <=22	8
		>22	8

Looking at the consecutive formulas and the results displayed here you can see the logic behind them. In the last two examples the formulas use **array constant** as their **last** component (argument). You create the constants by entering a list of items within curly braces, {}. In the examples, the items are separated by semicolons, so the results are arranged vertically (in a column). If you separate the items using commas, the results will be arranged in a row (horizontally).

Following the examples, if you're dealing - in any real data analysis - with a high volume of numeric (or mixed) type of data, you can create similar array formulas with appropriate array constants to obtain **distribution list** with preselected boundaries (e.g., 1-10, 11-20, 21-30, 31-40...etc.), and use it in your analysis. If needed, the array constants can be entered in the worksheet cells and named, as any other range.

All can be done with just **one easily editable formula** that works with:

- numbers entered in any order and in discontinuous ranges (with some empty cells)
- numbers mixed with textual entries, and
- numbers resulting from regular Excel formulas.

The results of counting with array constants can be utilized e.g., for graphical presentation (chart):

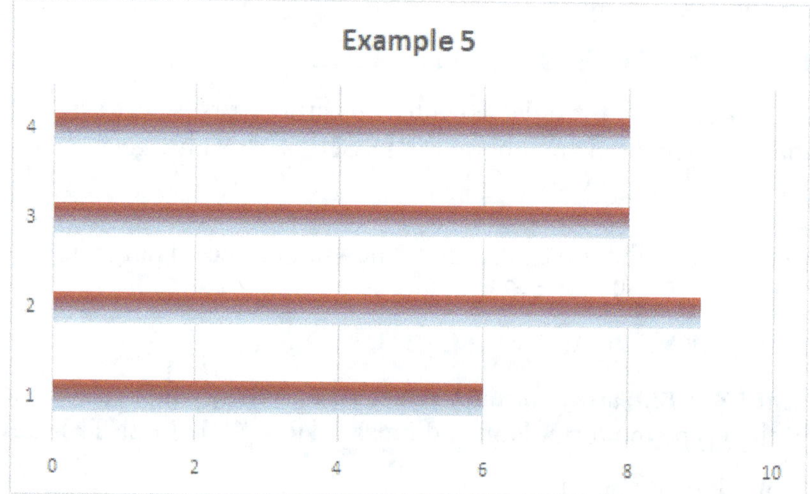

Important note: some dates are included on purpose (those coloured differently) in my example of data range used for counting.

Remember that if there are cells formatted as DATE or TIME in the selected range of your data, they are treated as **serial numbers** and included in the counting. So, you might need to exclude them from the analysis. Otherwise, they may distort the results.

How to Check If the Contents of Two Ranges/Worksheets is Different

You are not sure if some ranges of data in your worksheet, or in two different worksheets, contain the same data. How to figure it out? And if they are different, is the difference significant?

Use ARRAY formula to check it out. You can count the differing cells using e.g., this kind of array formula in Sheet1 to compare with cell contents in Sheet2:

=SUM(IF(B2:G100=Sheet2!B2:G100,0,1))

Remember that to enter it you need to simultaneously hold down the **CTRL** and the **SHIFT** keys as you press **ENTER**. The formula will show up in the formula bar, surrounded by curly brackets.

Also, make sure that the size of compared ranges is the same. Location, however, can be different, like e.g. A2:F20 in one worksheet and C5:H23 in another.

If there are no differences, the formula displays **0** (zero). If there are differences, the **total number of differing cells** is provided by the formula.

If needed, you can now investigate further, e.g., by selecting **both** ranges/worksheets and using the Excel **conditional formatting** feature to format current selection in Sheet2 (e.g., B2:D10) by applying this kind of rule:

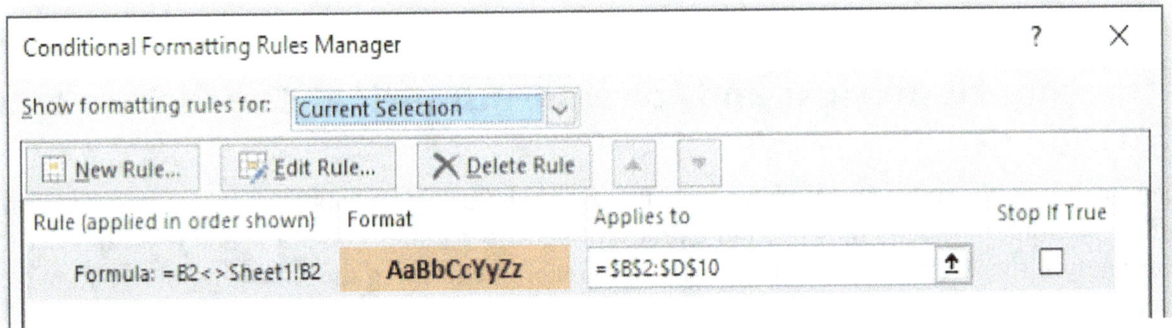

The formatting marks specific cells in Sheet2 that differ from those in Sheet1, as in the example below:

<table>
<tr><td></td><td colspan="3">In Sheet1</td><td colspan="3">In Sheet 2</td></tr>
<tr><td>1</td><td></td><td></td><td></td><td></td><td></td><td></td></tr>
<tr><td>2</td><td></td><td>30.5</td><td>-10</td><td></td><td>30.5</td><td>-10</td></tr>
<tr><td>3</td><td></td><td>20.05</td><td>0</td><td></td><td>20.05</td><td>0</td></tr>
<tr><td>4</td><td>rama</td><td>40</td><td>10</td><td>rama</td><td>-7</td><td>10</td></tr>
<tr><td>5</td><td>sara</td><td>21</td><td>20</td><td>sara</td><td>21</td><td>20</td></tr>
<tr><td>6</td><td>mart</td><td>8</td><td>30</td><td>mart</td><td>15</td><td>11</td></tr>
<tr><td>7</td><td>aroma</td><td>-3</td><td>40</td><td>aroma</td><td>-3</td><td>40</td></tr>
<tr><td>8</td><td>noc</td><td>234</td><td>50</td><td>nocka</td><td>234</td><td>50</td></tr>
<tr><td>9</td><td>osiem</td><td>7</td><td>60</td><td>osiem</td><td>7</td><td>60</td></tr>
<tr><td>10</td><td>berta</td><td>50</td><td></td><td>berta</td><td>50</td><td></td></tr>
</table>

Problem solved.

To COUNT Any Characters or Strings in Any Range of Cells

Use an **ARRAY** formula. You can find out the number of occurrences of anything (e.g., BS, 2016, s, graph, three days, 50%, etc.) within a given cell or a range of cells.

Assuming that your data range is e.g. A2:D100, select any cell outside that range and type the formula analogous to this one:

=SUM((LEN(A2:D100)-LEN(SUBSTITUTE(A2:D100,"Fig.","")))/LEN("Fig."))

and simultaneously hold down the **CTRL** and the **SHIFT** keys as you press **ENTER**. The formula will show up in the formula bar, surrounded by curly brackets. And the cell, where you array-entered the formula, will show the result, like here in cell G1:

```
{=SUM((LEN(A2:D100)-LEN(SUBSTITUTE(A2:D100,"Fig.","")))/LEN("Fig."))}
```

E	F	G	H	I	J	K
		3				

Obviously, you could use also this 'normal' formula: **=COUNTIF(A2:D100,"*Fig.*")** for the same purpose. However, it would show erroneous result in those cases where the counted string appears multiple times in a single cell, because it counts only the number of cells that meet a criterion, not the number of occurrences of the string.

Another, related to the first one, **ARRAY** formula, as in this example: **=SUM(LEN(A2:D100))**, **counts** (sums) **all characters** in a given range of cells (or in a single cell). Just remember to enter it as **ARRAY** formula, i.e., press CTRL+SHIFT+ENTER keys.

Extracting Numerical and/or Non-numerical Characters from a String

When dealing with data in Excel, there are situations, where you have both numbers and text in the same cells. Sometimes you may need to extract (or show separately) numbers and text, in order to easier analyse those values. In such cases I would recommend using the following macro to make such a task more efficient.

```
Sub ExtractBoth()
'Extracts separately numerical & non-numerical characters from a string in an active cell
Dim exTxt As String
Dim exNum As Double
Dim myStr As String
myStr = ActiveCell.Value
Dim outp As String
For i = 1 To Len(myStr)
        If Val(Mid(myStr, i, 1)) Or Mid(myStr, i, 1) = "0" Then
            exNum = exNum & Mid(myStr, i, 1)
        Else
            exTxt = exTxt & Mid(myStr, i, 1)
        End If
Next i
ActiveCell.Offset(, 1).Value = exNum
ActiveCell.Offset(, 2).Value2 = exTxt
outp = MsgBox("Extracted number: " & exNum & vbNewLine & "Extracted text: " & exTxt, , "Extracted digits and text")
End Sub
```

If your active cell is located e.g., in cell **A1** and contains string like this one:

ab&400er=29--23sdrk@j89:?

then the macro separates it into two parts like these:

400292389 and **ab&er=--sdrk@j:?**

and displays them in cells **B1** and **C1**. Then, optionally, it shows them for you in a message box.

The macro code can be easily adapted to your specific needs.

Extract Formulas to External File

If your workbook/worksheet is full of Excel formulas it may be worth to keep track of them in one place, in a compact listing, in a separate text file. Here is a short macro that serves the purpose:

```
Sub ListFormulas()
Dim rng As Range
'Extracts all formulas from a worksheet to a text file (Notepad/Wordpad)
Open "C:\Users\Adam\Desktop\XFormulas.txt" For Output As #1
For Each rng In Sheets("Formulas").UsedRange.Cells
        If rng.Formula <> "" And Left(rng.Formula, 1) = "=" Then
                Print #1, rng.Address; Tab; rng.Formula
        End If
```

Next
Close #1
End Sub

Just copy it and paste into one of the VBE modules of your workbook (*I'd recommend Personal workbook*), to make the macro easily available for copying - whenever you need it - to any of your workbooks.

Remember to replace the **path** to *your* text file and the **sheet name** in the macro, with your own.

It extracts all formulas from a worksheet and writes them into a text file, in the following format (*example*):

```
$A$2    =INDEX(FREQUENCY((A3:A10),20),2)
$C$2    =AVERAGE(LEN(A3:B9))
$D$2    =SUM(LEN(A3:A9))
$E$2    =INDEX(B4:B9,MATCH(MAX(LEN(B4:B9)),LEN(B4:B9),0),1)
$F$2    =MAX(IF(ISERROR(A3:A9),"",A3:A9))
$G$2    =SUM(IF(B4:B9=C4:C9,0,1))
$H$2    =ADDRESS(MIN(IF(A3:A9=MAX(A3:A9),ROW(A3:A9),"")),COLUMN(A3:A9))
$I$2    =AVERAGE(IF(A3:A9>0,A3:A9,FALSE))
```

If your formulas are spread over multiple worksheets of your workbook, the macro can be modified to loop through all of the worksheets.

Create/Record a Macro

If you have tasks in Microsoft Excel that you do repeatedly, you can record a macro with the Macro Recorder to automate those tasks. A macro is an action or a set of actions that you can run as many times as you want. When you create a macro, you are recording your mouse clicks and keystrokes. After you create a macro, you can edit it to make minor changes to the way it works.

When you record a macro, the Macro Recorder records all the steps in Visual Basic for Applications (VBA) code. These steps can include typing text or numbers, clicking cells or commands on the ribbon or on menus, formatting cells, rows, or columns, or even importing data from an external source, say, Microsoft Access. Visual Basic Application (VBA) is a subset of the powerful Visual Basic programming language, and is included with most Office applications. Although VBA gives you the ability to automate processes within and between Office applications, it is not necessary to know VBA code or computer programming if the Macro Recorder does what you want.

The Macro Recorder captures almost every move you make. So, if you make a mistake in your sequence, for example, clicking a button that you did not intend to click, the Macro Recorder will record it. The resolution is to re-record the entire sequence, or modify the VBA code itself. This is why whenever you record something, it's best to record a process with which you're highly familiar. The more smoothly you record a sequence, the more efficiently the macro will run when you play it back.

Macros and VBA tools can be found on the **Developer** tab, which is hidden by default, so the first step is to enable it. To do that, go to **File > Options > Customize Ribbon**. Then, in the **Customize the Ribbon** section, under **Main Tabs**, check the **Developer** box, and press **OK**.

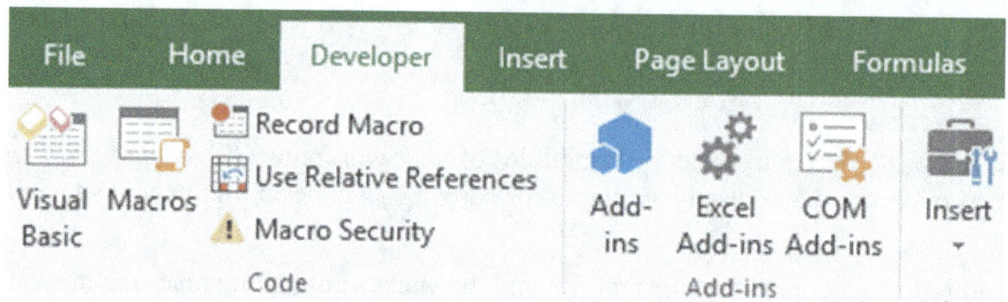

To record your macro - in the **Code** group on the **Developer** tab, click **Record Macro, or** press **Alt+T+M+R**. Optionally - enter a name for the macro in the **Macro name** box (make the name as descriptive as possible so you can quickly find it if you create more than one macro}, enter a shortcut key in the **Shortcut key** box, and a description in the **Description** box.

Note: The first character of the *macro name* must be a letter. Subsequent characters can be letters, numbers, or underscore characters. Spaces cannot be used in a macro name; an underscore character works well as a word separator. If you use a macro name that is also a cell reference, you may get an error message that the macro name is not valid.

To assign a *keyboard shortcut* to run the macro, in the **Shortcut key** box, type any letter (both uppercase or lowercase will work) that you want to use. It is best to use **Ctrl + Shift** (uppercase) key combinations, because the macro shortcut key will override any equivalent default Excel shortcut key while the workbook that contains the macro is open. For instance, if you use **Ctrl+Z** (Undo), you will lose the ability to Undo in that Excel instance.

In the **Store macro in** list, select where you want to store the macro. In general, you'll save your macro in the **This Workbook** location, but if you want a macro to be available whenever you use Excel, select **Personal Macro Workbook**. When you select **Personal Macro Workbook**, Excel creates a hidden personal macro workbook (Personal.xlsb) if it does not already exist, and saves the macro in this workbook.

Click **OK** to start recording. Perform the actions you want to automate, such as entering boilerplate text or filling down a column of data. When completed the actions, click **Stop Recording** on the **Developer** tab. **Take a closer look at the macro.** You can learn a little bit about the Visual Basic programming language by editing a macro.

To edit a macro, in the **Code** group on the **Developer** tab, click **Macros**, select the name of the macro, and click **Edit**. This starts the Visual Basic Editor. You can also open the Visual Basic Editor by pressing **Alt+F11**.

See how the actions that you recorded appear as code. Some of the code will probably be clear to you, and some of it may be a little mysterious. Experiment with the code, close the Visual Basic Editor, and run your macro again.

There are a few helpful things you should know about macros:

- When you record a macro for performing a set of tasks in a range in Excel, the macro will only run on the cells within that range. So, if you add an extra row to the range, the macro will not run the process on the new row, but only on the cells within the range.

- If you have planned a long process of tasks to record, plan to have smaller relevant macros instead of having one long macro.

- It is not necessary that only tasks in Excel can be recorded in a macro. Your macro process can extend to other Office applications, and any other applications that support Visual Basic Application (VBA). For example, you can record a macro where you first update a table in Excel and then open Outlook to email the table to an email address.

Working with Macros in Excel

In the **Developer** tab, click **Macros** to view macros associated to a workbook. Or press **Alt+ F8**. This opens the **Macro** dialog box.

Be careful. Macros cannot be undone. Before you run a recorded macro for the first time, make sure that you've either saved the workbook where you want to run the macro, or better yet work on a copy of the workbook to prevent unwanted changes. If you run a macro and it doesn't do what you want, you can dose the workbook without saving it.

You can run a macro in many ways:
- From the Developer tab: click on the "Macros" button in the "Developer" tab, select the macro you want to run and click on the "Run" button.
- By pressing a combination shortcut key (if you have assigned a shortcut prior to macro recording).
- By clicking a button on the Quick Access Toolbar (QAT). But first, you need to add your macro to the QAT by right-clicking on the QAT and selecting Customize the QAT. In the Excel Options dialog box, select Macros in the Choose commands from dropdown and add your macro to the QAT.
- By clicking a button in a custom group on the ribbon. But first, you need to add your macro to the Ribbon by customizing it. Go to File - Options - Customize Ribbon and create a new tab or group. Then, add your macro to the group.
- From the Visual Basic Editor (VBE). Simply place the cursor inside the macro code and press the F5 key or click on the Run button in the toolbar.
- By configuring a macro to run automatically upon opening a workbook; just name your macro as Auto_Open.
- By clicking an area on any graphic object (right-click it and select "Assign Macro…" from the menu) or on Excel button; either Form Control button or ActiveX Command button.

  To add the **Form Control button** to your worksheet, follow these steps:

  - Go to the Developer tab and click on Insert.
  - Under the Form Controls section, select the **Button** .
  - Click and drag on the worksheet to draw the button.
  - In the Assign Macro dialog box that appears, select the macro you want to run from the list and click OK.

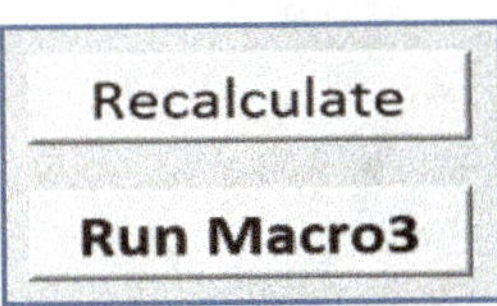

  - If you want to change the text on the button, right-click on it and select Edit Text. You can then enter the desired text, as shown here in these two examples.
  - To specify the **control properties** of the button, right-click the button, and then click **Format Control**.
  - Click on the button to run the macro.

To add the **ActiveX Command button** to your worksheet, follow these steps:

- Go to the Developer tab and click on the Insert button in the Controls group. Choose a button control from the **ActiveX Controls** section, and draw the button on the worksheet. You can format it to your liking, as shown here in the two examples.

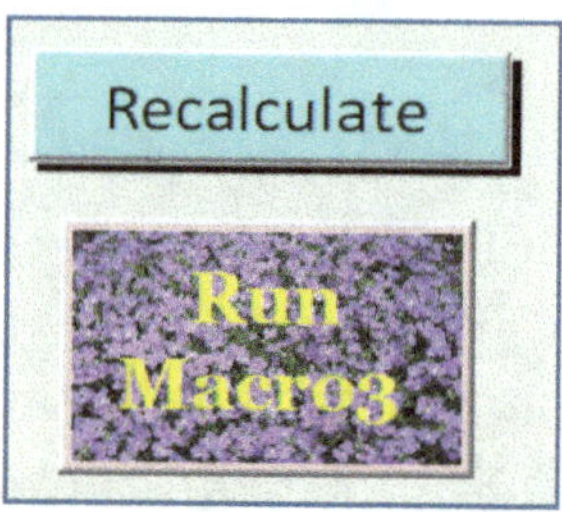

- Right-click the button and select View Code. This will open the Visual Basic Editor. In the code window, type the name of the macro you want to run. E.g., if your macro is named "MyMacro", the code could look like this:

```
Private Sub CommandButton1()
    MyMacro
End Sub
```

- Close the Visual Basic Editor and save the changes to the workbook.
- Test the button: click it to run the macro.

You can move the button to any location on the worksheet, and it will continue to work.

Open Workbook with Startup Worksheet

If you create a workbook that will be opened and used frequently by yourself and - especially - if you design it for sharing with other users, you may want to start it in a compelling, attractive way.

I'm presenting here an example of initializing a worksheet which you might want to appear when the workbook is being started. The workbook is macro-driven, so it must be saved as Macro-Enabled Workbook. This is how the worksheet looks like after loading with a randomly selected photo (this is a screenshot of the left part of my computer screen):

If you'd like to experiment with your own workbook, you can copy the following macro and paste it into '**This Workbook**' window of your VBA Project in your workbook.

```vba
Private Sub Workbook_Open()
'The macro will run automatically after opening the workbook in which it resides
'Displays designated worksheet (front page), following the macro instructions
Dim xPhoto As Variant
Dim folder As Object, file As Variant
Dim fs, f, s
Dim fIndex As Long
Dim fList() As String, i As Long
Worksheets("Main").Activate
With Application
    .ExecuteExcel4Macro "show.toolbar(""Ribbon"",False)"
    .ActiveWindow.DisplayGridlines = False
    .ActiveWindow.DisplayHeadings = False
    .DisplayFormulaBar = False
End With
DisplayStatusBar = False
DisplayWorkbookTabs = False
Cells.Select
With Selection.Interior
    .Pattern = xlPatternLinearGradient
    .Gradient.Degree = 270
    .Gradient.ColorStops.Clear
End With
With Selection.Interior.Gradient.ColorStops.Add(1)
    .ThemeColor = xlThemeColorAccent1
    .TintAndShade = -0.250984221930601
End With
Application.ScreenUpdating = False
On Error Resume Next
fromPath = "D:\Photos\Garden\"
Set fs = CreateObject("Scripting.FileSystemObject")
Set folder = fs.GetFolder(fromPath)        '(folder spec)
ReDim fList(1 To folder.Files.Count)
f = folder.Files.Count
Randomize  'Initialize random-number generator
fIndex = Int(Rnd * folder.Files.Count) + 1
For Each file In folder.Files
    i = i + 1
    If i = fIndex Then fList(i) = file.Name: Exit For
Next file
Set file = folder.Files(CStr(fList(fIndex)))
xPhoto = file
Range("B2").Select
If xPhoto <> "" Then
    ActiveSheet.Pictures.Insert(xPhoto).Select
```

```vba
        Selection.ShapeRange.LockAspectRatio = msoTrue
        Selection.ShapeRange.Height = 700#
        Selection.ShapeRange.PictureFormat.Brightness = 0.5
        Selection.ShapeRange.PictureFormat.Contrast = 0.5
        Selection.ShapeRange.PictureFormat.ColorType = msoPictureAutomatic
    End If
    Range("C3").Select
    Application.ScreenUpdating = True
    currenttime = Mid(Now(), 12, 5)
    If currenttime < "12:00" Then
        g01 = "Morning" & vbCrLf & "It's " & currenttime
    Else
        If currenttime >= "18:00" Then
            g01 = "Evening" & vbCrLf & "It's " & currenttime
        Else
            g01 = "Afternoon" & vbCrLf & "It's " & currenttime
        End If
    End If
    Beep
    MsgBox "Good " & g01 & "." & Chr$(10) & Chr$(10), vbOKOnly + vbInformation, "WELCOME
BACK!"
    Application.Wait (Now + TimeValue("0:00:01"))
    Application.ScreenUpdating = True
    ActiveSheet.Pictures.Select
    Selection.Delete  'Remove Photo
    Cells.Select
    With Selection.Interior
        .Pattern = xlNone
        .TintAndShade = 0
        .PatternTintAndShade = 0
    End With
    With Application
        .ExecuteExcel4Macro "show.toolbar(""Ribbon"",True)"
        .ActiveWindow.DisplayGridlines = True
        .ActiveWindow.DisplayHeadings = True
        .DisplayFormulaBar = True
    End With
    DisplayStatusBar = True
    DisplayWorkbookTabs = True
    Range("A1").Select
End Sub
```

The macro runs at the opening of the workbook. It does several things:

- activates worksheet named "Main"
- changes some of the worksheet settings
- selects *randomly* one of the photos located in "D:\Photos\Garden\" path on my computer
- inserts the selected photo into the selected worksheet
- determines current time of the day

- uses MsgBox to display some greeting expressions and the time
- when the user clicks OK in the message box, removes the photo and switches all initial settings back to normal

Before running the macro, you'd need to change the **worksheet name** and the **path to the photos** (or any other pictures) location to your own selections.

These or similar features can be included e.g., in a workbook template. Such a template could, in addition, contain some formats, styles, more worksheets, print settings, text, shapes, data, graphics, formulas, charts, hyperlinks, forms, etc.

Function N() = Insert Comment: TRUE or FALSE

When we return to our workbook created some time ago and try to revive/use it, it quite often happens that we've forgotten what we had intended to achieve by composing some complex formulas or entering even simple data points. We can avoid such situations in the future by adding *comments* or *notes* to some selected cells.

The **Insert Comment** feature is OK, but in most cases the better choice is to use the **N() function**, as illustrated below:

=SQRT(43)-G3+N("Enter any note/reminder here")

	E	F	G	H	I
	5.55744		TRUE		

As you can see, the N() function added to the formula in cell E2 is visible in the Formula Bar above, but hidden in the cell, so it doesn't distract your attention. Whatever text/reference you enter within the N function parentheses is converted to 0 (zero), so it doesn't affect the cell value.

This way we can easily see our reminder. It's a very good replacement for the Insert Comment feature.

By the way, the **TRUE** value entered in G3 and referenced in the E2 formula, returns **1**, so cell E2 displays *5.55744* instead of *6.55744*.

You may also find interesting that when you enter the formula =100-2*TRUE into a cell, it returns **98**, but =100-2*FALSE returns **100**.

VLOOKUP Function and the UDF

Normally you use the **VLOOKUP function** to find things in a table or a range by row. E.g., look up a price of a mower part by the part number The function works fine for a single table in a given worksheet.

But, let's say, you have a workbook with related several tables located in different worksheets. You might need to check all worksheets to find a match for your lookup value. In such a case you would need to use the VLOOKUP repeatedly in each of the worksheets. Much more efficient would be using this UDF (User Defined Function) I've created to make the task easier:

Function VLOOKUPinWBK(lookup_value As Variant, table_array As Range, _
col_index_num As Integer, Optional range_lookup As Boolean)
'This UDF looks in ALL worksheets in your workbook and finds the

```vba
' first match for lookup_value.
Dim wSh As Worksheet
Dim wks As String
Dim vLooked
On Error Resume Next
For Each wSh In ActiveWorkbook.Worksheets
    With wSh
        wks = wSh.Name
        Set table_array = .Range(table_array.Address)
        vLooked = WorksheetFunction.VLookup(lookup_value, table_array, _
            col_index_num, range_lookup)
    End With
If Not IsEmpty(vLooked) Then vLooked = vLooked: Exit For
Next wSh
Set table_array = Nothing
VLOOKUPinWBK = vLooked & " (found in '" & wks & "')"
End Function
```

You can use it just once to get the first match of your lookup_value *in any of the worksheets*. The result also informs you in which of the worksheets the match has been found.

To use this code, press ***ALT+F11*** and go to **Insert-Module**, then copy and paste the code into the open window. Press ***ALT+Q*** to return to your worksheet.

Example of using the VLOOKUPinWBK function follows.

I have two somewhat different tables, one in Sheet1:

Id	Nam1	Nam2	Position	Value
1	Bart	Agata	Porter	280
2	Lone	Karina	Salesman	1050
3	Bert	Lech	Manager	800
4	Remi	Barb	President	390
5	Carter	Mesa	Worker	1260
6	Emma	Albin	Pilot	1349
7	Dor	More	Techn1	400
8	Kon	Kamil	Techn2	580
10	Lost	Rob	Plumber	890

and another in Sheet2:

Id	Nam1	Nam2	Positio	Value
1	Bart	Agata	Porter	280
2	Lone	Karina	Salesman	1050
3	Bert	Lech	Manager	800
4	Artek	Barb	President	870
5	Sam	Tesa	Secretary	5000
6	Emma	Albin	Pilot	1349
7	Dor	More	Techn1	400
8	Kon	Kamil	Techn2	580
10	Lost	Rob	Plumber	890

I need to find a match for **'Sam'** (col. B) **in col. D** (Position), so I enter in any empty cell of Sheet1 the following formula using the UDF (with arguments as in normal VLOOKUP function):

=VLOOKUPinWBK("Sam",$B$1:$E$200,3,0)

The result is displayed as: **Secretary (found in 'Sheet2')**

Average Numbers, Kind of

There are many meanings and uses of *Average* number. The two formulas presented here refer to the most common average, i.e., **arithmetic mean**, not geometric, harmonic or any other.

To get AVERAGE - excluding 0s and blank cells - for values located e.g., in column A, in first 100 cells, you can use the following formula:

=AVERAGEIFS(A1:A100,A1:A100,"-0",A1:A100,"<>""")

To Get SIMPLE MOVING AVERAGE for some last cells in the column A, you can use formula like this one:

=AVERAGE(OFFSET(A$1,COUNTA(A:A)-1,0,-5,1))

This kind of Average is commonly used in financial sector as a type of technical indicator available to traders, but in many other applications as well. The average can be calculated for any number of last cells (or time frame) in a column. In this example the formula provides average for the last *five* cells in the column.

If you need any other number of last cells for your calculations, replace "5" in the formula with that other number, as needed.

Generate Unique Random Alphanumeric Characters and Strings

If you play lottery games of lotto type or want to get a list of some *unique* random numbers, letters or expressions, Excel is very helpful in generating them. There are many ways to accomplish that. Here are just couple of them.

To create a list of unique random numbers using an array formula:

first, format the selected cell, e.g. A1, as **Text**. Enter a range of numbers from which to draw, in this format: **1-50**. Next, enter in cell A2 the following **array** formula:

=SMALL(IF(COUNTIF(C$1:C1,ROW($1:$50))<>1,ROW($1:$50)),1+INT(RAND()*(RIGHT(C$1,LEN(C$1)-FIND("-",C$1))-LEFT(C$1,FIND("-",C$1)-1)+1-ROW()+ROW(C$2))))

To enter it correctly, hold **CTRL+SHIFT** and press **ENTER** key on your keyboard. If you need to generate random unique numbers from a different range, you must replace the numbers (1 and 50) in both A1 and A2 cells.

Now you need to copy cell A2 and paste it to as many rows as many random numbers you are expecting to obtain (up to 50 in the example).

To create a list of unique random numbers using UDF (User Defined Function):

- Press ALT+F11 on your keyboard to open up the VB Editor.
- If no Module is available within your Project, then right-click within the VBA **Project Explorer** and select **Insert**, then choose **Module** from the menu.
- Enter the following code in the Module:

```vba
Function GetUnique(Lo As Integer, Hi As Integer, Nr As Integer) As String
'Generates x unique random numbers between any 2 numbers you specify
'e.g. =GetUnique(1,50,8) produces 8 unique random numbers between 1 and 50
    Dim iArr As Variant
    Dim i As Integer
    Dim r As Integer
    Dim temp As Integer
    Application.Volatile
    ReDim iArr(Lo To Hi)
    For i = Lo To Hi
        iArr(i) = i
    Next i
    For i = Hi To Lo + 1 Step -1
        r = Int(Rnd() * (i - Lo + 1)) + Lo
        temp = iArr(r)
        iArr(r) = iArr(i)
        iArr(i) = temp
    Next i
    For i = Lo To Lo + Nr - 1
        If i = Lo Then GetUnique = GetUnique & "" & iArr(i)
        If i > 1 Then GetUnique = GetUnique & " * " & iArr(i)
    Next i
    GetUnique = Trim(GetUnique)
End Function
```

- Use the function in any selected cell by entering it in the format shown above on the comment lines.

To create a random letter of alphabet (either Upper or Lowercase):

use this formula:

=IF(RAND()<=0.5,CHAR(RANDBETWEEN(65,90)),CHAR(RANDBETWEEN(97,122)))

It generates a random letter from **a** to **z** and **A** to **Z** characters.

To create a string of random _letters_, like in this example:

etO	sis	Nkr	bCZ	KEx	yCO	QAO
Csn	hGP	UJq	NVC	tph	Ofs	RKH
HOS	uKQ	LAK	mSp	RfP	Ooz	ZMq

you need to use "&" character to add the letters together:

**=IF(RAND()<=0.5,CHAR(RANDBETWEEN(65,90)),CHAR(RANDBETWEEN(97,122)))&IF
(RAND()<=0.5,CHAR(RANDBETWEEN(65,90)),CHAR(RANDBETWEEN(97,122)))&IF(R
AND()<=0.5,CHAR(RANDBETWEEN(65,90)),CHAR(RANDBETWEEN(97,122)))**

This specific formula generates a string of **three** random letters. If you drag the cell fill handle over to some range you want to cover with this formula, you will get the range filled with random 3-letter strings. The formula can be quite easily modified to get _unique_ random strings including any and many (more than three) alphanumeric characters.

Counting unique cell entries in a worksheet

Sometimes you may want to be sure that your large Excel dataset contains unique entries only, i.e., none of the entries appears more than once. How would you check it?

There are some array formulas and advanced filtering methods available for such occasion, but the most convenient way is probably using the UDF (User Defined Function) presented here:

```
Function Count1time(cRng As Range) As Variant
'Counts each cell with a value in the selected range
'Excludes any repeats!
'example of usage: Count1time(A1:C100)
        Dim cVal As Variant
        Dim uniq As New Collection
        Application.Volatile
        On Error Resume Next
        For Each cVal In cRng
            uniq.Add cVal, CStr(cVal)
        Next
        Count1time = "Found " & uniq.Count & " unique entries"
End Function
```

To use it in your workbook - open the Visual Basic Editor (VBE) by pressing **ALT+F11** shortcut, right-click within **Project Explorer**, select **Insert > Module** (if not inserted there yet). Copy and paste the function code in the Module window.

Switch back to your Excel worksheet and test the function on any selected set of data. If the function counting result is equal to the number of cell entries within the tested range, it confirms that all data in your set are de facto unique. If not - some values are entered more than once.

Reference the Last Cell in a Column

If you need to reference the **last cell value** in a column, use the following **array** formula:

```
=INDIRECT("G"&MAX(ROW(1:1048576)*(G:G<>"")))
```

It returns the value held in the last filled cell in column **G**.

If you need to find out also what the **row number** of the cell keeping the value is, then this **array** formula can be used:

```
=CELL("row",INDIRECT("G"&MAX(ROW(1:1048576)*(G:G<>""))))
```

You may want to get **both the value and location / row number** of the last cell. In such a case you can combine the above formulas into one, like in this example:

```
=INDIRECT("G"&MAX(ROW(1:1048576)*(G:G<>"")))&" ==> "&"Row
"&CELL("row",INDIRECT("G"&MAX(ROW(1:1048576)*(G:G<>""))))
```

Sometimes the formula can return an **error value**. It may happen, if any of the cells in the column displays an error. To make you aware of such an error, you can include error checking part, e.g.:

```
=IFERROR(INDIRECT("G"&MAX(ROW(1:1048576)*(G:G<>"")))&" ==> "&"Row
"&CELL("row",INDIRECT("G"&MAX(ROW(1:1048576)*(G:G<>"")))),"Error in the
column!")
```

Replace **G** in the formulas with your actual column of interest, as needed, and keep in mind that those are all ARRAY formulas, so you need to hold simultaneously **CTRL+SHIFT** keys and press the **ENTER** key to create them.

How to Find Something with FIND Function

While working in Excel we're always looking for something. The FIND function can be very helpful in our searches.

Remember two things: the FIND is **case-sensitive** (differentiates between "a" and "A") and **doesn't work with Date** format (cells formatted as dates).

Used by itself, it just finds position of a character or text within a longer string. However, when used in combination with some other functions, it can be very useful in solving complex tasks. Here is summary of some examples of the FIND usage, described beneath the table.

Given string	Formula used	Output
C:\Users\Artur\Desktop\ [Micron.xlsm]Sheet2	=IF(CELL("Filename",A1)>"",LEFT(CELL("Filename",A1),FIND("[",CELL("Filename",A1))-1),"")	C:\Users\Artur\ Desktop\
Home/active/Avisible	=MID(A1,FIND("/",A1,FIND("/",A1,1)+1)+1,4)	Avis
cells%point%Min123% Maxi	=MID(A1,FIND("%",A1,FIND("%",A1)+1)+1,FIND("%",A1,FIND("%",A1)+1)+2)-FIND("%",A1,FIND("%",A1)+1)-1)	Min123
repeatSentence	=FIND(CHAR(10),SUBSTITUTE(A1,"e",CHAR(10),3))	8
cor>name it	=RIGHT(A1,LEN(A1)-FIND(">",A1))	name it
Start Sim	=FIND("S",A1,FIND("S",A1,1)+1)	7
5008$+6410£let	=MID(A1,FIND("$",A1)+1,FIND("£",A1)-FIND("$",A1)-1)	+6410

1: **Find the directory/folder** name of the file, you are using currently, with this formula:

=IF(CELL("Filename",A1)>"",LEFT(CELL("Filename",A1),FIND("[",CELL("Filename",A1))-1),"")

2: **Extract some number of characters** (e.g., **4**) following the second occurrence of "/":
=MID(A1,FIND("/",A1,FIND("/",A1,1)+1)+1,4)

3: **Return all characters** between 2nd and 3rd "%":

=MID(A1,FIND("%",A1,FIND("%",A1)+1)+1,FIND("%",A1,FIND("%",A1,FIND("%",A1)+1)+2)-FIND("%",A1,FIND("%",A1,+1)-1)

4: **Find position of any of (2nd,3rd,4th...) occurrences** of a given character in a string (e.g., 3rd occurrence of "e"):

=FIND(CHAR(10),SUBSTITUTE(A1,"e",CHAR(10),3))

5: **Find some substring of the string** after a given character (e.g., after ">"):

=RIGHT(A1,LEN(A1)-FIND(">",A1))

6: **Find position of the second occurrence of some character** in a string (e.g., "S"):

=FIND("S",A1,FIND("S",A1,1)+1)

7: **Find text between two characters** (can be the same or different); in this example, between "$" and "£":

=MID(A1,FIND("$",A1)+1,FIND("£",A1)-FIND("$",A1)-1)

Pull Number from Alphanumeric String in a Cell

Sometimes you may need to pull the numbers from alphanumeric strings in your worksheet cells. The User Defined Function (UDF), presented here, separates numbers from a cell containing numbers and text characters. The referenced cell can contain any string, including spaces, decimal points, or negative numbers.

```vba
Function PullNum(rng As Range, _
    Optional Point As Boolean, Optional Negat As Boolean) As Double
'Pulls a number from a cell containing alphanumerics
'e.g. =PullNum(A1,,TRUE) pulls negative number
    Dim cnt As Integer, i As Integer, sLen As Integer
    Dim sTxt As String, sMinus As String, sDP As String, sN As String
    Dim sV As Variant
    sTxt = rng
    If Point = True And Negat = True Then
        sMinus = "-": sDP = "."
    ElseIf Point = True And Negat = False Then
        sMinus = vbNullString: sDP = "."
    ElseIf Point = False And Negat = True Then
        sMinus = "-": sDP = vbNullString
    End If
    sLen = Len(sTxt)
    For cnt = sLen To 1 Step -1
    sV = Mid(sTxt, cnt, 1)
        If IsNumeric(sV) Or sV = sMinus Or sV = sDP Then
            i = i + 1
            sN = Mid(sTxt, cnt, 1) & sN
            If IsNumeric(sN) Then
                If CDbl(sN) < 0 Then Exit For
            Else
                sN = Replace(sN, Left(sN, 1), "", , 1)
            End If
        End If
    If i = 1 And sN <> vbNullString Then sN = CDbl(Mid(sN, 1, 1))
    Next cnt
    PullNum = CDbl(sN)
End Function
```

To use the function, copy its code to any of the Modules in your workbook (add a Module, if not included yet in the workbook). The function can be used in several formats, depending on your optional needs, e.g.:

```
=pullnum(A1)
=pullnum(A1,TRUE)
=pullnum(A1,TRUE,TRUE)
=pullnum(A1,,TRUE)
=pullnum(A1,FALSE,TRUE)
```

Here are some examples of output obtained with the function:

Cell content	Extracted number	Function format
james09 456\&$	9456	=pullnum(M10)
$8977tim7.56	89777.56	=pullnum(M11,TRUE)
arka0.5678902	0.5678902	=pullnum(M12,TRUE)
on-457,230tim	-457230	=pullnum(M13,,TRUE)
f-456om1.48sa05c@	-4561.4805	=pullnum(M14,TRUE,TRUE)
19AA+8888WWd1	1988881	=pullnum(M15)
+/-145.ton00120	145.0012	=pullnum(N16,TRUE,FALSE)

COUNTING Selectively, in a Range

Excel is primarily for counting and calculations, so let's see couple of examples.

Count UNIQUE values only

Use the following **array** formula to get the count of unique values in e.g. *A1:A100* range:

=SUM(1/COUNTIF(A1:A100,A1:A100))

If you don't need the count, but just want to make sure that your list (or range) of values contains unique items only (i.e., none of them is repeated) then you can get the answer with this **array** formula:

=IF(COUNTA(A1:A100)-SUM(1/COUNTIF(A1:A100,A1:A100))>0,"Not unique","Unique")

These are *array* formulas, so to enter them, you need to simultaneously hold down the **Ctrl** and the **Shift** keys as you press **Enter** key.

Count ODD or EVEN values only

The SUMPRODUCT function can be utilized for this counting.

To count **ODD** values only in the A1:A100 range, use this formula:

=SUMPRODUCT(--(MOD(A1:$A$100,2)=1),--(A1:$A$100<>""))

To count **EVEN** values only in the same range, use this formula:

=SUMPRODUCT(--(MOD(A1:$A$100,2)=0),--(A1:$A$100<>""))

The double-negative (--) used in the formulas coerce True and False into 1s and 0s, which are needed (in some cases) to properly interpret them.

SUMPRODUCT is a quite versatile function, working nicely with up to 255(!) array arguments. By default, it multiplies arrays of values, but can be used also for addition, subtraction, and division of arrays; just replace the commas separating arguments with the operators you need (+,-,*). I've provided above just couple of examples with default multiplication of two arrays.

Flipping the Content of a Cell

If you need for some reason to reverse (flip) the content of any cell in your worksheet, either number or text, the following UDF (User Defined Function) would be helpful. Just copy it to any Module (add it if not there yet) in your workbook. The function works fine in *most* cases.

Remember that for cells containing text or numbers ending with zero digit, you need to use it in this format: **=RevOrder(A1,TRUE)**.

```vba
Function RevOrder(rcell As Range, Optional isText As Boolean)
'Reverses the content of any cell, but remember to use it properly
'=RevOrder(A1,TRUE) for text or for numbers ending with 0 digit
'=RevOrder(A1,FALSE) or =RevOrder(A1) for other numbers
    Dim i As Integer
    Dim sNew As String
    Dim sOld As String
    sOld = Trim(rcell)
    For i = 1 To Len(sOld)
        sNew = Mid(sOld, i, 1) & sNew
    Next i
    If isText = False Then
        RevOrder = CLng(sNew)
    Else
        RevOrder = sNew
    End If
End Function
```

Here are some examples of the results obtained with the function:

Cell content	Reversed cell content	Function format
1245678900	0098765421	=revorder(M10,TRUE)
234.567	765.432	=revorder(M11,TRUE)
765432.560	65.234567	=revorder(M12,TRUE)
123456	654321	=revorder(M13,FALSE)
800,056	650008	=revorder(M14,FALSE)
800,056	650008	=revorder(M15)
07ofERta	atREfo70	=revorder(N16,TRUE)
0.56789	98765.0	=revorder(N17,TRUE)
climate	etamilc	=revorder(N18,TRUE)
-0.6708	8076.0-	=revorder(N19,TRUE)

Generate Unique Random Codes

The following macro will create random 5-digits codes. No code will be duplicated.

```vba
Sub GenerateUniqueAccessCodes()
'Creates and records (in selected column) random 5-digit codes (without duplication)
'The codes can be used for any purpose, wherever unique codes must be applied (procedures,
'locations, parts, etc.)
    Dim rng As Range
    Dim code As String
    Dim lastRow As Long
    Dim i As Integer
    Dim n As Integer
    n = 10    'number of codes you want to create; change as needed
    For i = 1 To n
        lastRow = Cells(Rows.Count, "A").End(xlUp).Row    'change "A" to the column letter of the
column you want to use
        Set rng = Range("A" & (lastRow + 1))    'change this to the cell where you want to start
generating the codes
```

```vba
    Do Until WorksheetFunction.CountIf(Range("A1:A" & rng.Row - 1), code) = 0 'change "A" to
another column, if changed above
        code = Format(Application.WorksheetFunction.RandBetween(10000, 99999), "00000")
        'change to a different number of digits, as required
    Loop
    rng.Value = code
  Next i
End Sub
```

Protect All Workbooks in a Folder/Directory

The following macro will protect all your workbooks in the folder you specify in the Input Box ("myPath"). Change the "Password" entry in the macro to your own choice.

```vba
Sub ProtectAllWorkbooks()
'Protects all workbooks in your specific folder
'Change (and remember!) the Password below to your liking
    Dim wbk As Workbook
    Dim myPath As String
    Dim sFile As String
    wFormat = "*.xl*"
    myPath = InputBox("Enter your Directory path", "Directory path",
"C:\Documents\ExcelFiles\")
    sFile = Dir(myPath & wFormat)
    Do While sFile <> ""
        Set wbk = Workbooks.Open(myPath & sFile)
        With wbk
            Application.DisplayAlerts = False
            wbk.SaveAs Filename:=.FullName, _
              Password:="rr" 'Change to your password
            Application.DisplayAlerts = True
        End With
        Set wbk = Nothing
        Workbooks(sFile).Close False
        sFile = Dir
    Loop
End Sub
```

EVENTS / TRACKING

How to Create Activity Tracker / Timer

If you'd like to keep in Excel the record of your common daily tasks, in terms of disciplined use of your valuable time, then the solution I'm presenting here can be helpful. It makes easy recording of duration of any routine daily activities and provides basis for further analysis of any kind.

This is how it looks like in an exemplary edition:

	A	B	C	D	E
1					
2		**Start Time**	**Activity / Event**	**End Time**	**Duration**
3		18:38:52	Activity/Topic 1	18:56:27	**0hrs 17min 35sec**
4		18:39:03	Activity/Topic 2	18:56:30	**0hrs 17min 27sec**
5		18:39:20	Activity/Topic 3	18:56:34	**0hrs 17min 14sec**
6		18:49:19	Activity/Topic 4		
7		18:49:32	Activity/Topic 5	18:56:01	**0hrs 6min 29sec**
8		18:49:41	Activity/Topic 6	18:55:05	**0hrs 5min 24sec**
		18:57:09	Activity/Topic 7		
		18:57:47	Activity/Topic 8	22:08:28	**3hrs 10min 41sec**
			Activity/Topic 9		

It's similar to using a stopwatch or timer, with one big advantage: you enter the times without typing/entering them. It happens automatically when you just click corresponding cells within the table. At the start of your task, you enter the **'Start Time'** by selecting/clicking on a cell in column B. Then, when your task is completed, you just click on a cell in the same row in column D (**'End Time'**). These are the *time stamps*. Depending on your needs, they could be transformed to the *date stamps*. And the 'Duration' of the task is displayed automatically for you in column E.

Follow these steps to create a similar activity monitor in your workbook:

- rename one of the worksheets in your new workbook to e.g., *'Tracker'*
- insert/create Excel table with headers as shown above
- define the Names for the table columns (using **Formulas>Define Names** in the ribbon), like shown here:

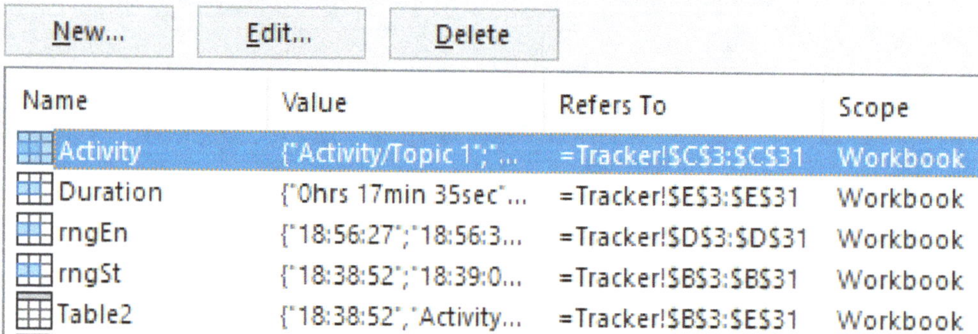

Name Manager

	New...		Edit...		Delete	

Name	Value	Refers To	Scope
Activity	{"Activity/Topic 1";"...	=Tracker!$C$3:$C$31	Workbook
Duration	{"0hrs 17min 35sec"...	=Tracker!$E$3:$E$31	Workbook
rngEn	{"18:56:27";"18:56:3...	=Tracker!$D$3:$D$31	Workbook
rngSt	{"18:38:52";"18:39:0...	=Tracker!$B$3:$B$31	Workbook
Table2	{"18:38:52","Activity...	=Tracker!$B$3:$E$31	Workbook

- enter your list of tasks/actions you want to monitor in column C
- use **ALT+F11** keyboard shortcut to display the VBA editor window, then select **View>Project Explorer**
- select the **'Tracker'** worksheet (*double-click* to display it) listed in your VBA Project
- paste (or enter) the following macro into displayed editor window:

Private Sub Worksheet_SelectionChange(ByVal myCell As Range)

```vba
'Example of activity tracker with time stamps
'It's using worksheet event - SelectionChange
Dim rngSt As Range
Dim startRow As Integer, rngRows As Integer
Dim en As Variant, st As Variant
Static entryTime As Variant
Set Strts = Worksheets("Tracker").Range("rngSt")
startRow = 3      'The first row of the range
rngRows = Strts.Rows.Count
If ActiveCell.Row >= startRow And ActiveCell.Row < (rngRows + startRow) Then
    If ActiveCell.Column = 2 Or ActiveCell.Column = 4 Then
      entryTime = Now()
      ActiveCell.Value = entryTime
      If ActiveCell.Column = 4 Then
        en = ActiveCell.Value
        st = ActiveCell.Offset(0, -2).Value
        ActiveCell.Offset(0, 1).Value = Hour(en - st) & "hrs " & Minute(en - st) & "min " _
        & Second(en - st) & "sec"
      End If
    Else
      If ActiveCell.Column = 1 Then ActiveCell.FormulaR1C1 = "©"
      If ActiveCell.Column > 5 Then
        ActiveSheet.Pictures.Insert( _
        "https://cdn.hubblecontent.osi.office.net/icons/publish/icons_zebra/zebra.svg").Select
        Range("$G$1").Select
      End If
      If ActiveCell.Column = 3 Then ActiveCell.Select
    End If
End If
End Sub
```

Now, close the window and return to the 'Tracker' worksheet. If everything went well with the setup, then you should be able to test the 'Tracker' with your clicks/entries.

When you click a cell in column B of your table, start time should appear. Clicking in column D displays end/stop time and duration of your activity in Column E. If you click in any row above or below the table, nothing happens (the cell is just selected).

If you click a cell to the left of the table (column A), copyright character will appear, and clicking anywhere to the right of the table will display the picture of zebra...☺

	A	Start Time	Activity / Event	End Time	Duration
3	©	18:38:52	Activity/Topic 1	18:56:27	0hrs 17min 35sec
4	©	18:39:03	Activity/Topic 2	18:56:30	0hrs 17min 27sec
5	©	18:39:20	Activity/Topic 3	18:56:34	0hrs 17min 14sec
6		18:49:19	Activity/Topic 4		
7	©	18:49:32	Activity/Topic 5	18:56:01	0hrs 6min 29sec
8	©	18:49:41	Activity/Topic 6	18:55:05	0hrs 5min 24sec
9		18:57:09	Activity/Topic 7		
10	©	18:57:47	Activity/Topic 8	22:08:28	3hrs 10min 41sec
11		22:08:41	Activity/Topic 9		
12			Activity/Topic 10		

Now you can create/modify the table to fit your specific needs. Obviously, the macro and definitions of Names would require some editing as well (including the choice of the picture, in such a case.

Have some fun!

Workbook Events: Printing - Speech - Alerts

When printing in Excel, one quite frequently makes mistakes. Sometimes the printout does not look as expected and we may waste more paper than necessary. To reduce such outcomes to minimum we can utilize Excel **event** feature called **BeforePrint**.

You can use the following **workbook event** procedure (VBA code) that will - just before printing your worksheet/selection - alert you with **speech feature** by asking if you are sure that your workbook and the print settings are OK; if not, printing is cancelled.

```
Private Sub Workbook_BeforePrint(Cancel As Boolean)
For Each wk In Worksheets   'Make sure that worksheets are recalculated before printing
    wk.Calculate
Next
vbOption = MsgBox("Are you sure that all settings are OK and print can be started?", vbYesNo)
If vbOption = 7 Then        '6=Yes, 7=No
    Cancel = True
    Application.Speech.Speak "Printing is cancelled."
'   MsgBox ("Print is cancelled.")   'optional
Else
    Application.Speech.Speak "Recalculation is completed and now printing takes place."
End If
End Sub
```

To implement this procedure, select the **Developer** tab in the ribbon and select **Visual Basic** from the menu, then select the **View tab>Project Explorer**. In **VBAProject** of <u>your</u> workbook click on **ThisWorkbook**, then copy the code provided here and paste it into the space located directly under the **Workbook** field there. Save your workbook as **Excel Macro-Enabled Workbook**.

Try to print something to see if the event procedure works as intended.

DATES / TIME / CALENDAR

WeekDay and BirthDay

You know your birthday date, no problem. Do you know on which day of the week you were born? **If not**, you can find it out quite easily in Excel. There are many ways to do it, but probably the simplest one is to use the **WEEKDAY** function, as shown in this snip:

	A	B	C
1	**Date**	**Day of the week**	**Formula in B2**
2	04/12/2001	TUESDAY	=WEEKDAY(A2)

The syntax for WEEKDAY function in Excel is: WEEKDAY(serial_number,[return_type]),

where **serial_number** practically means a serial number (like e.g., *40232*) or an entry in any acceptable DATE format, e.g., *15 Nov 2021*, and the **return_type** can be omitted (defaults to **1**). This looks OK; you get a correct day of the week in return.

However, when you try to use different *return_types*, things may become a bit confusing. Here is an example:

Return_type	Number returned	Formula used	Result
1 (or omitted)	1 (Sun) to 7 (Sat)	=WEEKDAY(A2)	**Tuesday**
2	1 (Mon) to 7 (Sun)	=WEEKDAY(A2,2)	**Monday**
3	0 (Mon) to 6 (Sun)	=WEEKDAY(A2,3)	**Sunday**
11	1 (Mon) to 7 (Sun)	=WEEKDAY(A2,11)	**Monday**

Custom format used for the **Result**:   dddd

So, to avoid an erroneous result and make sure that the weekday of your birth (or whatever event) is correct, it's safer to use more reliable custom formats, like these ones:

dd/mm/yyyy ddd   *or*   **dd mmmm yyyy, dddd**

If needed, add them to your list of custom formats in **Format Cells... >Number >Custom** category and then select the format for some cell(s). When you enter the date like **04/12/2001** (or simply **=A2**, based on example provided above) into the formatted cells, you'll see the following results displayed for the two formats:

```
04/12/2001 Tue
04 December 2001, Tuesday
```

You can be sure now, without using the WEEKDAY function, that the day of the week the event took place was **Tuesday**.

Date and Time STAMP

There are many ways of creating a date stamp or/and time stamp in Excel. You can check them e.g., in these web pages:

ExcelChamps, TrumpExcel, and **ExtendOffice**

However, in most cases - unless you need a time stamp which displays **seconds** - you can use Excel *shortcuts* for both date and time:

CTRL+SHIFT+: (colon) shortcut for your time stamp,

`14:09`

and

CTRL+; (semicolon) shortcut for the date stamp.

`05/09/2021`

These two shortcuts provide *STATIC* (non-refreshable) stamps; they are not updated whenever anything changes in your worksheet.

The NOW() function is OK, but it inserts DYNAMIC (refreshable) stamp, so it requires conversion from function to a value format to become static.

How to DATE in Excel

This is about dating with the Excel **DATE... function**, and with its versatile formats and forms of uses. It's syntax is simple but the results of its application can be sometimes a bit confusing or unexpected.

Confusing - because the DATE function with its syntax **DATE(year,month,day)** doesn't object some strange parameters and accepts numbers such as:

- negative, 0, and -12 integers for a month,
- higher number of days than the number of days allowable for a given month, as well as 0 days,
- negative numbers for a day,
- number lower than 1900 for a year.

So, e.g., entering accidentally month number **14** would set the date to February of the following year. Entering month number **0** would set the date to December of the previous year. Entering year number **1888** would set the date to the year 3788.

Normally, i.e., in General format, DATE function returns a serial number starting from January 01, 1900, represented by number **1**, which was **Sunday**, and increasing by 1 for every next calendar day. September 05, 2021 is the **44444** special day in this sequence, and it's **Sunday** as well.

If you need to deal with dates before the year 1900 you can access relevant information the web page of **MrExcel**.

When using the DATE function, it's important to remember that whenever you need to use WEEKDAY function in combination with DATE, weekday number depends on the "return-type". If you are used to consider e.g., **Sunday** as the first day of the week, the return-type **1** must be used. If you use **Monday** as the first day of the week then return-type **2** must be used with the WEEKDAY function.

Let's have a look at some examples of using the DATE and related functions/formulas, formats and outcomes shown in this table:

Year	Month	Day	Excel Formula	Cell/Date Format	Result Returned	Comments
2011	2	15	=DATE(B3,C3,D3)	General	40589	Serial number representing the date.
2015	1	-2	=DATE(B3,C3,D3)	14/03/2012	15/02/2011	Standard format
2020	-3	24	=DATE(B3,C3,D3)	2012-03-14	2011-02-15	Standard format
			=DATE(B3,C3,D3)	14 March 2012	15 February 2011	Standard format
			=DATE(B3,C3,D3)	dd-mm-yy	15-Feb-11	Custom format
			=DATE(B3,C3,D3)	dd-mm	15-Feb	Custom format
			=DATE(B3,C3,D3)	mmm-yy	Feb-11	Custom format
			=DATE(B3,C3,D3)	dd/mm/yyy ddd	15/02/2011 Tue	Custom format
			=DATE(B3,C3,D3)	dd	15	Custom format
			=DATE(B3,C3,D3)	ddd	Tue	Custom format
			=DATE(B3,C3,D3)	dddd	Tuesday	Custom format
			=DATE(B4,C4,D4)	14/03/2012	29/12/2014	Negative day in D4 moved date back 2 days.
			=DATE(B3,C3,D3)-16	Standard format	30/01/2011	Subtracted number (16) moved date back 16 days.
			=DATE(YEAR(TODAY()),MONTH(TODAY()),1)	Standard format	01/09/2021	Returned the 1st day of the current month and year.
			=NOW()	dd/mm/yyy hh:mm	04/09/2021 16:42	Custom format
			=TEXT(DATE(B3,C3,D3),"dddd")	General, or Text	Tuesday	Day of the Date converted to Text format.
			=TEXT(F4,"ddd, mmmm yyyy")	General, or Text	Wed, March 2012	Date converted to custom date format.
			=TEXT(F4,"d-mmm-yyyy")	General, or Text	14-Mar-2012	Date converted to custom date format.
			=TEXT(F4,"dddd, mmmm d, yyy")	General, or Text	Wednesday, March 14, 2012	Date converted to custom date format.
			=WEEKDAY(DATE(B3,1,3),2)	General, or Text	1	Returned "1", Monday as the 1st day of the week.
			=DATEVALUE("14-03-2021")	General, or Text	44269	Returned serial number representing the date.
			=DAY(G3) or =DAY(G4)	General, or Text	15	Returned day of the month from the date.
			=MONTH(G3) or =MONTH(G4)	General, or Text	2	Returned month number from the date
			=MONTH(DATE(B4,C4,D4))	General, or Text	12	Negative day in D4 moved date back 2 days, from Jan to Dec.
			=YEAR(G3) or =YEAR(G4)	General, or Text	2011	Returned year number from the date
			=DATE(B5,C5,D5)	General, or Text	24/09/2019	Negative month in C5 moved date back 3 months, from end of the year to Sep.
			=DATE(B5,0,D5)	General, or Text	24/12/2019	Month "0" in the formula set date to the last month of previous year.

The yellow-coloured column shows the results of formulas entered and how they depend on formats selected for display in a worksheet.

It doesn't matter in what format a given full date is displayed (used), you can get (extract) from that date a day, month or year by using DAY, MONTH and YEAR functions.

Date to Date

Date functions in Excel can answer a whole plethora of questions we are dealing with in everyday life. Some of them are quite straightforward, and some not quite, but all have practical applications.

Couple of notes, before you try to use any of the formulas:

- **MONDAY** is designated here as the first day of the week

- Cells with the formulas shown here must be in **General** format, not Date format.
- Cells A2:C2 are presented in Custom format: **"dddd dd/mm/yyyy"**

<u>Useful tip</u>: you can enter **Current date** using this shortcut: **CTRL+;** (semicolon)

With a setup in your worksheet like this one:

	A	B	C
1	**Current date**	**Future or Past date**	**Date of Birth**
2	Tuesday 27/04/2021	Friday 01/04/2022	Thursday 15/09/1983
3		248 *Number of days left in current year.*	

examples of formulas presented below can help you to find many of your questions answered.

➤ **How many days** left in this calendar year: **=DATE(YEAR(A2),12,31)-A2**

➤ **Number of specific week days** between two dates, the second date inclusive. Use the following formulas for the number of:

Mondays: **=SUMPRODUCT((WEEKDAY(ROW(INDIRECT(A2&":"&B2)),2)=1)*1)**

Tuesdays: **=SUMPRODUCT((WEEKDAY(ROW(INDIRECT(A2&":"&B2)),2)=2)*1)**

Wednesdays:
=SUMPRODUCT((WEEKDAY(ROW(INDIRECT(A2&":"&B2)),2)=3)*1)

Thursdays: **=SUMPRODUCT((WEEKDAY(ROW(INDIRECT(A2&":"&B2)),2)=4)*1)**

Fridays: **=SUMPRODUCT((WEEKDAY(ROW(INDIRECT(A2&":"&B2)),2)=5)*1)**

Saturdays: **=SUMPRODUCT((WEEKDAY(ROW(INDIRECT(A2&":"&B2)),2)=6)*1)**

Sundays: **=SUMPRODUCT((WEEKDAY(ROW(INDIRECT(A2&":"&B2)),2)=7)*1)**

➤ **Number of weekdays** (Monday-Friday) between two dates, the second date inclusive:

=SUMPRODUCT((WEEKDAY(ROW(INDIRECT(A2&":"&B2)),2)={1,2,3,4,5})*1)

➤ **Number of weekend days** (Saturday-Sunday) between two dates, the second date inclusive:

=SUMPRODUCT((WEEKDAY(ROW(INDIRECT(A2&":"&B2)),2)={6,7})*1)

➤ **Number of business days**, with holidays excluded:

=NETWORKDAYS.INTL(A2,B2,1,Freedays), where 'Freedays' represents a **range** of holiday dates set up and named so in your worksheet (if needed).

➤ **Number of days survived** since somebody's birthday (entered in cell C2):

=SUMPRODUCT((WEEKDAY(ROW(INDIRECT(C2&":"&A2)),2)={1,2,3,4,5,6,7})*1)-1

➤ **Number of days left** till the end of this century (including 31 Dec, 2100):

=SUMPRODUCT((WEEKDAY(ROW(INDIRECT(TODAY()&":"&DATE(2100,12,31))),2)={1,2,3,4,5,6,7})*1)

Conditional Formatting, About Time

Let's assume, we have in a worksheet a range of Start and Stop times formatted as "hh:mm:ss", and we want to format somehow the cells, so that the *times falling outside some time frame,* e.g., outside 6:00 AM and 3:00 PM, are clearly highlighted.

To do that we need to get Values of that two Times, using formulas like these:
=VALUE("06:00:00") resulting in 0.25, and =VALUE("15:00:00") resulting in 0.625 .
Knowing these values, you now use Conditional Formatting feature of Excel to format the outlying Times:

- First, select your range of cells with times entered.
- In the ribbon, select **Conditional Formatting>Highlight Cells Rules. More Rules...**
- In displayed window select options and enter limiting numbers as shown in the figure below:

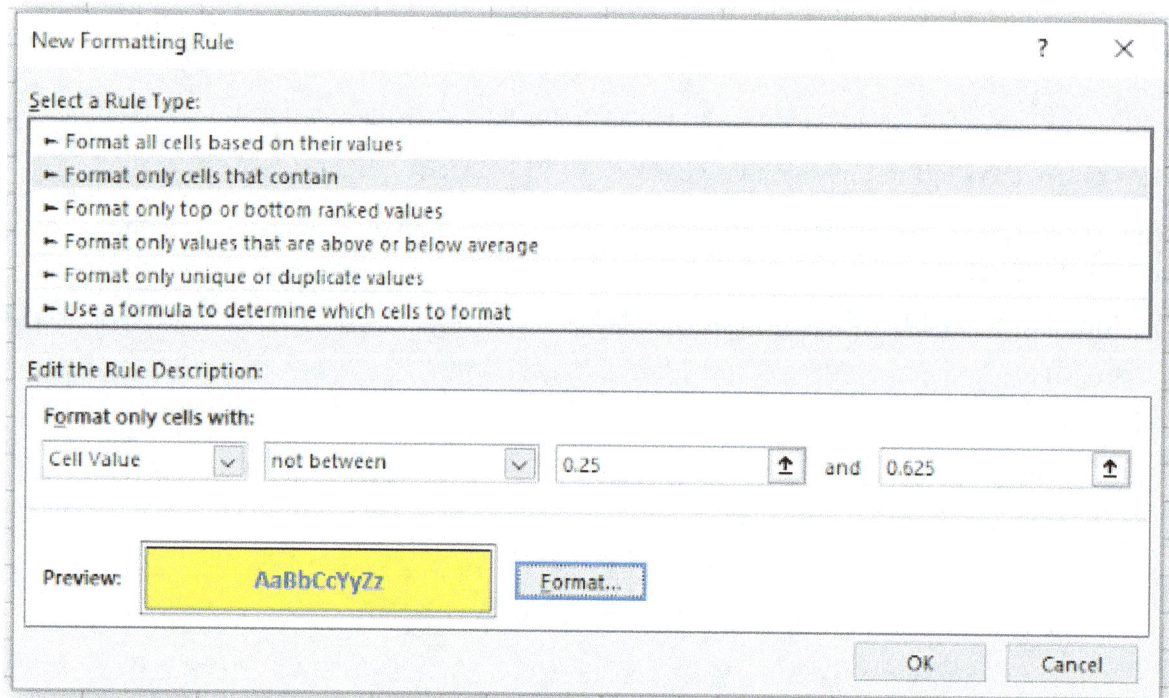

- Then select formatting options you want to, e.g., Bold font or/and Blue colour, outline border, cell background colour.

Example of formatting result is shown here (*just random times entered*):

Start time	Stop time
07:17:34	11:47:05
21:38:20	05:06:37
23:40:13	15:34:16
05:34:49	14:56:26
16:45:08	00:00:35
12:42:07	12:01:08
15:58:53	11:45:33
04:39:25	22:01:05
06:56:02	13:08:02
07:41:34	15:07:19
02:07:45	11:00:12
16:00:45	05:54:51
02:42:44	08:30:55
11:50:23	17:21:47
22:49:33	04:51:40

Happy conditioning!

Record Specific Time of Events or Steps of Some Process

Time, and time again…

When you organize your work, in Excel or elsewhere, at some point you may want to keep track of your activities/processes/events in your workbook. Here you'll find two helpful ways of recording time spent on whatever you do. The first one allows you to record just a point in time, like a stamp of current time. The second one shows you elapsed time, difference between starting of some activity and then stopping it.

Time stamp

To create a Time stamp like this one:

- Insert any shape or **Command Button** in your worksheet, by clicking **Developer - Insert - Command Button (ActiveX Control)**.
- Right-click the button and select **Properties** to change its Caption to "Time Stamp"; change any other properties as needed.
- Right click the Command Button again, then click **View Code** from the context menu. When VBA window pops up, enter the following VBA script:

```
Sub TimeStamp()
    ActiveCell.Value = Time
    ActiveCell.NumberFormat = "hh:mm:ss AM/PM"
End Sub
```

- Now press the **Alt + Q** keys simultaneously to close the VBA window.

Select a cell where you want to place the current time stamp, then click the Command Button. You've got your stamp placed in the selected cell. Subsequently, you can select consecutive cells to record time of events as they follow, one after another.

Time watcher

To create a timer (to get elapsed time), kind of time watcher, like this one:

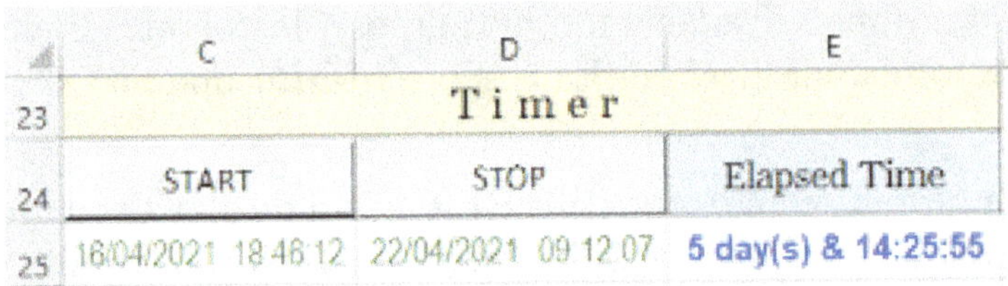

- Select some range of cells for your timer (3 rows by 3 columns).
- Insert two Command Buttons (side by side), by clicking **Developer > Insert > Command Button (ActiveX Control)**. Format them to your liking.
- Right-click one of them and select **Properties** to change its caption to "Start"; change any other properties, as needed. Repeat that for the second button and change its caption to "Stop".
- Right click any of the Command Buttons and click **View Code** from the context menu. When VBA window pops up, enter the following VBA scripts:

```
Private Sub StartNow()
    Dim Rcell As Range 'Replace "C25" below with your selected range
    Range("C25").NumberFormat = "dd/mm/yyyy  hh:mm:ss"
```

```vba
    Set Rcell = Range("C25")
    Rcell.Value = Now()
End Sub


Private Sub StopNow()
    Dim Rcell As Range 'Replace "C25","D25","E25" below with your selected ranges
    Range("D25").NumberFormat = "dd/mm/yyyy  hh:mm:ss"
    Set Rcell = Range("D25")
    Rcell.Value = Now()
    Range("E25").Select
    Selection.NumberFormat = "d"" day(s) &"" hh:mm:ss"
    Selection.Value = Range("D25").Value - Range("C25").Value
End Sub


Private Sub CommandButton1_Click()    'Replace "1" with actual number, if necessary
    StartNow
End Sub


Private Sub CommandButton2_Click()    'Replace "2" with actual number, if necessary
    StopNow
End Sub
```

- Now press the **Alt + Q** keys simultaneously to close the VBA window.
- In your worksheet, format (*optional*) the cells with "Timer" and "Elapsed Time" text.

Now you can use your time watcher as needed. Click on "Start" button to start timing. Click on "Stop" button to end timing, whenever needed (even after days, weeks, months). Elapsed time will be displayed in cell E25 (in this example), including the number of days passed.

You can also **show elapsed time** without any VBA coding, by using a simple formula. However, prior to that you need to format cells A1:C1 according to your needs (any custom format) and enter Start and Stop times in required format. Assuming that you store **Start** time in A1, and **Stop** time in B1 (which can be entered with help of formula =**NOW()**), enter in C1 the formula: =**B1-A1**. This will show the elapsed time.

Determine Zodiac Sign on Demand for Any Birth Date

If you need frequently and quickly find out which Zodiac sign people were born under, built a table as shown below within A2:D14 range. In column A you can enter either emoji symbols for the Zodiac signs or any other symbols available for this purpose. In columns B and C add Start and End dates for the signs. Date format for these entries is set to **14-Mar** option. Date entry is set to **dd-mmm** format.

Cell A1 will be used for birth date entry and cells B1, C1 will display the corresponding Zodiac symbol and its name. To get the correct result you need to enter two formulas:

First one in cell B1:

```
=IFS(A1-DATE(YEAR(A1),1,0)<=C14-DATE(YEAR(C14),1,0),A14,AND(A1-
DATE(YEAR(A1),1,0)-=B3-DATE(YEAR(B3),1,0),A1-DATE(YEAR(A1),1,0)<=C3-
DATE(YEAR(C3),1,0)),A3,A1-DATE(YEAR(A1),1,0)<=C4-DATE(YEAR(C4),1,0),A4,A1-
DATE(YEAR(A1),1,0)<=C5-DATE(YEAR(C5),1,0),A5,A1-DATE(YEAR(A1),1,0)<=C6-
DATE(YEAR(C6),1,0),A6,A1-DATE(YEAR(A1),1,0)<=C7-DATE(YEAR(C7),1,0),A7,A1-
DATE(YEAR(A1),1,0)<=C8-DATE(YEAR(C8),1,0),A8,A1-DATE(YEAR(A1),1,0)<=C9-
DATE(YEAR(C9),1,0),A9,A1-DATE(YEAR(A1),1,0)<=C10-DATE(YEAR(C10),1,0),A10,A1-
DATE(YEAR(A1),1,0)<=C11-DATE(YEAR(C11),1,0),A11,A1-DATE(YEAR(A1),1,0)<=C12-
DATE(YEAR(C12),1,0),A12,A1-DATE(YEAR(A1),1,0)<=C13-
DATE(YEAR(C13),1,0),A13,A1-DATE(YEAR(A1),1,0)-=B14-DATE(YEAR(B14),1,0),A14)
```

Second one in cell C1:

=OFFSET(IFS(A1-DATE(YEAR(A1),1,0)<=C14-DATE(YEAR(C14),1,0),A14,AND(A1-
DATE(YEAR(A1),1,0)-=B3-DATE(YEAR(B3),1,0),A1-DATE(YEAR(A1),1,0)<=C3-
DATE(YEAR(C3),1,0)),A3,A1-DATE(YEAR(A1),1,0)<=C4-DATE(YEAR(C4),1,0),A4,A1-
DATE(YEAR(A1),1,0)<=C5-DATE(YEAR(C5),1,0),A5,A1-DATE(YEAR(A1),1,0)<=C6-
DATE(YEAR(C6),1,0),A6,A1-DATE(YEAR(A1),1,0)<=C7-DATE(YEAR(C7),1,0),A7,A1-
DATE(YEAR(A1),1,0)<=C8-DATE(YEAR(C8),1,0),A8,A1-DATE(YEAR(A1),1,0)<=C9-
DATE(YEAR(C9),1,0),A9,A1-DATE(YEAR(A1),1,0)<=C10-DATE(YEAR(C10),1,0),A10,A1-
DATE(YEAR(A1),1,0)<=C11-DATE(YEAR(C11),1,0),A11,A1-DATE(YEAR(A1),1,0)<=C12-
DATE(YEAR(C12),1,0),A12,A1-DATE(YEAR(A1),1,0)<=C13-
DATE(YEAR(C13),1,0),A13,A1-DATE(YEAR(A1),1,0)-=B14-
DATE(YEAR(B14),1,0),A14),0,3)

	A	B	C	D
1	**28-Nov**	↗	**Sagittarius: Archer**	
2	**Zodiac sign (emoji)**	**Start date**	**End date**	**Zodiac sign name**
3	♒	20-Jan	17-Feb	Aquarius: Water-Bearer
4	♓	18-Feb	19-Mar	Pisces: Fish
5	♈	20-Mar	19-Apr	Aries: Ram
6	♉	20-Apr	20-May	Taurus: Bull
7	♊	21-May	20-Jun	Gemini: Twins
8	♋	21-Jun	22-Jul	Cancer: Crab
9	♌	23-Jul	22-Aug	Leo: Lion
10	♍	23-Aug	22-Sep	Virgo: Maiden (or Virgin)
11	♎	23-Sep	22-Oct	Libra: Scales
12	♏	23-Oct	21-Nov	Scorpio: Scorpion
13	♐	22-Nov	21-Dec	Sagittarius: Archer
14	♑	22-Dec	19-Jan	Capricorn: Goat

Enter couple of dates in cell A1 to make sure that you get expected results. Then, you can hide rows 2 to 14, if you wish, to make your solution look more mysterious.

Calculate person's age

Use this formula to determine somebody's age accurately:

=(NOW()-DATE(yyyy,mm,dd))/365.25

E.g., person born on April 14, 1973 was 49.97 years old on April 01, 2023.

PERSONAL FINANCES

Stock Portfolios Tracking with Yahoo Finance in Excel – Part 1

Do you want to manage your stock portfolio in *Yahoo Finance* and follow its performance in your private Excel workbook rather than somewhere in a cloud? If so, here it is, step by step procedure, how to do it.

If you are actually not the user of the Yahoo Finance site, then you need to sign up there with user Id. and password.

Create your own portfolio, if you don't have any yet, by clicking on **Create Portfolio** in the menu, entering portfolio name (e.g., "*BestView*") and selecting the currency. Click on **Submit** button.

At this stage you can select either one of the available **Views**, e.g., *"DayWatch"*, or use **Create New View** option to make your own selection of portfolio columns you want to include in your View. Having done the selections, now enter your stock symbols you need to follow.

When you finish, your portfolio could look like this in the "*BestView*" (View using your own selections of columns):

Symbol	Last Price	Price/Book	Forward Annual Div Rate	Change	Open	Low	High	Chg %	Volume	Earnings Date	Trailing P/E	1yr Target Est	Currency
ACBI	24.54	1.41	-	-0.10	24.89	24.54	24.78	-0.41%	123,445	Oct 20, 2021 - Oct 25, 2021	11.67	28.50	USD
TSLA	711.20	28.21	-	+2.71	707.03	704.07	716.97	+0.38%	12.646M	Oct 19, 2021 - Oct 25, 2021	374.91	713.15	USD
CNQ.TO	40.90	1.42	1.88	-0.04	40.94	40.70	41.23	-0.10%	7.251M	Nov 04, 2021 - Nov 04, 2021	11.87	55.00	CAD
MRD.TO	12.62	0.39	0.48	+0.08	12.60	12.56	12.67	+0.64%	9,353	Nov 09, 2021 - Nov 09, 2021	185.59	10.75	CAD
GSK.L	1,481.12	482.13	0.80	-1.68	1,475.00	1,474.80	1,484.80	-0.11%	752,206	Oct 27, 2021 - Oct 27, 2021	17.06	-	GBp
VOD.L	122.85	62.14	0.08	-0.13	122.56	122.00	123.06	-0.11%	7.731M	Nov 16, 2021 - Nov 16, 2021	409.50	-	GBp

If you change your mind, you can still edit the table after clicking on **Edit View**).

When finished with editing, *right-click* within the table and click on **Table to Excel > Display inline** item in the displayed menu. Next click on **To Excel** in the new open box. When another small window appears, select **Excel** (default) in the box beside *Open with* text. Click **OK**.

Now Excel file opens and, after a second or so, a warning message will be displayed. Ignore it and click on **Yes** button. Excel opens a new worksheet page (with [**Protected View**] in its name). Click on Enable Editing (if displayed) at the top bar.

With cell selection within the table press **CTRL+T** to create *Excel Table*. Format it to your liking using **Table Tools > Design** in the menu, so it looks e.g., like this one:

	A	B	C	D	E	F	G	H	I	J	K	L	M	N
1	Symbol	Last Price	Price /Book	Forward Annual Div Rate	Change	Open	Low	High	Chg %	Volume	Earnings Date	Trailing P/E	1yr Target Est	Currency
2	ACBI	24.65	1.42	-	0.01	24.89	24.54	24.78	0.0004	94.381k	Oct 20, 2021 - Oct 25, 2021	11.7	28.5	USD
3	TSLA	711.47	28.37	-	2.98	707.03	704.07	716.97	0.0042	11.056M	Oct 19, 2021 - Oct 25, 2021	377.02	713.15	USD
4	CNQ.TO	40.99	1.42	1.88	0.05	40.94	40.7	41.23	0.0012	1.419M	Nov 04, 2021 - Nov 04, 2021	11.91	55	CAD
5	MRD.TO	12.62	0.39	0.48	0.08	12.6	12.56	12.67	0.0064	9.353k	Nov 09, 2021 - Nov 09, 2021	185.29	10.75	CAD
6	GSK.L	1482.8	482.68	0.8	-1	1478	1476.8	1485.67	-0.0007	3.901M	Oct 27, 2021 - Oct 27, 2021	17.08	-	GBp
7	VOD.L	122.98	62.21	0.08	0.58	122.54	121.84	123.53	0.0047	32.962M	Nov 16, 2021 - Nov 16, 2021	409.93	-	GBp
8														
9	Link to my YahooFinance Portfolio													

Below the table (or at its side) enter <u>link</u> to the Yahoo Finance web site by copying the web page address, which may look similar to this one:

https://finance.yahoo.com/portfolio/p_2/view/view_5

and pasting it into the worksheet cell. You'll use this link later to update your portfolio table as your portfolio growth (you add new stocks or remove some of them in your Yahoo Portfolio) and as its value fluctuates in time.

Now it's time to save your work.

To **update the table** at any time, you need to follow these steps:

- Click on the link created already for the table and find/view your portfolio in the Yahoo Finance site.
- Right-click within the portfolio table and select **Table to Excel...**, next click on **To Excel**.
- New small window appears. Select **Excel**(default) in the box beside *Open with* text. Click **OK**.
- Wait a second and click on **Yes** button within the displayed warning message band. Excel opens a new worksheet page (with [**Protected View**] in its name).
- Select the table **data** only - without the headers row - and copy the selection.
- Go back to your worksheet containing the original formatted table, select cell A2 (in this example) and paste the data with *Matching destination formatting* option selected.

Your portfolio table has been updated with fresh data. Now delete the page with *[Protected View]* in its name. Save your workbook.

In **Part 2** of the Stock Portfolios Tracking... I'm demonstrating how to make use of the imported raw data for recording and tracking your trades (buys and sales), and evaluating performance of your individual positions.

Stock Portfolios Tracking with Yahoo Finance in Excel – Part 2

In Part 1 we've created exemplary Excel Table for your Portfolio of stocks and provided steps you need to follow in order to update the table, as you'll need from time to time.

Now add a new worksheet in your workbook. Let's call it "**Trades**".

In this worksheet, based on the raw data in your created **Portfolio** table you can create Excel Tables for keeping track of your stock trading, buying, and selling.

Let's say, you just started with couple of records in your Yahoo Finance portfolio and created this Excel Table:

	A	B	C	D	E	F	G	H	I	J	K	L	M
1	Symbol	Last Price	Price /Book	Forward Annual Div Rat	Change	Open	Low	High	Chg %	Volume	Earnings Date	Trailing P/E	1yr Target Est
2	ACBI	24.65	1.42	-	0.01	24.89	24.54	24.78	0.0004	94.381k	Oct 20, 2021 - Oct 25, 2021	11.7	28.5
3	TSLA	711.47	28.37	-	2.58	707.03	704.07	716.97	0.0042	11.056M	Oct 19, 2021 - Oct 25, 2021	377.02	713.15
8													
9	Link to my YahooFinance Portfolio												

Now you'll reference this table and create two tables for keeping track of your trades. Here is an example of such tables:

Tracking the Portfolio Value and Gain/Loss, US$ Today: 27-Aug-21

Bought

Stock Symbol	# of Shares Owned	Avg Unit Cost	Commission	Purchase Date	Original Expense	Current Value	Gain/Loss	Gain/Loss %	Day Avg Price	Day Close Price	Hold (days)
ACBI	1500	$24.65	$29.95	08-May-19	$37,004.95	$37,042.55	$37.60	0.1	$24.72	$24.65	842
TSLA	50	$711.47	$29.95	05-Mar-20	$35,603.45	$35,464.30	-$139.15	-0.4	$709.89	$711.47	540
...					$0.00	$0.00	$0.00	#DIV/0!	$0.00	$0.00	
...					$0.00	$0.00	$0.00	#DIV/0!	$0.00	$0.00	
...					$0.00	$0.00	$0.00	#DIV/0!	$0.00	$0.00	
...					$0.00	$0.00	$0.00	#DIV/0!	$0.00	$0.00	
				Sum	$72,608	$72,507	-$102				

Sold

Stock Symbol	# Shares	Avg Unit Cost	Purchase Commission	Purchase Date	Original Expense	SalePrice	Sale Commission	Sale Date	Net Gain/Loss	True Weekly Gain/Loss (%)	Hold (days)
TSLA	30	$452.82	$29.95	15-Jun-18	$13,614.55	$481.25	$29.95	04-May-20	$793.00	0.06%	689
...					$0.00				$0.00		0
							Net Gain/Loss, US$	$793			

As you can see, I've used cell formatting to differentiate between data entry cells and cells containing formulas. Green cells are for your data entry, all other cells contain formulas. The **Gain/Loss %** column is conditionally formatted for visual comparison of relative performance of stock positions. I've selected for that purpose Green-Yellow-Red option from **Color Scales** of Conditional Formatting menu in the ribbon.

To clarify functioning of the "Trades" tables I'm providing their view with all the **Formulas** shown, so you can see their structure for your specific use:

Tracking the Portfolio Value and Gain/Loss, $US Today =TODAY()

Bought

Stock Symbol	# of Shares Owned	Avg Unit Cost	Commission	Purchase Date	Original Expense	Current Value	Gain/Loss	Gain/Loss %	Day Avg Price	Day Close Price	Hold (days)
ACBI	1500	24.65	29.95	43593	=B4*C4+D4	=B4*J4-D4	=G4-F4	=100*(G4-F4)/F4	=(Data!B2+Data!F2+Data!G2+Data!H2)/4	=Data!B2	=IF(E4>0,$K$1-E4,"…..")
TSLA	50	711.47	29.95	43895	=B5*C5+D5	=B5*J5-D5	=G5-F5	=100*(G5-F5)/F5	=(Data!B3+Data!F3+Data!G3+Data!H3)/4	=Data!B3	=IF(E5>0,$K$1-E5,"…..")
...					=B6*C6+D6	=B6*J6-D6	=G6-F6	=100*(G6-F6)/F6	=(Data!B4+Data!F4+Data!G4+Data!H4)/4	=Data!B4	=IF(E6>0,$K$1-E6,"…..")
...					=B7*C7+D7	=B7*J7-D7	=G7-F7	=100*(G7-F7)/F7	=(Data!B5+Data!F5+Data!G5+Data!H5)/4	=Data!B5	=IF(E7>0,$K$1-E7,"…..")
...					=B8*C8+D8	=B8*J8-D8	=G8-F8	=100*(G8-F8)/F8	=(Data!B6+Data!F6+Data!G6+Data!H6)/4	=Data!B6	=IF(E8>0,$K$1-E8,"…..")
...					=B9*C9+D9	=B9*J9-D9	=G9-F9	=100*(G9-F9)/F9	=(Data!B7+Data!F7+Data!G7+Data!H7)/4	=Data!B7	=IF(E9>0,$K$1-E9,"…..")
				Sum	=SUM(F4:F9)	=SUM(G4:G9)	=SUM(H4:H9)				

Sold

Stock Symbol	# Shares	Avg Unit Cost	Purchase Commission	Purchase Date	Original Expense	SalePrice	Sale Commission	Sale Date	Net Gain/Loss	True Weekly Gain/Loss (%)	Hold (days)
TSLA	30	452.82	29.95	43266	=B16*C16+D16	481.25	29.95	43955	=IF(G16>0,G16*B16-F16-H16, D16)	=IF(G16>0,((G16*B16-H16)/(B16*C16+D16))/(Y(7/)/16-E15+1)) 1,"…")	=I16-E16
...					=B17*C17+D17				=IF(G17>0,G17*B17-F17-H17, D17)	=IF(G17>0,((G17*B17-H17)/(B17*C17+D17))/(Y(7/)/17-E17+1)) 1,"…")	=I17-E17
								Net Gain/Loss, $US	=SUM(J16:J17)		

Obviously, this is just an example. You can edit and modify the tables to your specific needs and liking.

In Part 3 of the "**Stock Portfolios Tracking...**" I'm presenting a simple approach for summarising the performance of the Yahoo Finance portfolio in Excel, also graphically.

Stock Portfolios Tracking with Yahoo Finance in Excel - Part 3

After completing Excel tables (in Part 2) for tracking trades in your account, it's time for creating some summary of your Portfolio performance. For this purpose, you can create another Excel Table (e.g., called "Portfolio Status") and a chart based on the table content. This will allow you to conduct a quick and easy visual evaluation of your investment positions.

Start with adding a new worksheet named e.g., "Performance". First, create the table. Here is an exemplary format and content:

	A	B	C	D	E	F	G	H	I
1	**Portfolio Status**					Date of Record:	27-Aug-21		
2						Projected Dividends per Year:	$103		
4	Stock Symbol	# of Shares Owned	Share Price Paid	Share Price Now	Gain/Loss $	Share Price Target	% Yield	Original Cost of Shares	Gain/Loss %
6	ACBI	1500	$24.65	$24.72	$37.60	$28.50	0.20	$36,975.00	0.1
7	TSLA	50	$711.47	$709.89	-$139.15	$737.31	0.08	$35,573.50	-0.4
8	...	0	...	$0.00	$0.00	$0.00	0.00	#VALUE!	#VALUE!
9	...	0	...	$0.00	$0.00	$0.00	0.00	#VALUE!	#VALUE!
10									

As in previous tables the cells filled with green colour indicate *data entry* cells. The remaining cells contain formulas filled automatically after entering all necessary data. Cells in column E are conditionally formatted, so that cells showing *gains* are filled with yellow background.

The stock symbols are *linked* with corresponding Yahoo quote pages, e.g., ACBI symbol is linked to "**https://finance.yahoo.com/quote/ACBI/?p=ACBI**" page. This way you get direct and easy access to a valuable information on your investments.

The formulas used in the table are shown in the following table, so you can follow the format illustrated above or create your own, depending on your needs:

	A	B	C	D	E	F	G	H	I
1	**Portfolio Status**					Date of Record:	=TODAY()		
2						Projected Dividends per Year, $:	=0.01*(G7*D7*B7+ G8*D8*B8+G9*D9*B9)		
4	Stock Symbol	# of Shares Owned	Share Price Paid	Share Price Now	Gain/Loss $	Share Price Target	% Yield	Original Cost of Shares	Gain/Loss %
6	ACBI	1500	24.65	=IF(Trades!J4="",0,Trades!J4)	=Trades!H4	431.33	0.2	=B6*C6	=100*E6/H6
7	TSLA	50	711.47	=IF(Trades!J5="",0,Trades!J5)	=Trades!H5	737.31	0.08	=B7*C7	=100*E7/H7
8	...	0		=IF(Trades!J6="",0,Trades!J6)	=Trades!H6	0	0	=B8*C8	=100*E8/H8
9	...	0		=IF(Trades!J7="",0,Trades!J7)	=Trades!H7	0	0	=B9*C9	=100*E9/H9

Having the table ready you can now create your chart reflecting the status of your positions, gains or losses on individual positions. Here is an example of such chart built on just two stocks used in the exemplary portfolio:

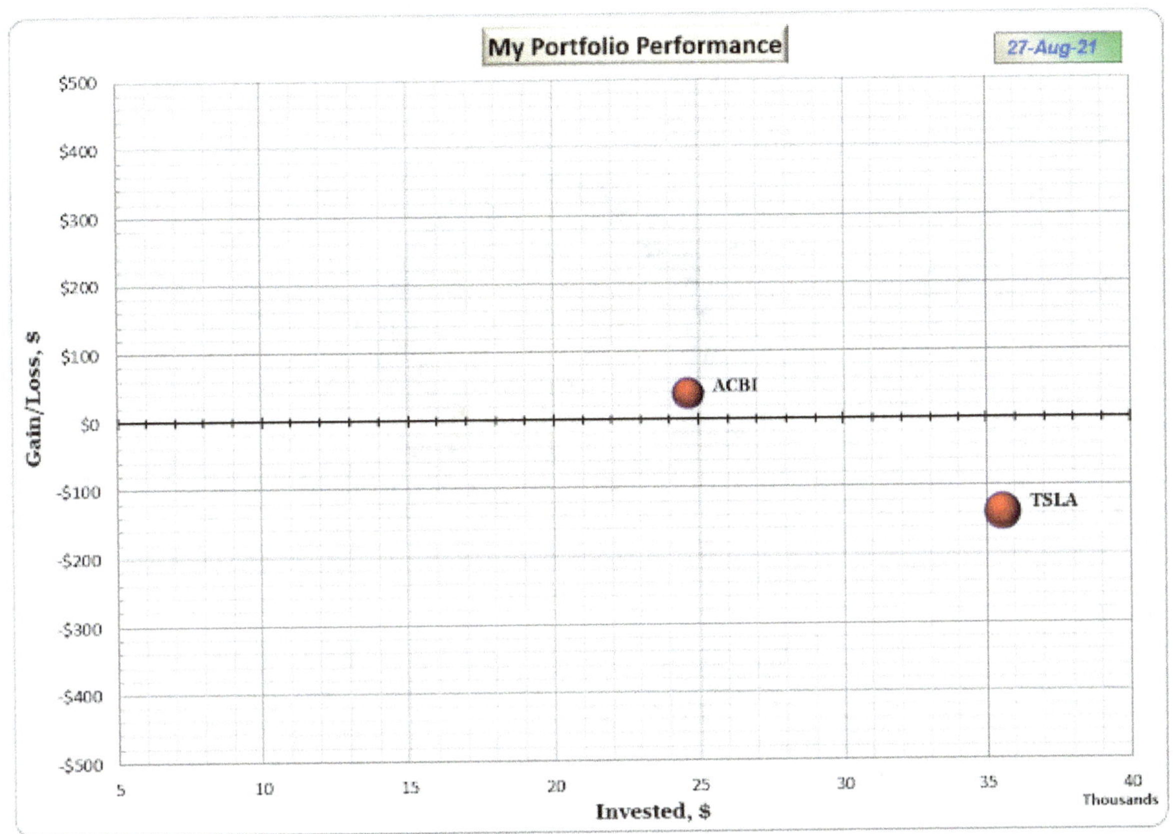

Hope this will help you in managing your personal portfolio.

GRAPHICS / ARTS / GAMES

Picture in Picture in Excel Worksheet

What if you need to highlight/call attention to any fragment of your worksheet, be it a piece of data table or a picture/chart, for a presentation or just for printing a report?

You can do it quite easily in Excel. Let's consider a picture. You may need to overlay an enlarged small fragment of your picture onto the original whole picture. To do that you can use the Windows **"Snip & Sketch"** utility (the shortcut to invoke it, is: **Windows Logo key + SHIFT + S**). You can select either *rectangular* or *free-form* snip. After getting the snip, format/enlarge it as needed, in a way attracting attention to it, and move it to a desired position. This is an example of the 'picture in picture':

The same can be done also with any chart/graphics.

If you want e.g., to cut out a small fragment of a table and format/enlarge it, then the simple way to do it is by copying the fragment and paste it over the table (or anywhere else) **as a picture** (use this shortcut: **ALT+H+V+U** for pasting). It is a *FLOATING* picture, so it can be moved around and formatted at your will. Here's an example:

Jan	Feb	Mar	Apr	May	Jun	Jul	Aug
87.00	77.00	17.00	80.00	72.00	82.00	18.00	81.00
50.00	13.00	94.00	75.00	49.00	31.00	64.00	30.00
93.00	60.00	90.00	92.00	79.00	40.00	81.00	38.00
44.00	15.00	56.00	72.00	71.00	11.00	68.00	76.00
11.00	14.00	13.00	15.00				
66.00	30.00	28.00	37.00				
99.00	55.00	32.00	41.00				
83.00	84.00	100.00	4.00				
50.00	81.00	99.00	82.00				
86.00	74.00	63.00	73.00				
24.00	76.00	73.00	61.00				
91.00	98.00	67.00	96.00				
13.00	72.00	59.00	55.00	22.00	99.00	32.00	77.00
66.00	95.00	100.00	95.00	45.00	72.00	51.00	96.00

The floating (enlarged) fragment overlaid on the table above:

93.00	60.00	90.00
44.00	15.00	56.00
11.00	14.00	13.00
66.00	30.00	28.00
99.00	55.00	32.00

Colourful Randomized Worksheet Creations

Using some Excel functions and conditional formatting you can create unusual graphics, backgrounds, images etc. Here are some of my creations.

Labyrinth

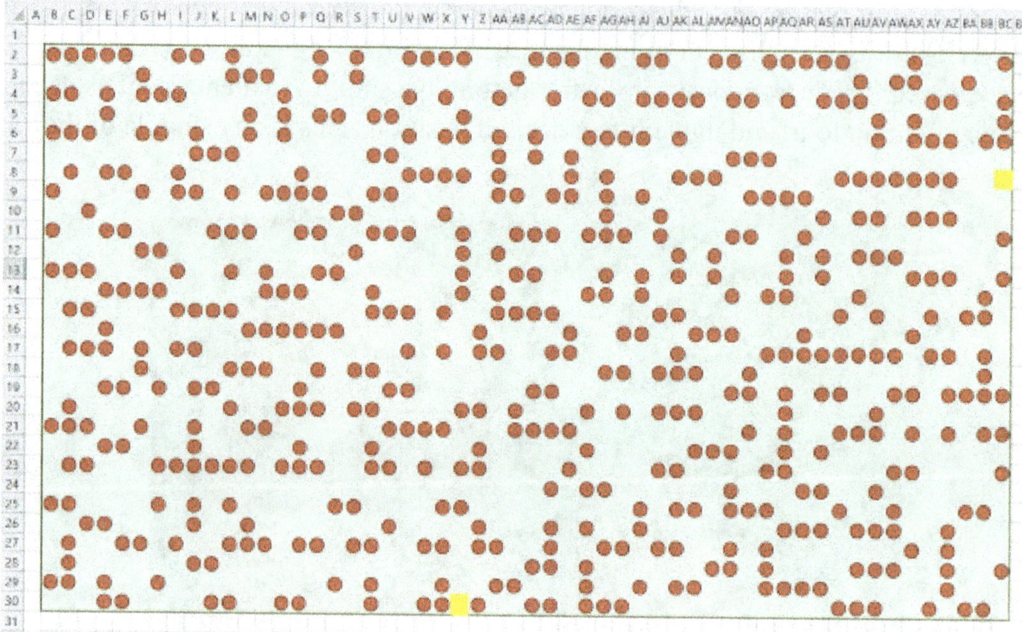

I followed these steps to create that example:

- selected the sheet and set column width to 2
- entered in cell B2 this formula: **=IF(SUM(A1:C1)=INT(RAND()+0.5),1,"")**
- copied the formula to B2:BC30 range
- used Conditional Formatting to display the icons, namely: selected the range and set formatting rule to show icon when cell value is -=1, and no icon when cell value is <1 and -=0
- filled the range with green background colour

Sierpiński Triangle

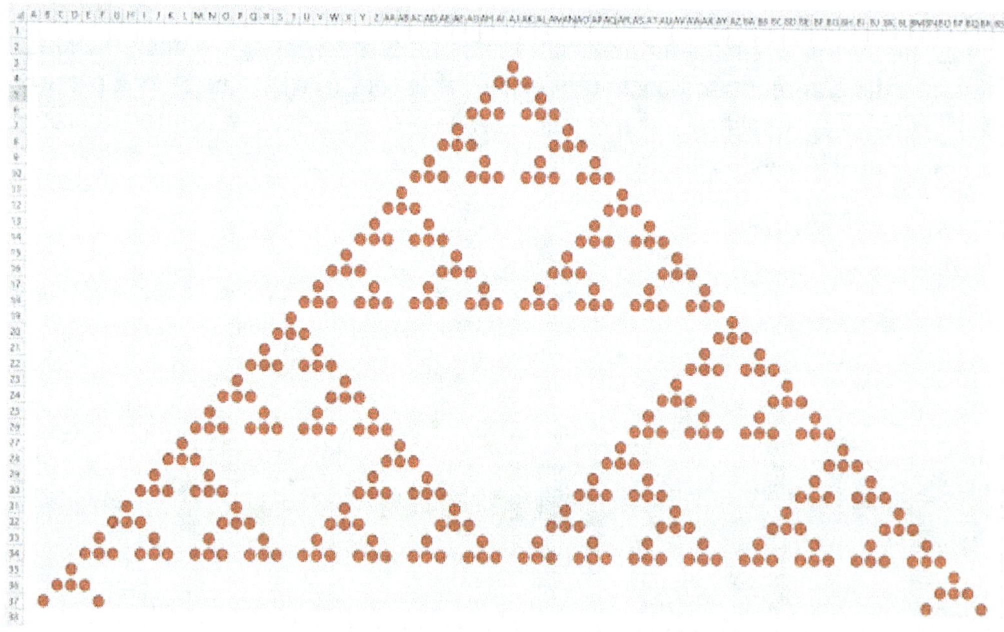

This triangle was created as described here:

- selected the sheet and set column width to 2
- entered in cell B2 this formula: =IF(SUM(A1:C1)=1,1,"")
- copied the formula to B2:BR37 range
- entered "1" in cell AJ3
- used Conditional Formatting to display the icons, namely: selected the range and set two formatting rules:

1. Format based on Icon Sets style when cell value **is -=1**, and
2. Format only cells containing cell value **=""** to selected Colour and Pattern

Random Paths

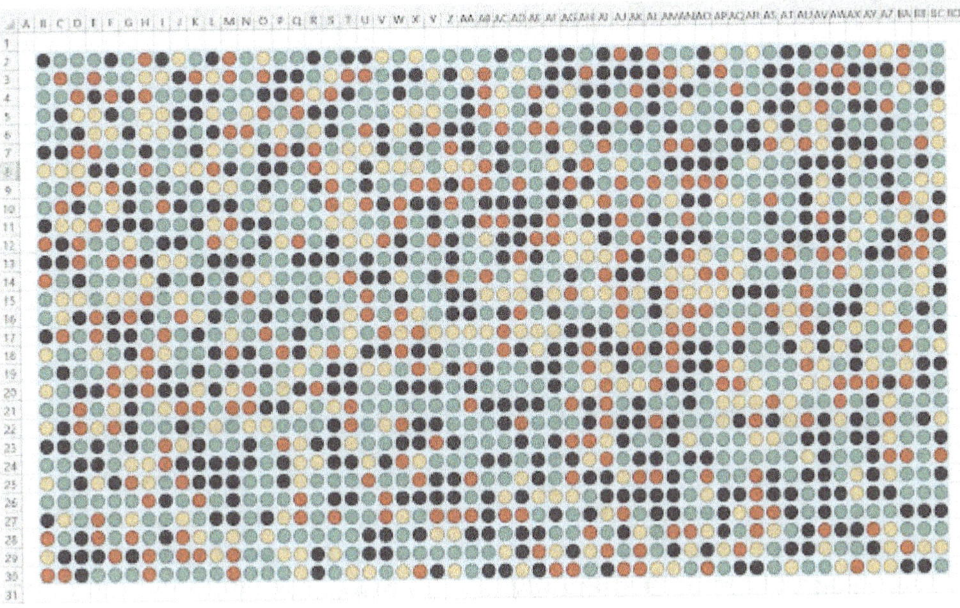

This random pattern has been created, after setting column width to 2, with the following formula:

=IF(SUM(A1:C1)-0,SIN(RAND()*45),COS(RAND()*45))

entered in cell B2 and copied to B2:BC30 range. In Conditional Formatting I used formatting rule with Icon Set, when cell values are >=75 percent, <75 and >=50 percent, and <50 and >=25 percent.

Mosaic

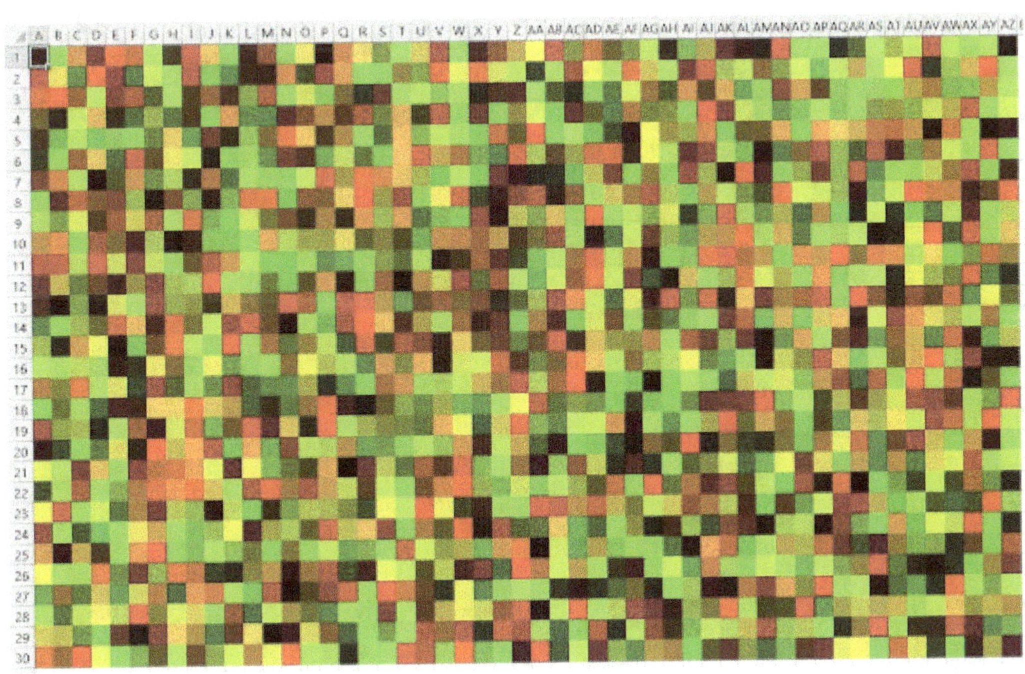

To create a similar mosaic of colours in certain range of quadratic cells, set the column width to 2 and then use the following macro code. You need to copy and paste the code into open VBE space (press **ALT+F11** to get there).

```vba
Sub RandomColors()
Dim rng As Range
Dim WorkRng As Range
Dim xRed As Byte
Dim xGreen As Byte
Dim xBlue As Byte
On Error Resume Next
xTitleId = "MyColors"
Set WorkRng = Application.Selection
Set WorkRng = Application.InputBox("Range", xTitleId, WorkRng.Address, Type:=8)
For Each rng In WorkRng
xRed = Application.WorksheetFunction.RandBetween(0, 255)
xGreen = Application.WorksheetFunction.RandBetween(0, 255)
xBlue = Application.WorksheetFunction.RandBetween(0, 255)
rng.Pattern = xlSolid
rng.PatternColorIndex = xlAutomatic
rng.Interior.Color = VBA.RGB(xRed, xGreen, xBule)
Next
End Sub
```

Creating Graphs Based on Data Table; the Easy Way

Whatever your Excel data source (entered or generated using a formula), convert the range of cells, they occupy, into Excel table. Simply select the range and use **CTRL+T** shortcut to do that. This way - when you later expand your data entries (add new data) or contract the table (remove some data) - your chart will get updated automatically (dynamically).

Here is kind of a template I've used to organize my data for charting:

	A	B	C	D	E	F	G	H	I
1	X	Y1	Y2	Y3	Y4				
2	-10.000	0.198	-1.000	0.408		Functions			
3	-9.900	0.200	-1.000	0.581		Y1 =	-2*x/(1+x^2)		
4	-9.800	0.202	-1.000	0.731		Y2 =	2*exp(-0.1*x^2)-1		
5	-9.700	0.204	-1.000	0.852		Y3 =	cos(2*x)		
6	-9.600	0.206	-1.000	0.939		Y4 =			
7	-9.500	0.208	-1.000	0.989					
8	-9.400	0.210	-1.000	0.999					
9	-9.300	0.213	-1.000	0.969					
10	-9.200	0.215	-1.000	0.901					
11	-9.100	0.217	-0.999	0.796					
12	-9.000	0.220	-0.999	0.660					
13	-8.900	0.222	-0.999	0.498					
14	-8.800	0.224	-0.999	0.316					
15	-8.700	0.227	-0.999	0.121					
16	-8.600	0.229	-0.999	-0.079					
17	-8.500	0.232	-0.999	-0.275					
18	-8.400	0.235	-0.998	-0.461					

I could fill the table with any function data, like in this example, or with raw data and get a graph based on just one function or two, or even three or four. Sometimes, when I've plotted e.g., two functions that have had different orders of magnitude, I used a secondary axis for one of them to display results in relevant scales.

To create your graph, select X column and appropriate Y column(s), then go to **Insert** tab and in **Charts** group select whatever chart type you need. That's it.

Now format your chart as you want to. Excel provides for that the whole plethora of options. Here I'm providing just two formatting examples to show you variety of possible solutions:

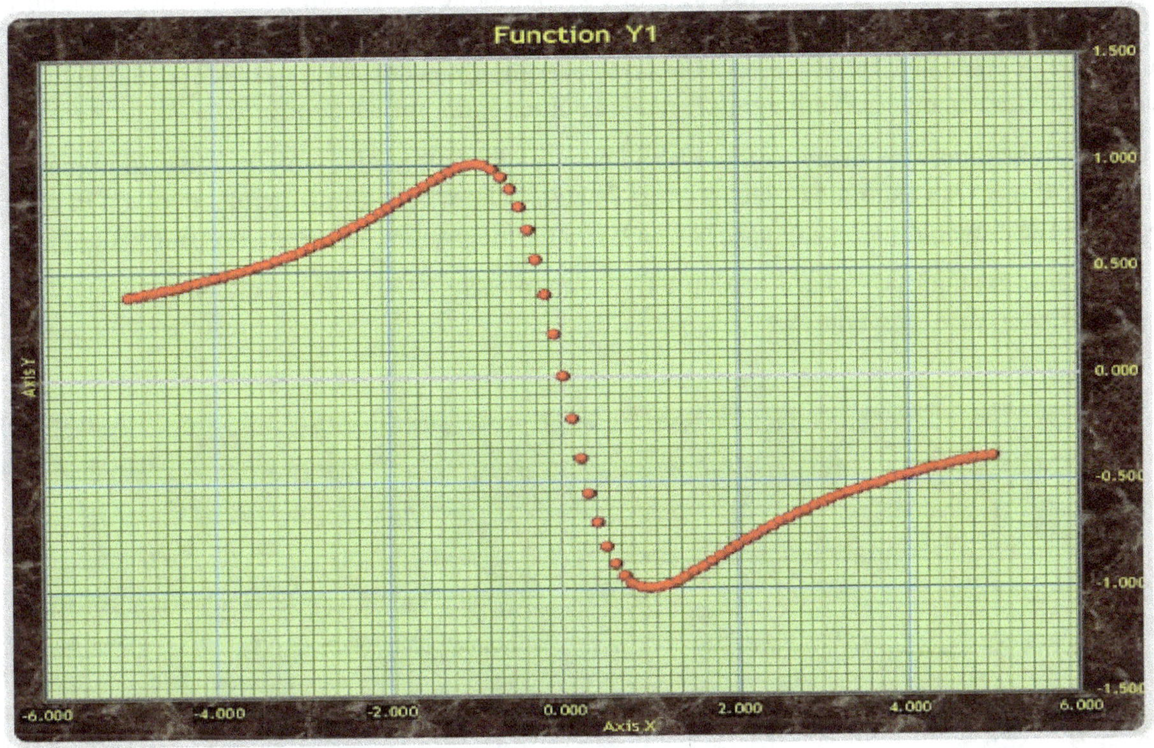

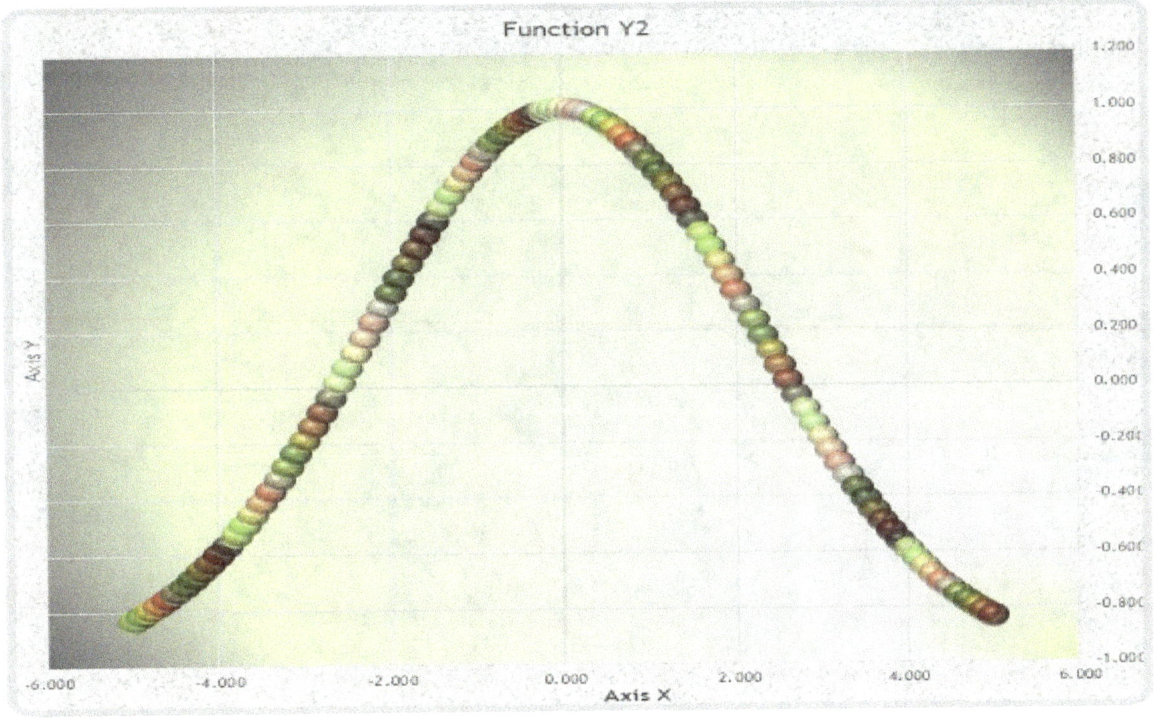

Enjoy Excel Charting!

World of Fractals - Beauty of Recursion

In my computer programming adventures, among other things, I've explored iteration and recursion.

Iteration is simpler, because it's basically just a **For** loop used in all common languages. It handles large number of steps consecutively. You go up or down, step by step, until you reach the top or the bottom.

Recursion is much more convoluted. It's a way of thinking and solving problems, because there is more than iteration to it. Steps are also repeated here, but you reduce the problem to smaller tasks and handle them separately; sort of divide-and-conquer strategy involving inheritance. You define the value of your function, which has more than one variable, by using other values of the same function, i.e., you change only one variable and keep all others constant, until some endpoint is reached, and then change something else, reach another endpoint, and so forth.

Recursive algorithms take many forms. It's the beauty of math, really, which shows up in many of those algorithms. One example of recursion is fractals. The whole art of fractals evolved in recent decades. Have a look at its beauty e.g., at this website: https://www.fractal-recursions.com/

Here are some examples of what I was able to create in early 1990s. No special software.... All done using just Excel VBA procedures.

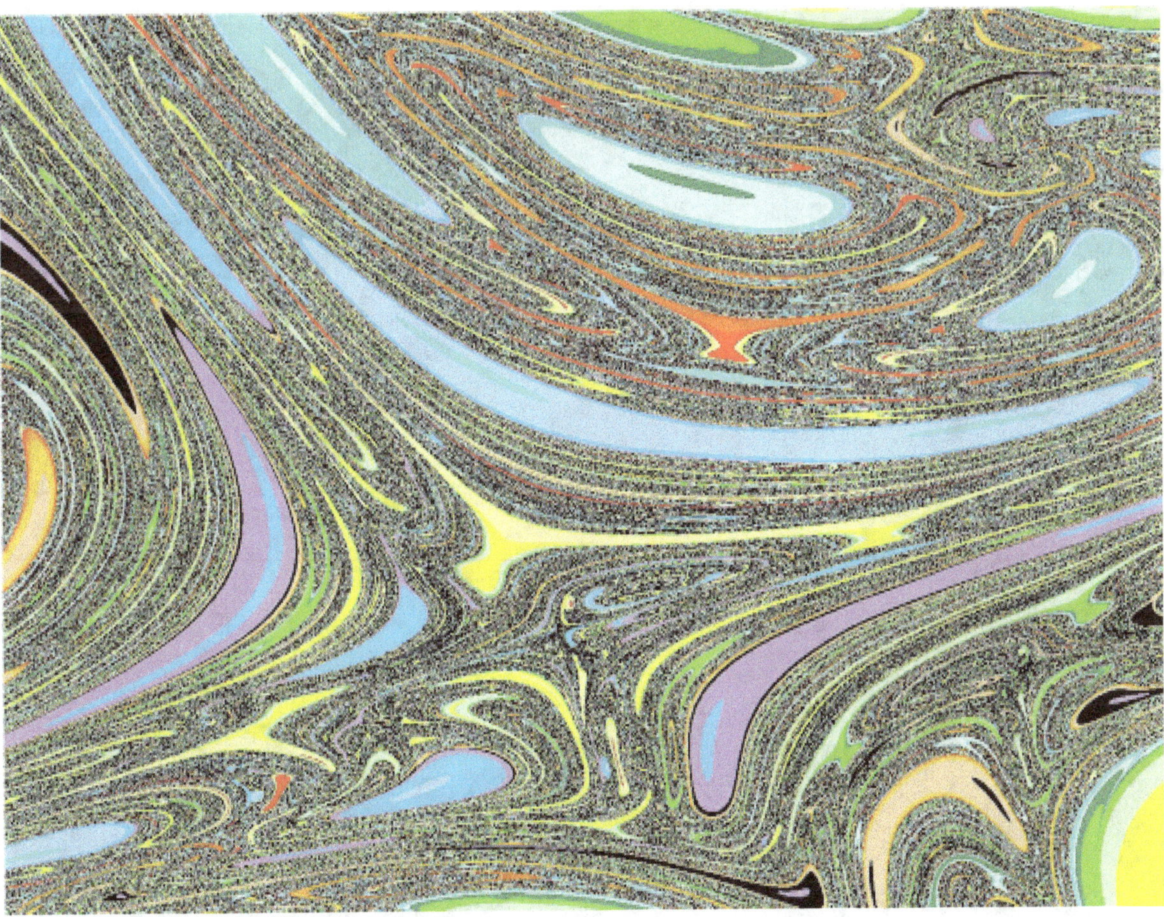

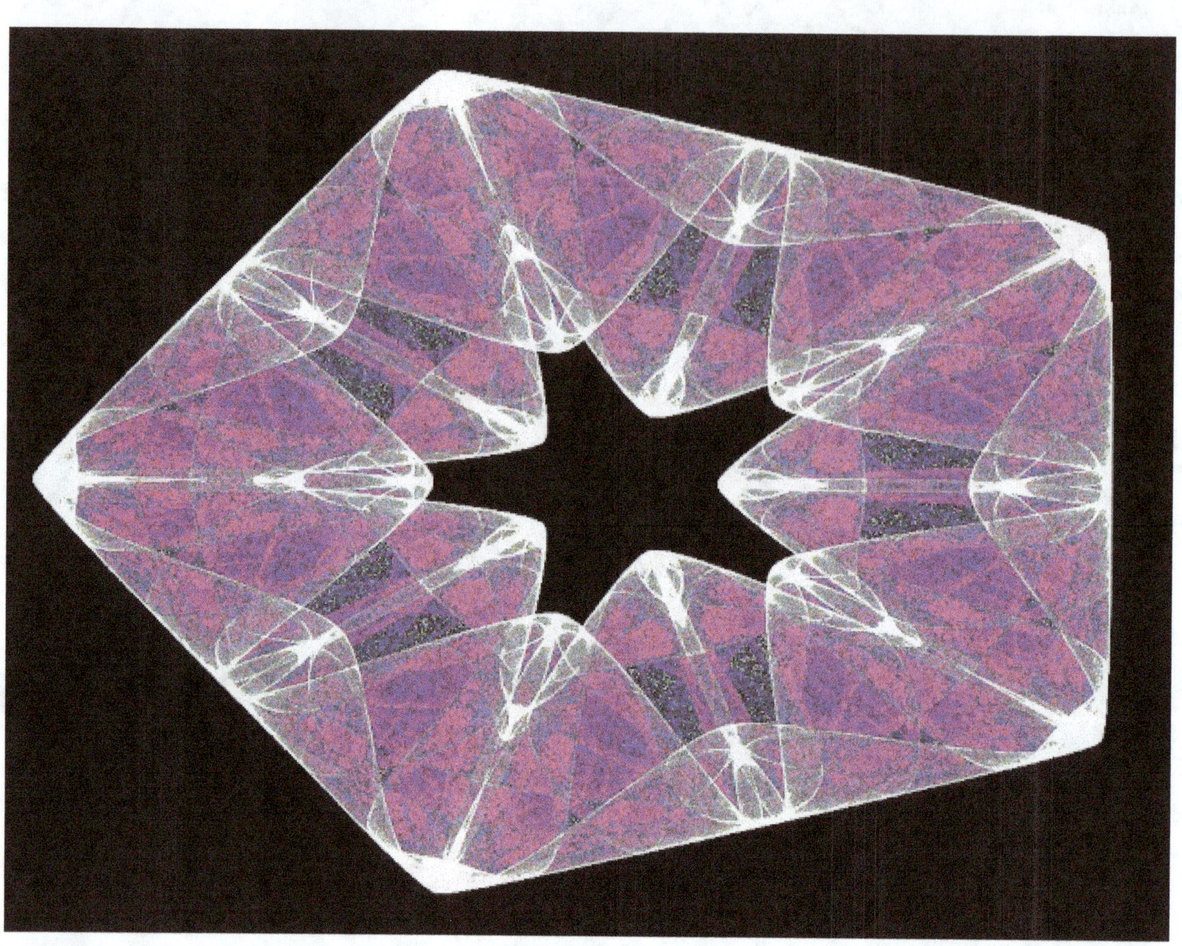

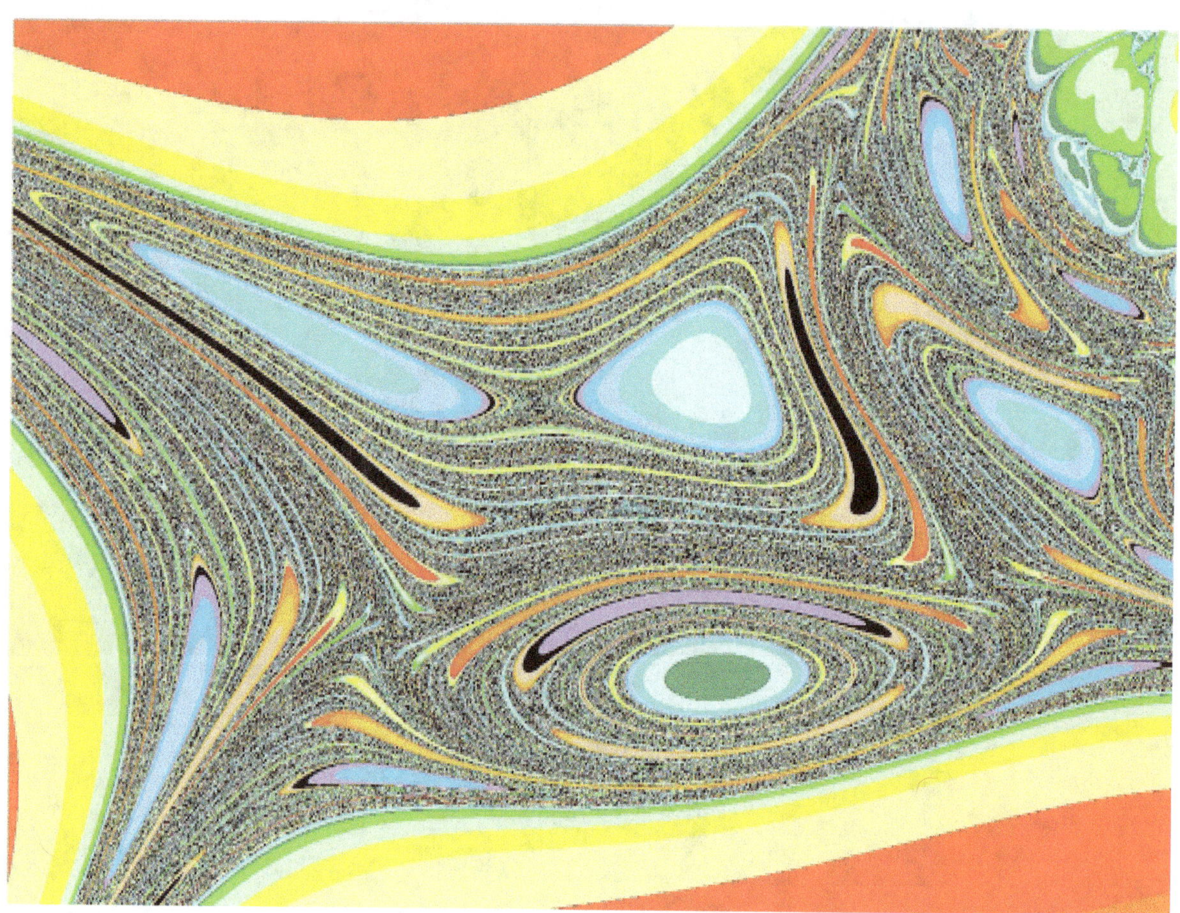

Create your own Lottery

Do you want to create and issue (distribute) randomly coded tickets to people - for any good reason you can think of? It could be e.g., some kind of a lottery or a game. Excel may be very helpful in achieving such a goal.

Let's say you've decided to issue tickets marked with codes like this: **A000** (one letter and three digits). This pattern creates 26,000 permutations, so you can issue 26,000 tickets with a different code each. Then, you build a list of only 5200 randomly selected codes in Excel worksheet (col. B in example shown below). You crate the list using this formula:

=CHAR(INT(RANDBETWEEN(65,90)))&MID(RAND(),3,3)

and then copying all 5200 positions and paste them (in place) as values. You can remove from the list any recurring codes by selecting **Data>Remove>Duplicates** (in col. B) in the ribbon.

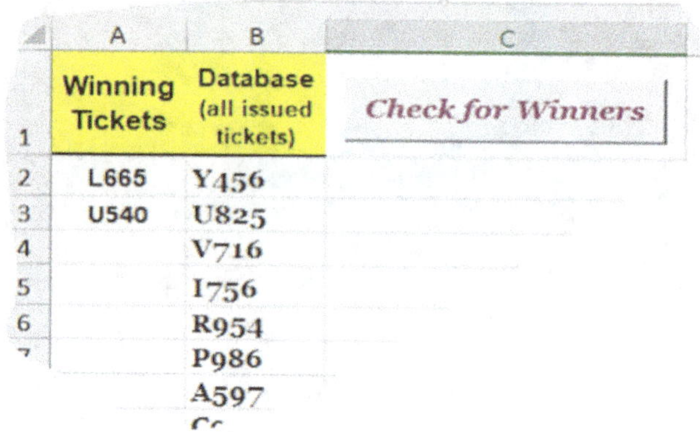

	A	B	C
	Winning Tickets	Database (all issued tickets)	Check for Winners
1			
2	L665	Y456	
3	U540	U825	
4		V716	
5		I756	
6		R954	
7		P986	
		A597	

Creating Pixel Art - Iterations

You can use Excel to create some work of art. Over 32000 iterations can be utilized, and this allows to produce lots of pixels in your worksheet and, practically, create unlimited number of 2D 'pictures' and 3D 'sculptures'.

To give you an idea what kind of 'art' I'm talking about, here are just couple of examples:

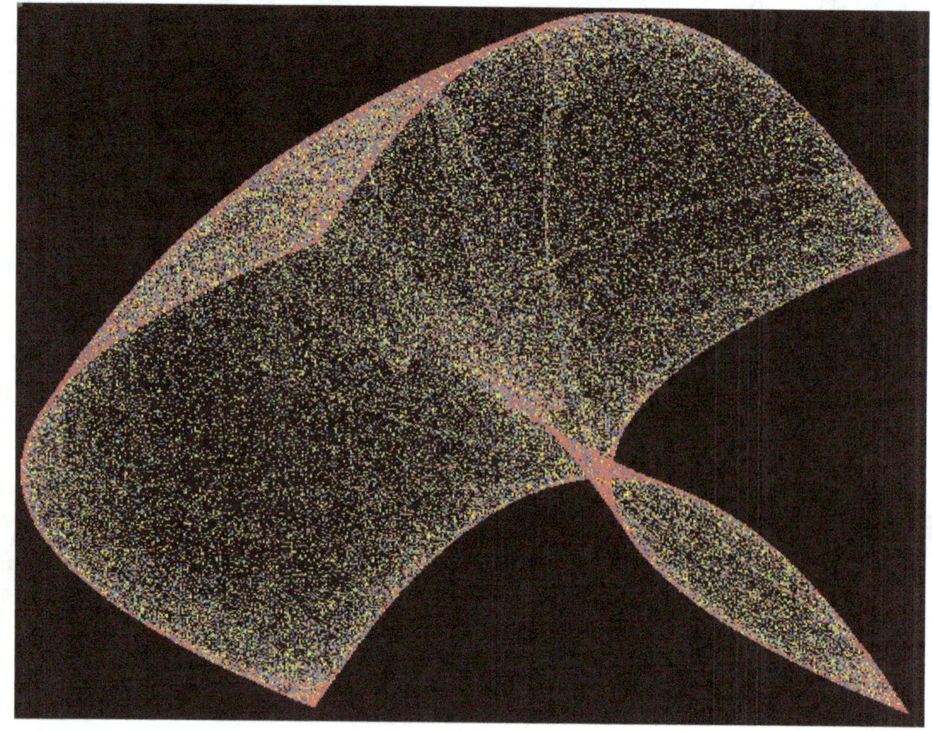

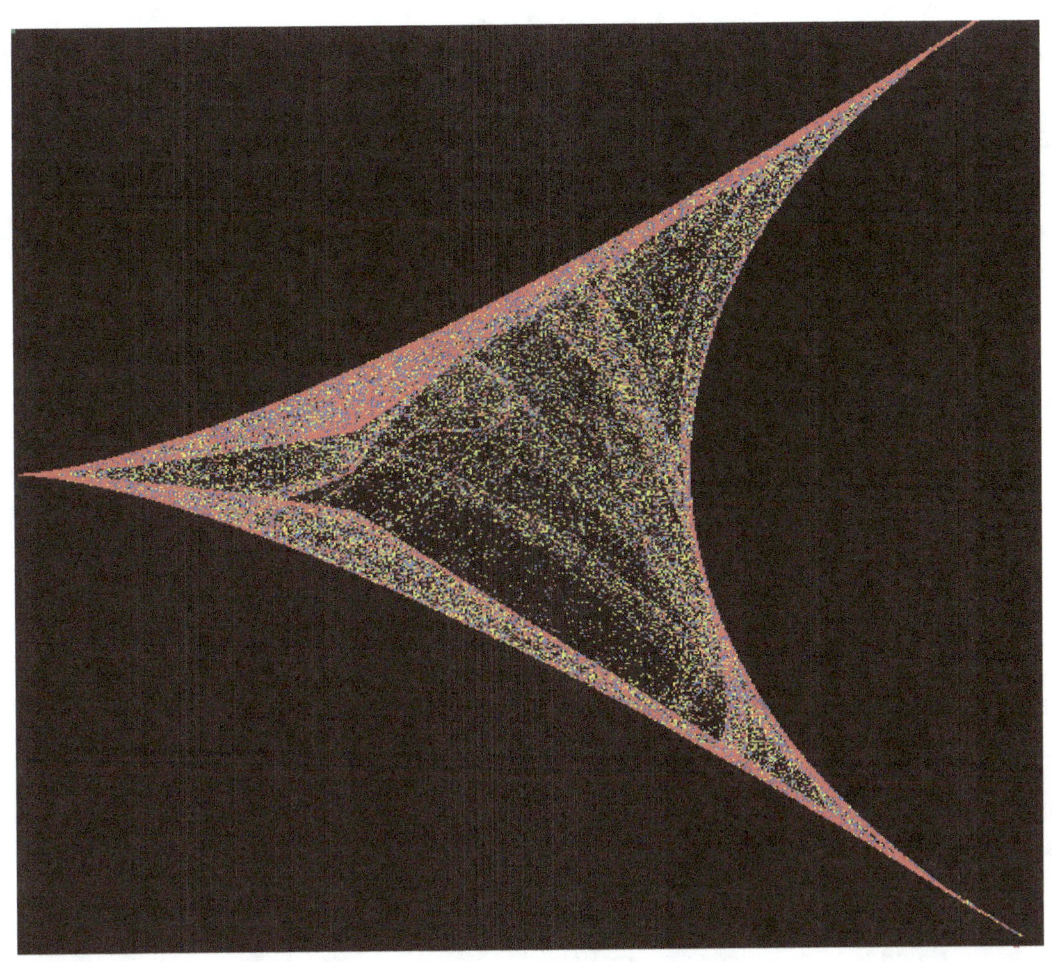

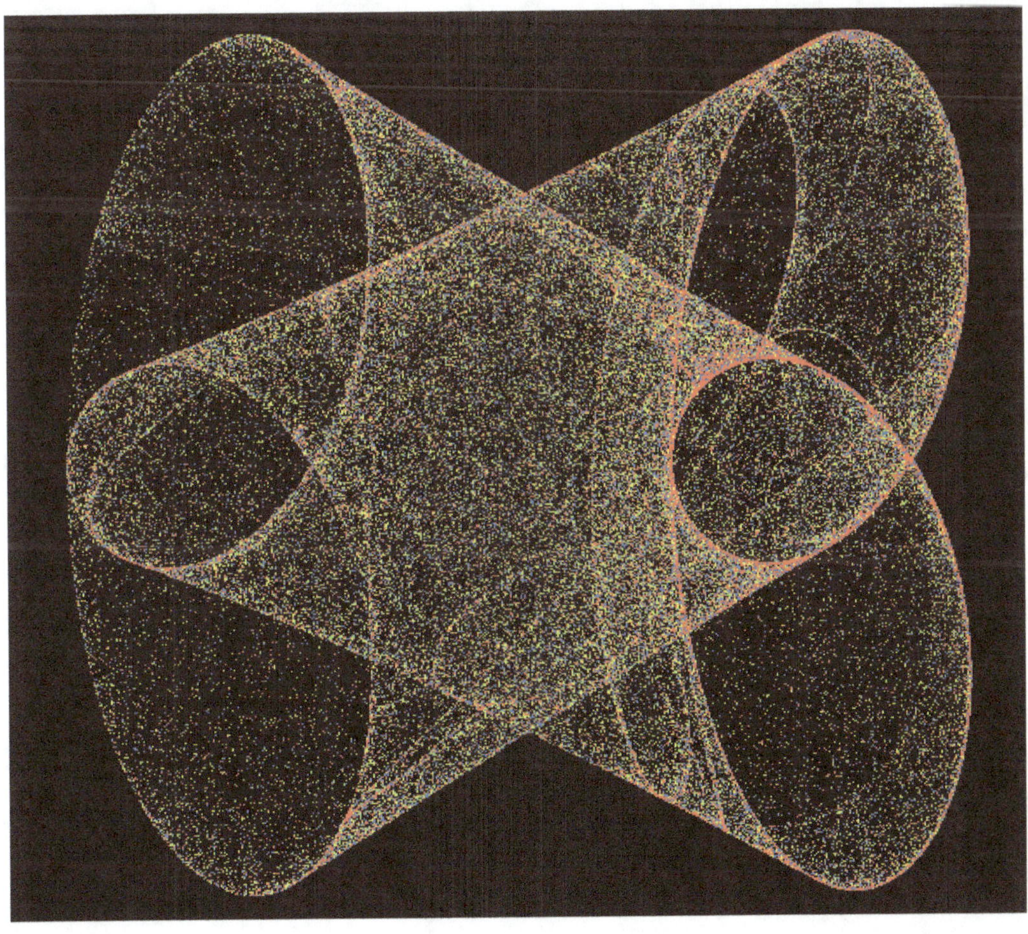

All you need to show your creativity is to use the two macros provided for you below (*one for drawing and the other for erasing*). Before starting your creative work, you need to determine some name for your picture. Go to **Formulas > Define Name** in your workbook and enter **"TRI"** in the **Name:** field and **"=Sheet1!$B$2:$ZZ$601"** in **Refers to:** field.

Next, insert and format two **Buttons** (Form Controls), like what you see here:

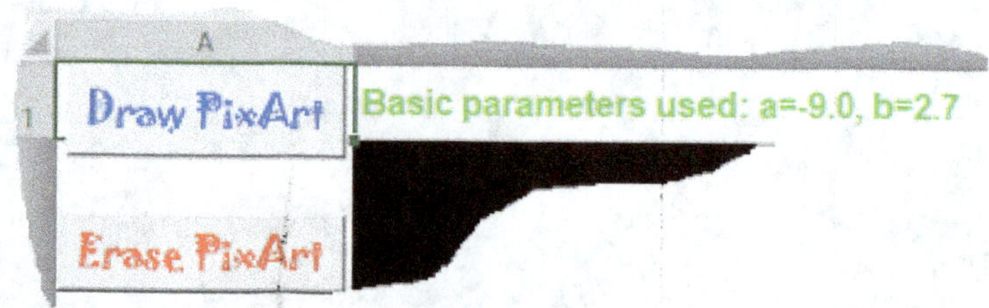

Go to **Developer > Insert > Button**, add the text (**Draw...**, **Erase...**) and assign the two macros to them. You'll use the buttons to create and erase the pictures.

Now you can copy the macros listed below to one of the modules inserted in your workbook (VBAProject). At this point you're ready to start experimenting with the pixel art. There are several parameters (variables), functions, formulas, equations, colours etc., that can be changed and manipulated within the first macro to obtain various drawing effects.

Here are the macros:

```
Option Explicit
Sub Sculpture()
'Produces graphics: from random mist to well defined pixel art
'Use provided parameters and translations to define "sculptures"
'It takes several seconds to produce some pixel art
Dim cP(3) As Long
Dim wid As Double
Dim myPts As Single
Dim myRange As Range
Dim cx As Double, cy As Double, rC As Double, iC As Double
Dim xUL As Double, xLL As Double, yUL As Double, yLL As Double
Dim y As Double, x As Double, c As Double, d As Double
Dim intW As Integer, intH As Integer, i As Integer, j As Integer
Dim a As Single, b As Single, sPercent As Single, co As Single
'Colour palette; change as you like
cP(0) = 65280      'green
cP(1) = 65535      'yellow
cP(2) = 13382400    'blue
cP(3) = 255      'red
On Error GoTo TheEnd
'Set your canvas range for square cells; here set to B2:ZZ601
Set myRange = Application.InputBox("Select a range in which to create square cells", ,
_"$B$2:$ZZ$601", Type:=8)
On Error Resume Next
If myRange.Cells.Count = 0 Then Exit Sub
GetWidth:   'Set the width of cells (0.08 is my screen pixel size)
wid = Val(InputBox("Input Column Width:", , "0.08"))
If wid < 0.08 Then
   MsgBox "Invalid column width value"
   GoTo GetWidth
```

```vba
End If
Application.ScreenUpdating = False
myRange.EntireColumn.ColumnWidth = wid
myPts = myRange(1).Width      'Set row height
myRange.EntireRow.RowHeight = myPts
xLL = -1.02: xUL = 3.02: yLL = -1.02: yUL = 2.59
intW = myRange.Columns.Count: intH = myRange.Rows.Count
Application.Goto reference:="TRI"     'TRI is the named range (=Sheet1!$B$2:$ZZ$601")
With Selection.Interior
    .Pattern = xlSolid
    .PatternColorIndex = xlAutomatic
    .Color = 0    'Background colour; set to black
End With
Range("A1").Select
x = 0: y = 0
cx = 1: cy = 0.5
a = Rnd() * (-10 - 10) + 10: b = Rnd() * (-10 - 10) + 10 'Random real numbers between -10 & 10
For j = 1 To 4      'Iterate by colours
    Select Case j
        Case 1
            co = cP(0)
        Case 2
            co = cP(1)
        Case 3
            co = cP(2)
        Case Else
            co = cP(3)
    End Select
    For i = 1 To 30000    'Number of iterations with each of the colours
        x = cx: y = cy
        c = Sin(a * x): d = Cos(b * y ^ 2)     'Use any other formulas to get desirable results
        cx = d + c * c + 0.6: cy = Sin(2 * a * x) - Sin(c) * d + 0.8 'As above
        iC = Int(intW * (cx - xLL) / (xUL - xLL)): rC = Int(intH * (cy - yLL) / (yUL - yLL))
        myRange.Cells(1 + rC, 1 + iC).Interior.Color = co
        If iC < 2 Then iC = 2: If iC - intW Then iC = intW
        If rC < 2 Then rC = 2: If rC - intH Then rC = intH
    Next i
Next j
Range("Sheet1!B1").Select
myRange.Cells(1, 1).Offset(-1, 0) = "Basic parameters used: a=" & Format(a, "#0.0;-#0.0") & ", _
b=" & _Format(b, "#0.0;-#0.0")
Application.ScreenUpdating = True
myRange.Cells(1, 1).Offset(-1, -1).Select
TheEnd:
Set myRange = Nothing
If Application.ScreenUpdating = False Then Application.ScreenUpdating = True
End Sub


Sub EraseSculpt()
'Clear the graphic and restore cell size
Dim TRI As Name
Application.ScreenUpdating = False
```

```vba
        Application.Goto reference:="TRI"
        Selection.Clear
        With Selection
            .ColumnWidth = 8.43
            .RowHeight = 12.75
        End With
        Range("B1").Select
        Selection.ClearContents
        Range("A2").Select
    Application.ScreenUpdating = True
End Sub
```

Animation - Flying Objects

The following VBA (Visual Basic Application) code makes Excel shapes and some other types of graphics flying. In this instance I'm shooting a rocket on my worksheet across the computer screen. This shape is based on Excel graphic named "Graphic 4".

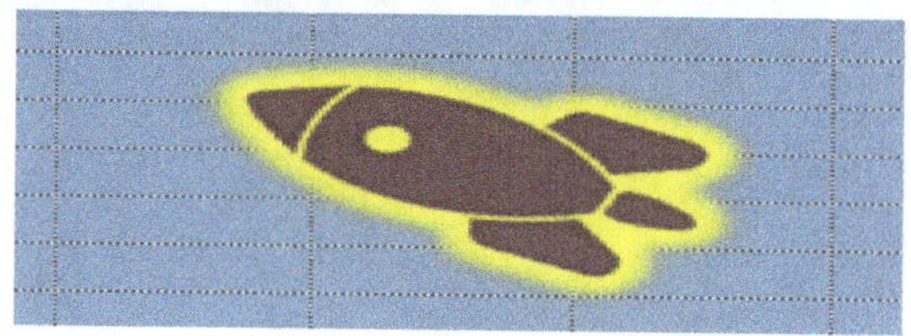

```vba
Option Explicit
Public Declare Sub Sleep Lib "kernel32" (ByVal iMilliseconds As Long)

Sub Flyer()
    Sheet1.Shapes("Graphic 4").Left = 1000        'Starting X
    Sheet1.Shapes("Graphic 4").Top = 450          'Starting Y
    MoveShp Sheet1.Shapes("Graphic 4"), 0!, 0!, #12:00:01 AM#      'Shape inserted
End Sub

Sub MoveShp(shp As Shape, ByVal coLeft As Single, ByVal coTop As Single, t As Date)
' Moves the shape from start to finish over the interval t
    Const xch = 0.018
    Const n1 As Long = 30        'Accelerate/decelerate steps
    Const n2 As Long = 60        'Coast steps
    Const n As Long = 2 * n1 + n2    'Total steps
    Dim i As Long            'Step index
    Dim stpv As Single            'Coasting, pixels/step
    Dim v As Single            'Velocity at current step
    Dim cLiLeft As Single, cLiTop As Single        'Left and Top num
    Dim cMi As Single                'Frctn denom
    Dim coLeftPr As Single, coTopPr As Single
    stpv = 1 / (n - n1)
    With shp
        coLeft = coLeft - .Left: coTop = coTop - .Top
        coLeftPr = .Left: coTopPr = .Top
        For i = 1 To n
            Select Case i
            Case 1 To n1            'Accelerate
```

```vba
        v = stpv * (1 + Cos(xch * 180 * (1 + i / n1))) / 2
    Case n1 + 1 To n - n1     'Constant velocity
        v = stpv
    Case Else     'Decelerate
        v = stpv * (1 + Cos(xch * 180 * (1 + (n - i) / n1))) / 2
    End Select
    .Left = .Left + v * (coLeft - cLiLeft) / (1 - cMi)
    .Top = .Top + v * (coTop - cLiTop) / (1 - cMi)
    cMi = cMi + v
    cLiLeft = .Left - coLeftPr: cLiTop = .Top - coTopPr
    DoEvents
    Sleep t * 86400000# / n
  Next i
  End With
End Sub
```

To use the code in Excel on your computer follow these steps:

- find and insert **Graphic 4** shape into your worksheet (*if you want to use any other Excel graphic, remember to change the shape name in the above code*)
- copy the code and paste it into any module of your project (workbook)
- select the **"Flyer"** macro from **Macros** in the ribbon to run it.

If you assign the macro to the shape (by right-clicking it and selecting "Assign Macro..." option), then just click on the shape and it will fly...

You can try to run the macro using some other shapes/objects.

Animation - Swinging Objects

In this example I'm presenting simulation of a swinging pendulum (Excel shape called "**3D Model 8**"), looking like this (in couple of positions):

Here is the VBA code used for creation of the pendulum effect:

```vba
Option Explicit
Public Declare Sub Sleep Lib "kernel32" (ByVal iMilliseconds As Long)

Sub Swing()
Do While Cells(1, 1).Value <> 2     ' Click the cell A1 to stop the macro
    Sheet1.Shapes("3D Model 8").Left = 912.132     'Starting X
    Sheet1.Shapes("3D Model 8").Top = 362.132     'Starting Y
    MoveShp Sheet1.Shapes("3D Model 8"), 0!, 0!, #12:00:01 AM#     'Call the procedure
Loop
End Sub
```

```vba
Sub MoveShp(shp As Shape, ByVal fLeft As Single, ByVal fTop As Single, t As Date)
'Moves the shape from original position, back & forth
    Const n As Long = 180   'Number of steps
    Const X = 700
    Const Y = 150
    Const r = 300     'Pendulum length
    Dim I As Long 'Step index
With shp
For I = 1 To n
    If I <= 0.25 * n Then
        .Left = X + r * Cos(WorksheetFunction.Radians(I + 45))
        .Top = Y + r * Sin(WorksheetFunction.Radians(I + 45))
    ElseIf I <= 0.5 * n Then
        .Left = X - r * Sin(WorksheetFunction.Radians(I - 45))
        .Top = Y + r * Cos(WorksheetFunction.Radians(I - 45))
    ElseIf I <= 0.75 * n Then
        .Left = X - r * Sin(WorksheetFunction.Radians(135 - I))
        .Top = Y + r * Cos(WorksheetFunction.Radians(135 - I))
    Else
        .Left = X + r * Sin(WorksheetFunction.Radians(I - 135))
        .Top = Y + r * Cos(WorksheetFunction.Radians(I - 135))
    End If
    If Selection.Address = "$A$1" Then End       'Clicking in cell A1 stops running the code
    DoEvents
    Sleep t * 8640000# / n
Next I
End With
End Sub
```

If you want to use the code and/or experiment with it, follow these steps:

- find and insert **3D Model 8** shape (*or some other, but remember to change the shape name in the above code*) into your worksheet
- copy the code and paste it into any module of your project (workbook)
- run the "**Swing**" macro; it will run continuously. To stop it - click in cell **A1**.

By the way, you can assign the "Swing" macro to the shape, by right-clicking it and selecting "Assign Macro..." option. After that, running the macro will be as easy as clicking on the shape.

You may wish to modify the code, using different shapes and to achieve different effects. Enjoy!

Pick Your Lucky Lotto Numbers

If you play Lotto, how do you pick your lucky numbers?

Everyone has their own method. Some people like to analyse past draws and study the statistics to select potential winning patterns. Others rely on totally random ways. My own experience shows that statistics helps a little bit with winnings at the **low end** only.

No method can guarantee a **big** win. Lotteries are completely random. To check out my 'independent' serendipity - years ago – I've created my own *Lotto number picker* coded with VBA. It's one of my oldest *Excel creations*. Here's its face in a worksheet:

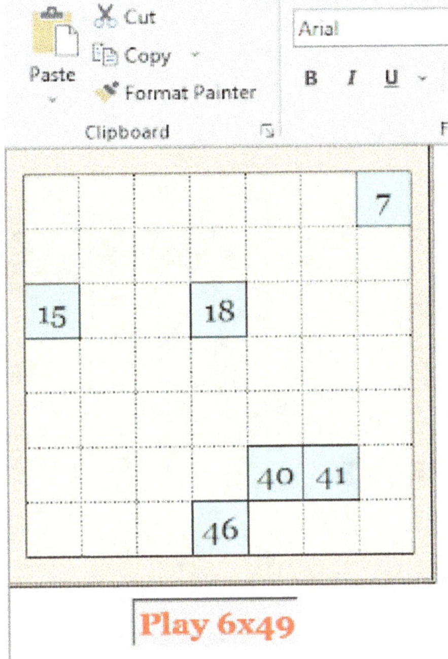

Simple and functional. It just picks six lucky numbers for you to play in a lottery like Lotto649 or something close to it. It can be modified quite easily for other lottery games based on random selections. You can get your *very own* quick picks on your own computer.

Copy the **VBA code** listed below and paste it to a **Module** in your VBA project (go there by using **ALT+F11** shortcut). Switch back to your worksheet and click on **Developer tab** to Insert (in the **Controls** group) the rectangular **Button** from **Form Controls**. Click he worksheet location where you want the button to appear and expand it there. The assign Macro window appears. Assign the **Draw649 macro** to the button and click OK. Right-click on it and then click **Format Control** to specify properties of the button.

Give it a try. Adjust the location of your control button, if necessary. Get your first lucky numbers. **Good luck!**

Here's the code:

```vba
Sub Draw649()
'Selects randomly 6 numbers from 1 to 49
Application.ScreenUpdating = False
    Range("B2:H8").Select
    Selection.RowHeight = 25
    Selection.ColumnWidth = 4
    With Selection
        .HorizontalAlignment = xlCenter
        .VerticalAlignment = xlCenter
    End With
    Selection.Borders(xlInsideVertical).LineStyle = xlNone
    Selection.Borders(xlInsideHorizontal).LineStyle = xlNone
    With Selection.Interior
        .ColorIndex = 36
        .Pattern = xlSolid
        .PatternColorIndex = xlAutomatic
    End With
    Range("A2").Select
    Selection.ColumnWidth = 1
    Range("I2").Select
    Selection.ColumnWidth = 1
    Range("A1:I9").Select
    With Selection.Borders(xlEdgeLeft)
```

```vba
      .LineStyle = xlDouble
      .Weight = xlThick
      .ColorIndex = xlAutomatic
   End With
   With Selection.Borders(xlEdgeTop)
      .LineStyle = xlDouble
      .Weight = xlThick
      .ColorIndex = xlAutomatic
   End With
   With Selection.Borders(xlEdgeBottom)
      .LineStyle = xlDouble
      .Weight = xlThick
      .ColorIndex = xlAutomatic
   End With
   With Selection.Borders(xlEdgeRight)
      .LineStyle = xlDouble
      .Weight = xlThick
      .ColorIndex = xlAutomatic
   End With
   Selection.Borders(xlInsideVertical).LineStyle = xlNone
   Selection.Borders(xlInsideHorizontal).LineStyle = xlNone
   With Selection.Interior
      .ColorIndex = 40
      .Pattern = xlGray50
      .PatternColorIndex = 2
   End With
   Range("B2:H8").Select
   With Selection.Font
      .Name = "Georgia"
      .Size = 14
      .Strikethrough = False
      .Superscript = False
      .Subscript = False
      .OutlineFont = False
      .Shadow = False
      .Underline = xlUnderlineStyleNone
      .ColorIndex = xlAutomatic
   End With
   With Selection.Interior
      .ColorIndex = 19
      .Pattern = xlGray50
      .PatternColorIndex = 2
   End With
   Selection.Borders(xlDiagonalDown).LineStyle = xlNone
   Selection.Borders(xlDiagonalUp).LineStyle = xlNone
   With Selection.Borders(xlEdgeLeft)
      .LineStyle = xlContinuous
      .Weight = xlThin
      .ColorIndex = xlAutomatic
   End With
   With Selection.Borders(xlEdgeTop)
      .LineStyle = xlContinuous
      .Weight = xlThin
      .ColorIndex = xlAutomatic
   End With
   With Selection.Borders(xlEdgeBottom)
      .LineStyle = xlContinuous
      .Weight = xlThin
      .ColorIndex = xlAutomatic
```

```
    End With
    With Selection.Borders(xlEdgeRight)
        .LineStyle = xlContinuous
        .Weight = xlThin
        .ColorIndex = xlAutomatic
    End With
    With Selection.Borders(xlInsideVertical)
        .LineStyle = xlContinuous
        .Weight = xlHairline
        .ColorIndex = xlAutomatic
    End With
    With Selection.Borders(xlInsideHorizontal)
        .LineStyle = xlContinuous
        .Weight = xlHairline
        .ColorIndex = xlAutomatic
    End With
    Range("B2").Select
CountN = 0
CountC = 0
CountR = 0
Numbr = 0
Randomize
Do While (CountN < 6)
    CountC = Int(Rnd() * 7 + 2)
    CountR = Int(Rnd() * 7 + 2)
    Cells(CountR, CountC).Select
    If Cells(CountR, CountC).Value = "" Then
        Numbr = (CountR - 2) * 7 + CountC - 1
        Select Case Numbr
            Case 1 To 49
                Cells(CountR, CountC).Value = Numbr
                With Selection.Borders(xlEdgeLeft)
                    .LineStyle = xlContinuous
                    .Weight = xlThin
                    .ColorIndex = xlAutomatic
                End With
                With Selection.Borders(xlEdgeTop)
                    .LineStyle = xlContinuous
                    .Weight = xlThin
                    .ColorIndex = xlAutomatic
                End With
                With Selection.Borders(xlEdgeBottom)
                    .LineStyle = xlContinuous
                    .Weight = xlThin
                    .ColorIndex = xlAutomatic
                End With
                With Selection.Borders(xlEdgeRight)
                    .LineStyle = xlContinuous
                    .Weight = xlThin
                    .ColorIndex = xlAutomatic
                End With
                With Selection.Interior
                .ColorIndex = 34
                .Pattern = xlSolid
                .PatternColorIndex = xlAutomatic
                End With
                CountN = CountN + 1
            Case Else
                Numbr = 0
```

```
        End Select
    End If
Loop
Application.ScreenUpdating = True
Range("AA1").Select
a = MsgBox("Clear the window?", vbOKOnly)
Range("A1:I9").Select
Range("A1:I9").Clear
Selection.RowHeight = 12.75
Selection.ColumnWidth = 8
Range("A1").Select
End Sub
```

SUDOKU Solver and Creator

If you are Sudoku solver you probably spent hours and hours trying to solve the puzzles. I'd like to show here that in Excel, with help of VBA macros, you can do it usually in seconds.

Create your own private Sudoku solver tool, which will not only solve the puzzle but also create your own, at different levels of difficulty. I'll guide you through all the steps.

In **the first step**, you'll need to design your worksheet structure/view. Start with Sudoku 9 x 9 cells square. Use any colours you like to create a pleasant display of the matrix. I've used RowHeight of 33 and ColumnWidth of 6 to make cells look like squares.

Here is my design shown in two stages: with blank fields (*before creating a puzzle*) and with filled fields (*after solving a puzzle*).

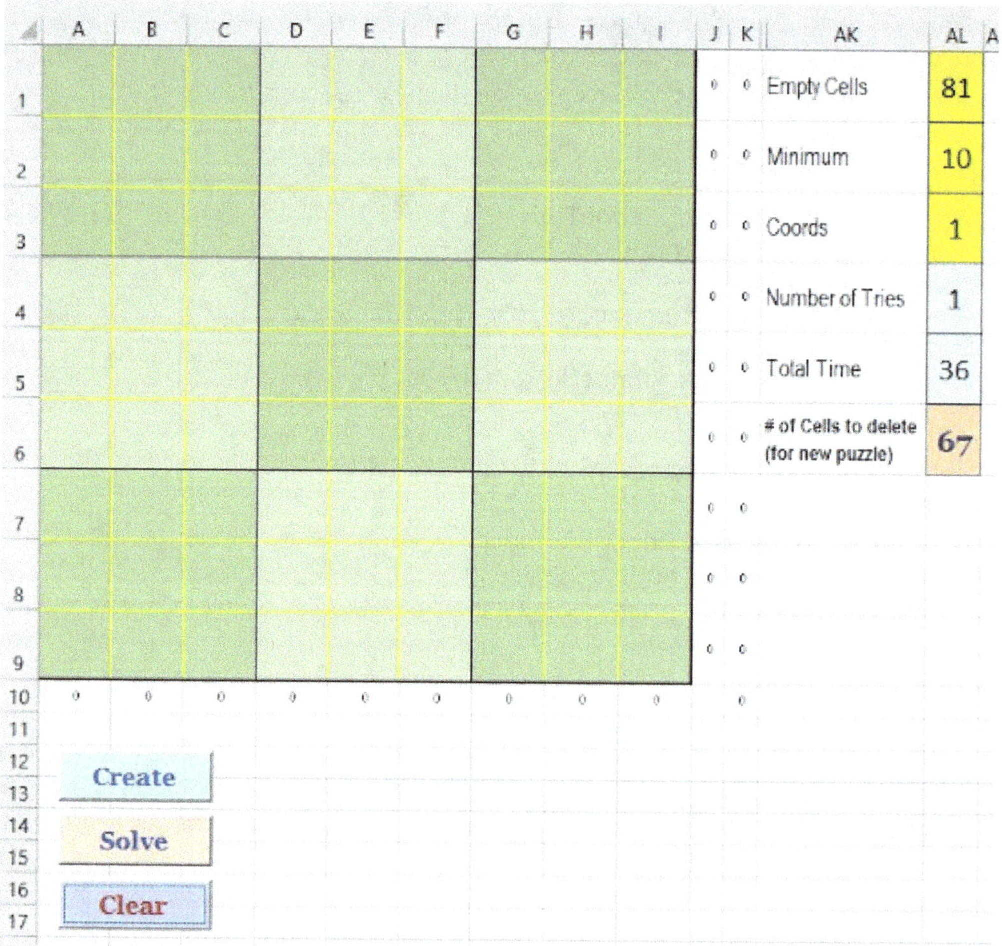

AK	AL
Empty Cells	81
Minimum	10
Coords	1
Number of Tries	1
Total Time	36
# of Cells to delete (for new puzzle)	67

Create

Solve

Clear

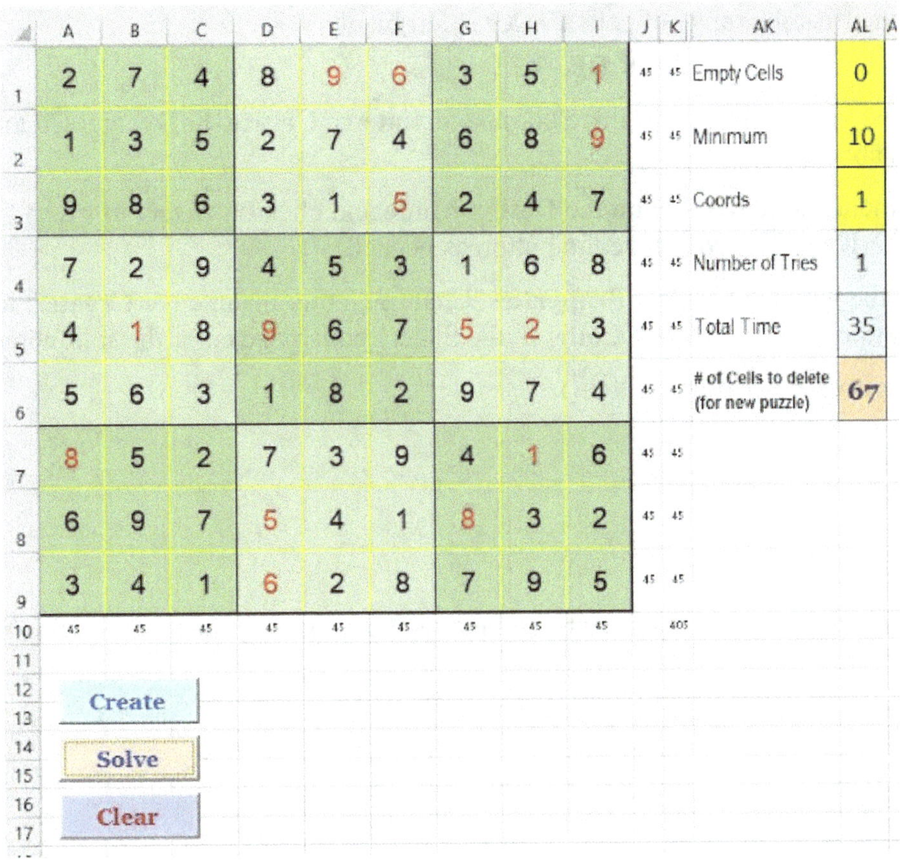

A	B	C	D	E	F	G	H	I	J	K	AK	AL
2	7	4	8	9	6	3	5	1	45	45	Empty Cells	0
1	3	5	2	7	4	6	8	9	45	45	Minimum	10
9	8	6	3	1	5	2	4	7	45	45	Coords	1
7	2	9	4	5	3	1	6	8	45	45	Number of Tries	1
4	1	8	9	6	7	5	2	3	45	45	Total Time	35
5	6	3	1	8	2	9	7	4	45	45	# of Cells to delete (for new puzzle)	67
8	5	2	7	3	9	4	1	6	45	45		
6	9	7	5	4	1	8	3	2	45	45		
3	4	1	6	2	8	7	9	5	45	45		
45	45	45	45	45	45	45	45	45	405			

Create

Solve

Clear

After formatting of the layout as presented in the example above, comes **the second step** - filling designated cells with formulas. Enter them as follows:

Cell	Formulas to enter
A10	=SUM(A1:A9); copy it to B10:I10
J1	=SUM(A1:I1); copy it to J2:J9
K1	=SUM(A1:C3)
K2	=SUM(D1:F3)
K3	=SUM(G1:I3)
K4	=SUM(A4:C6)
K5	=SUM(D4:F6)
K6	=SUM(G4:I6)
K7	=SUM(A7:C9)
K8	=SUM(D7:F9)
K9	=SUM(G7:I9)
K10	=SUM(A1:I9)
AL1	=COUNTBLANK(A1:I9)
AL2	=MIN(AN1:DP1)
AL3	=MATCH(AL2,AN1:DP1,0)
AL4	Constant, e.g. 1 or 2
AL5	No entry necessary
AL6	Constant, e.g. 70
AN1	=LEN(P1); copy it to AO1:AV1
AW1	=LEN(P2); copy it to AX1:BE1
BF1	=LEN(P3); copy it to BG1:BN1
BO1	=LEN(P4); copy it to BP1:BW1
BX1	=LEN(P5); copy it to BY1:CF1
CG1	=LEN(P6); copy it to CH1:CO1
CP1	=LEN(P7); copy it to CQ1:CX1
CY1	=LEN(P8); copy it to CZ1:DG1
DH1	=LEN(P9); copy it to DI1:DP1

- Make sure that the range of cells **P1:X9** is left blank.
- Hide Columns **L:AJ** and **AN:DP**.

Step three. Now you need to insert three command buttons: **Create**, **Solve**, and **Clear**, as you see in the example above.

In **Developer** menu **Controls** turn on the **Design Mode** and click on **Insert** to insert **Command Button** from **ActiveX Controls**. Size the button as needed.

Right-click on the button and select **Properties**. Change Caption Name to "**Create**". Right-click again on the button and select **View Code**. In the Sheet1 code page enter the following code:

```vb
Private Sub CommandButton1_Click()
'CommandButton "Create"
Range("sudoku").Font.Color = vbBlack
RrLogic = 1
MainCod
End Sub
```

Return to your worksheet and create next two buttons the same way, but name them "**Solve**" and "**Clear**".

For "**Solve**" button enter the following code:

```vb
Private Sub CommandButton2_Click()
'CommandButton "Solve"
'Dim CheckArray(9)
If Cells(1, 38) = 0 Then End      'Checks if the empty cells are 0(solved sudoku)
Range("sudoku").Font.Color = vbBlack
For x = 1 To 9        'checks if there are same numbers in row, column, box
  For y = 1 To 9
    rX = "a" & x & ":" & "i" & x 'Finds the coordinations of the range(row, column, box)
    rY = Chr(y + 64) & "1" & ":" & Chr(y + 64) & "9"
    xK = 1 + Int((x - 1) / 3) * 3
    yK = 1 + Int((y - 1) / 3) * 3
    rK = Chr(yK + 64) & xK & ":" & Chr(yK + 66) & xK + 2
    r = rX & "," & rY & "," & rK
    Set MyRange = Range(r)
    If Cells(x, y) = "" Then GoTo nextxy
    temp = Cells(x, y)
    Cells(x, y) = ""
    For Each c In MyRange.Cells
      If c.Value = temp Then
        Cells(x, y) = temp
        c.Font.Color = vbRed
        Cells(x, y).Font.Color = vbRed
        Message = MsgBox("Exits Sudoku", vbOKOnly)
        End
      End If
    Next
Cells(x, y) = temp
nextxy:
Next y, x
For x = 1 To 9    'Input data in an array
  For y = 1 To 9
```

```vba
        InputData(x, y) = Cells(x, y)
Next y, x
RrLogic = 2 ' If RrLogic =1 then Create Sudoku or If RrLogic =2 then Solve Sudoku
MainCod
End Sub
```

For "**Clear**" button enter this code:

```vba
Private Sub CommandButton3_Click()
'CommandButton "Clear"
Range("sudoku").Font.Color = vbBlack
For x = 1 To 9
  For y = 1 To 9
   Cells(x, y) = ""
Next y, x
End Sub
```

In **step four**, enter shortcut **ALT+F11** to open VBE page and click on the **View** in the menu to select **Project Explorer**. If there is no Module available within your VBA Project, then insert one by clicking on the **Insert** in the menu. Double-click on the **Module** and paste there the following Sub procedures:

```vba
Public InputData(9, 9), SpecialAr(), XCoords(), YCoords(), RrCount, RrLogic, CurNum As Integer
Public IsZero, AnyChanges As Boolean
Public x, y, MidNum, TempVar
Public MyRange As Range
Public TheSame As String

Public Sub MainCod()
Randomize Timer
wrongRep = 0: Xronos = Timer
1 IsZero = False
If RrLogic = 1 Then CreateSudoku Else SolveSudoku
wrongRep = wrongRep + 1      'Count of tries to solve sudoku
Do
CheckArea:
IsZero = False     'Becomes True when "123456789" is zero
If Cells(2, 38) = 1 Then GoTo 3     'Check if unique num in 2nd string array (in row, col or box)
ReDim SpecialAr(9), XCoords(4), YCoords(4)
AnyChanges = False        'True if any changes made after any check
For x = 1 To 9     'Row check
   For y = 1 To 9
   For k = 1 To Len(Cells(x, y + 15))
   If Cells(x, y + 15) = "0000000000" Then Exit For
   MidNum = Mid(Cells(x, y + 15), k, 1)
   SpecialAr(MidNum) = SpecialAr(MidNum) + 1        'Counts occurrence of a number in row
   Next k
  Next y
   For l = 1 To 9
     If SpecialAr(l) = 1 Then
        For y = 1 To 9     'Find cell with the unique number
          For k = 1 To Len(Cells(x, y + 15))       'Loop every char in the string
            MidNum = Mid(Cells(x, y + 15), k, 1)
```

```vb
                If Val(MidNum) = 1 Then
                    Cells(x, y) = 1     'The unique number in the 1st table
                    Cells(x, y + 15) = "0000000000"    'Set the string in the array for every completed
    cell 'in the 1st table
                    CurNum = Cells(x, y)  'Current cell investigated
                    RepairStr    'Calls the sub fixing the string table after cell is completed in 1st table
                    If IsZero = True Then GoTo 1    'Go back to the beginning if cannot go any further
                    GoTo CheckArea     'Make all the check if any change has been made
                End If
            Next k, y
        Else
        End If
    Next l
ReDim SpecialAr(9)
Next x
'Column check
For y = 1 To 9     'The same as above with exchanging the x and y coordinates
  For x = 1 To 9
    For k = 1 To Len(Cells(x, y + 15))
      If Cells(x, y + 15) = "0000000000" Then Exit For
      MidNum = Mid(Cells(x, y + 15), k, 1)
      SpecialAr(MidNum) = SpecialAr(MidNum) + 1
  Next k
  Next x
  For l = 1 To 9
    If SpecialAr(l) = 1 Then
      For x = 1 To 9
       For k = 1 To Len(Cells(x, y + 15))
        MidNum = Mid(Cells(x, y + 15), k, 1)
        If Val(MidNum) = 1 Then
        Cells(x, y) = 1: Cells(x, y + 15) = "0000000000"
        CurNum = Cells(x, y)
        RepairStr
        If IsZero = True Then GoTo 1
        GoTo CheckArea
        End If
       Next k, x
      Else
      End If
    Next l
  ReDim SpecialAr(9)
Next y
x = 0: y = 0
'Box check
For i = 1 To 6 Step 3        'The same as above but using the x and y coordinates of the box
  For j = 1 To 6 Step 3
    For n = 0 To 2
      For g = 0 To 2
        x = i + n: y = j + g
        For k = 1 To Len(Cells(x, y + 15))
          If Cells(x, y + 15) = "0000000000" Then Exit For
          MidNum = Mid(Cells(x, y + 15), k, 1)
```

```vba
              SpecialAr(MidNum) = SpecialAr(MidNum) + 1
            Next k
          Next g, n
      For l = 1 To 9
        If SpecialAr(l) = 1 Then
          For n = 0 To 2
            For g = 0 To 2
              x = i + n: y = j + g
            For k = 1 To Len(Cells(x, y + 15))
              MidNum = Mid(Cells(x, y + 15), k, 1)
              If Val(MidNum) = l Then
              Cells(x, y) = l: Cells(x, y + 15) = "0000000000"
              CurNum = Cells(x, y)
              RepairStr
              If IsZero = True Then GoTo 1
              GoTo CheckArea
              End If
            Next k
            Next g, n
            Else
            End If
        Next l
ReDim SpecialAr(9)Next j, i
'Check if there is a couple a triad or tetrad in the same row, column or box
If RrLogic = 1 Then GoTo 3
For x = 1 To 9     'row check
  For y = 1 To 8
    For k = y + 1 To 9
      If Cells(x, y + 15) = Cells(x, k + 15) And Len(Cells(x, y + 15)) < 5 Then
          YCoords(1) = y: TheSame = Cells(x, y + 15)
          For i = 2 To 4        'Give the Y coordinates of the same cells to the YCoords array
          If YCoords(i) = 0 Then YCoords(i) = k: Exit For
          Next i
      Else
      End If
    Next k
'If there are same cells, call the CheckSameY sub & keep the current row in the TempVar variable
If YCoords(1) <> 0 Then TempVar = x: CheckSameY: Exit For
Next y
If IsZero = True Then GoTo 1
If AnyChanges = True Then GoTo CheckArea
Next x
IsZero = False
For y = 1 To 9     'Column check
For x = 1 To 8
For k = x + 1 To 9
If Cells(x, y + 15) = Cells(k, y + 15) And Len(Cells(x, y + 15)) < 5 Then
XCoords(1) = x: TheSame = Cells(x, y + 15)
For i = 2 To 4     'Give the Y coordinates of the same cells to the YCoords array
If XCoords(i) = 0 Then XCoords(i) = k: Exit For
Next i
Else
```

```vb
End If
Next k
'If there are same cells then call the CheckSameY sub & keep the current row in the TempVar
variable
If XCoords(1) <> 0 Then TempVar = y: RemRepeats: Exit For
Next x
If IsZero = True Then GoTo 1
If AnyChanges = True Then GoTo CheckArea
Next y
'Take the returned value of match function which finds the string with the minimum length
3 synt = Cells(3, 38)
'Convert the coordinates of the 1x81 array to the 9x9 array
x = Int((synt - 1) / 9) + 1
y = synt - (Int((synt - 1) / 9) * 9)
PithNum = Cells(x, y + 15)        'Give to a var the string with possible number for the cell
'Return a random number from 1 to the length of the string
RndNum = Int(Rnd * Len(Cells(x, y + 15))) + 1
'Give to a var the corresponding number
CurNum = Mid(PithNum, RndNum, 1)
Cells(x, y) = CurNum
Cells(x, y + 15) = "0000000000"
RepairStr
If IsZero = True Then GoTo 1
Loop Until Cells(1, 38) = 0
Cells(4, 38) = wrongRep
Cells(5, 38) = Timer - Xronos
If RrLogic = 1 Then DelCells
End Sub

Public Sub CreateSudoku()
'Prepare the tables to start creating a new sudoku
For x = 1 To 9
For y = 1 To 9
Cells(x, y + 15) = "123456789"
Cells(x, y) = ""
Next y, x
End Sub

Public Sub SolveSudoku()
'Solve a sudoku given by the user or created from the program
For x = 1 To 9     'Gives all the combinations to the string table
  For y = 1 To 9
    Cells(x, y + 15) = "123456789"
Next y, x
For x = 1 To 9     'Insert all the given data from the array into the 1st table
  For y = 1 To 9
  If InputData(x, y) = 0 Then Cells(x, y) = "": GoTo 2
  Cells(x, y) = InputData(x, y)
  Cells(x, y).Font.Color = vbRed        'Cells with data become red
  CurNum = Cells(x, y) 'For any given num fix the corresponding string
  Cells(x, y + 15) = "0000000000"
  RepairStr
      If IsZero = True Then Message = MsgBox("Not Possible", vbOKOnly): End
```

```vba
2 Next y, x
End Sub

Public Sub RepairStr()
rX = "p" & x & ":" & "x" & x     'Make the range in 2nd table, for every cell of 1st table, which
'contains row, column and box
    rY = Chr(y + 79) & "1" & ":" & Chr(y + 79) & "9"
    xK = 1 + Int((x - 1) / 3) * 3
    yK = 1 + Int((y - 1) / 3) * 3
    rK = Chr(yK + 79) & xK & ":" & Chr(yK + 81) & xK + 2
    r = rX & "," & rY & "," & rK
    Set MyRange = Range(r)
    For Each c In MyRange.Cells     'Subtract the current number from any string of the range
       For j = 1 To Len(c.Value)
          If Mid(c.Value, j, 1) <> CurNum Then tempXY$ = tempXY$ + Mid(c.Value, j, 1)
       Next
       If tempXY$ = "" Then IsZero = True   'Check if the string with possible num is nothing that
'means that the sudoku cannot be solved
       c.Value = tempXY$
       tempXY$ = ""
    Next
End Sub

Public Sub CheckSameY()
'Subtract diads, triads and tetrads from the string in the same row
AnyChanges = False
x = TempVar: TempVar = ""     'Variable containing the current x coordinate
metritis = 0
If YCoords(Len(TheSame)) = 0 Then ReDim YCoords(4): Exit Sub
For k = 1 To 9
 If Cells(x, k + 15) = "0000000000" Then metritis = metritis + 1
 Next k
'Check if there are no more empty cells in the 1st table except the diads, triads or tetrads
 If Len(TheSame) + metritis = 9 Then ReDim YCoords(4): Exit Sub
For y = 1 To 9
   For i = 1 To Len(TheSame)
      If y = YCoords(i) Then GoTo 1       'Prevent the program from subtracting the numbers from
'the cells which contains the diads, triads or tetrads
   Next i
   For i = 1 To Len(TheSame)
     For k = 1 To Len(Cells(x, y + 15))
       MidNum = Mid(Cells(x, y + 15), k, 1)
       If MidNum <> Mid(TheSame, i, 1) Then TempVar = TempVar + MidNum
       If MidNum = Mid(TheSame, i, 1) Then AnyChanges = True
     Next k
   If TempVar = "" Then IsZero = True
   Cells(x, y + 15) = TempVar
   TempVar = ""
   Next i
 1 Next y
 ReDim YCoords(4)
 End Sub
```

```vba
Public Sub RemRepeats()    'Subtract diads, triads and tetrads from the string in the same row
AnyChanges = False
y = TempVar: TempVar = ""        'Variable containing the current y coordinate
metritis = 0
If XCoords(Len(TheSame)) = 0 Then ReDim XCoords(4): Exit Sub
For k = 1 To 9
If Cells(k, y + 15) = "0000000000" Then metritis = metritis + 1
Next k
'Check if there are no more empty cells in the s1 tables except the diads, triads or tetrads
If Len(TheSame) + metritis = 9 Then ReDim XCoords(4): Exit Sub
For x = 1 To 9
'Prevent the program from subtracting the numbers from the cells which contains the diads, triads
or 'tetrads
    For i = 1 To Len(TheSame)
       If x = XCoords(i) Then GoTo 1
    Next i
    For i = 1 To Len(TheSame)
       For k = 1 To Len(Cells(x, y + 15))
         MidNum = Mid(Cells(x, y + 15), k, 1)
          If MidNum <> Mid(TheSame, i, 1) Then TempVar = TempVar + MidNum
          If MidNum = Mid(TheSame, i, 1) Then AnyChanges = True
       Next k
     If TempVar = "" Then IsZero = True
     Cells(x, y + 15) = TempVar
     TempVar = ""
    Next i
1 Next x
ReDim XCoords(4)
End Sub

Public Sub DelCells()
'Delete cells randomly (get ready to play)
RrCount = 0
10 Do
x = Int((Rnd * 9) + 1)
y = Int((Rnd * 9) + 1)
'Stop
If Cells(x, y) <> "" Then
   Cells(x, y) = ""
Else
   GoTo 10
End If
RrCount = RrCount + 1
Loop Until RrCount = Cells(6, 38)
End Sub
```

Go back to your worksheet. Turn off the **Design Mode** and check if everything was entered correctly and works as intended. Finish any formatting and save your workbook as Macro-Enabled one.

Happy Sudoku-ing...

The End